Human Impact
on Ancient Environments

Human Impact on Ancient Environments

Charles L. Redman

The University of Arizona Press
Tucson

The University of Arizona Press
© 1999 The Arizona Board of Regents
All Rights Reserved

Library of Congress Cataloging-in-Publication Data
Redman, Charles L.
Human impact on ancient environments / Charles L. Redman.
    p. cm.
Includes bibliographical references and index.
ISBN 13: 978-0-8165-1962-0 (cloth : acid-free paper)—
ISBN 10: 0-8165-1962-5
ISBN 13: 978-0-8165-1963-7 (pbk. : acid-free paper)—
ISBN 10: 0-8165-1963-3
1. Nature—Effect of human beings on—History. 2. Human ecology—
History. 3. Paleoecology. 4. Environmental archaeology. 5. Environmental
degradation—History. 6. Extinction (Biology)—History. I. Title.
GF75.R42   1999
304.2'09—dc21
99-6237

Manufactured in the United States of America on acid-free, archival-quality
paper containing a minimum of 50% post-consumer waste and processed
chlorine free.

11   10   09   08   07   06   9   8   7   6   5   4

Contents

Illustrations

Figures

Table

Preface

From the earliest years of their profession, archaeologists have been concerned with how humans were able to adapt successfully to their surroundings, but it is only in recent years that they have begun to focus on how these adaptations may have degraded the environment. The results of these studies, taken from many parts of the world, have provided us with surprisingly clear examples of serious human impacts on the environment reaching back thousands of years. A careful review of this newly available literature finds that the environmental crisis is not a new problem, but its basic human-environmental relationships have been with us for millennia. It is only the technology with which we operate, the size of the population, and the extent of the impact that have changed since prehistory.

Recognition of the past as a new and rich source of information to help understand today's environmental crisis has already begun to reinvigorate archaeology. The archaeological record is populated with thousands of communities that for varying lengths of time maintained a balance with their environment, yet over time, virtually all developed practices that degraded their surroundings and undermined their continued existence. Happily, the categories of data that illuminate these processes — climatic reconstruction, environmental characteristics, food resources, population estimates, and chronology of occupations — are exactly the kind of information archaeologists are most successful at retrieving.

This volume brings together numerous archaeological case studies from all over the globe into a single, coherent volume. The objective is to portray the nature of human-environmental relations under a wide range of conditions as they existed in many parts of the world and at various periods of time. The early chapters of the book introduce the reader to a history of human attitudes towards the environment and how these have affected human actions (chapter 2), as well as to basic ecological and archaeological concepts that help shape the way we understand and analyze our materials (chapter 3). The book concludes with a chapter that puts the information into a perspective through which readers can develop their own views on the lessons to be learned from the past (chapter 8).

Recent archaeological discoveries are assembled into four chapters according to the major categories of human impacts: animal extinctions and habitat destruction (chapter 4), agricultural practices (chapter 5), urban growth (chapter 6), and implications of increasingly complex society (chapter 7). Each of these chapters will begin by briefly discussing how the natural systems we are concerned with operate, how humans can affect the operation of those systems, and what kinds of archaeological evidence can be found to document these impacts. The balance of each of these chapters will be a presentation of archaeological case studies that have revealed the existence of these types of impacts in prehistory. I divided this background material and these case studies into four separate chapters to emphasize the key impacts of the human activities on the natural systems in terms of similar contemporary environmental threats. However, it will become immediately obvious to the reader that the operations of the natural systems in question are strongly interdependent and that each of the human impacts may have elements that rightly belong in the other three chapters. The same is true of the case studies themselves; none are pure examples of one type of impact alone, but each touches on two or more of the factors emphasized here. As with the presentation of all information relating to systems, it is best to communicate by breaking an otherwise complex phenomenon into artificially discrete, yet more understandable, units. The reader is urged at all times to keep in mind the underlying interrelatedness of the phenomena, and the text will include cross references highlighting the linkages that occur in the real situation.

The decision to organize the book in this manner was not made lightly, since as an archaeologist I have been most comfortable with presenting data by regions of the world and according to developmental time periods. This reflects the broadly held assumption that changes in human activities can be best understood in specific regional contexts and as having occurred according to a chronologically ordered developmental sequence. In some of my own writing, I have found it useful to look at a cultural process as a series of stages that may occur in numerous regions at differing time periods (for my treatment of the origin of complex society, see Redman 1978). There is no question in my mind that there would be benefits to using either of these frameworks for the presentation of data in this book. The case studies themselves were undertaken in regional projects that worked in closely controlled chronological contexts to demonstrate the environmental changes in question. Many aspects of human impacts on the environment are certainly related to stages of cultural and technological development and occurred in specific geographical regions, and hence, would be comprehensible in that framework of presentation.

The overriding reason that the book is not organized according to regions of the world and developmental time periods is that I do not want the reader to assume that the human-environmental interactions we are investigating are limited to specific regions or cultures, or that they have only evolved into a problem in recent times. One hundred years ago George P. Marsh was telling anyone who would listen that humans were devastating their environment; 2000 years ago Cicero in Rome and Mencius in China were writing of the degradation of once-productive lands; and I expect that one of the messages being portrayed by the cave painters of 20,000 years ago in southwest Europe was about conservation of the environment.

Although there are specific technologically related aspects to the human-environmental relationship that have only become salient in the twentieth century, I strongly believe that many of the fundamental aspects of this relationship are much older than the first Earth Day in 1970 and can be best examined in a cross-cultural, multitemporal framework. The perspective I believe to be most useful is that the *environmental crisis* is not strictly a recent problem uniquely tied to contemporary politics, economics, or technology, but rather centers more on the nature of human decision-making and the forces that help shape those decisions. Human-environmental relations have been around as long as humans, and in most aspects, these relations have been in place for centuries, if not millennia. I see the contemporary political and economic situation as being the end product of thousands of years of a slowly changing, fundamentally similar set of human-environmental interactions. The presentation of information in this volume is sufficiently objective to allow the readers to accept, reject, or not be certain of whether they agree with this position. The primary goal of this book is not to win over adherents to a new way of thinking about environmental relations, but rather to enlarge the perspective and broaden the sources of data used for understanding the issues that confront us, in order for us to make better decisions for the future.

There are many people who have contributed to this book; foremost among them are the archaeologists who have conducted the pioneering studies reported here. Colleagues kind enough to read and make helpful comments on the manuscript include Nancy Grimm, Don Rice, and Paul Minnis. I have also had substantial help from Shearon Vaughn for drawings, Kim Savage for permissions and index, Helen Hayes and Heather Hopkins for editing, and Ramon Ortiz for bibliography. I thank my family for being supportive throughout this endeavor. I also thank those who generously allowed me to use their illustrations, as cited in the figure captions. Susan McIntosh encouraged me to take the initial step toward writing this book by inviting me to speak at an international conference on human impact on the environment held at Rice University; it led to my first article on the subject (1992). Since then, I've been involved in organizing three symposia on this general topic. The participants in those symposia had exciting stories to tell and convinced me that we, as archaeologists, could contribute to this most fundamental of contemporary issues.

*Human Impact
on Ancient Environments*

1
Lessons from
a Prehistoric "Eden"

Perhaps the greatest challenge facing humans today is for us to live in concert with our environment. For people to seek creature comforts, economic prosperity, and maximum enjoyment sometimes seems to be in direct conflict with preserving the richness of the natural environment, maintaining human health, and even insuring the continuity of life on Earth. Is humankind on a fast track to self-destruction? Is there a realistic balance that can be reached? Or, in fact, are the problems not as grave as some would have us believe? Scholars, philosophers, and lay people of all persuasions are asking these questions, and their resolution will affect people in every part of the globe.

Recognition of the gravity of the *environmental crisis* has become widespread over the past thirty years, galvanizing scientists from diverse disciplines into a pursuit of urgently needed answers. *Science,* the prestigious journal of the American Association for the Advancement of Science, recently devoted an entire section to the latest findings on how humans are impacting virtually all of Earth's ecosystems. Among their startling revelations are that more than half of the accessible fresh water on Earth is used by humans, nearly half the land surface of the globe has been transformed by human action, more atmospheric nitrogen is fixed by human activities than by all natural terrestrial sources combined, and about one-quarter of the bird species on Earth have been driven to extinction (Vitousek et al. 1997:494). Nevertheless, almost all research by ecologists and other natural scientists has attempted to understand the operation of the biological and physical systems in isolation from human impacts and have focused their investigation only on current situations. The articles in *Science* are a clear admission that "most aspects of the structure and functioning of Earth's ecosystems cannot be understood without accounting for the strong, often dominant influence of humanity" (ibid.:494).

Further complicating the limited perspective of many former studies is the fact that, for many of the processes being studied, a significant time period is required to differentiate human impacts from natural cycles. There is a frustration among many scientists who feel unable to fully understand ecological processes or to determine the true magnitude of human impacts on the environment. In response to this, the National Science Foundation established in 1980 an entire research division to address long-term studies. As successful as these studies have been, they are severely limited by their great expense and the fact that many processes may not become clear until after decades or even centuries. This presented an intractable problem until researchers recognized that some of the problems they were interested in have been occurring for a long time and that they might be able to learn from experiences in the past, not just from studies of this particular instant in time. An integral element of this new perspective is that ecological cycles, including those dominated by humans, operate on differing time scales. Some processes may act over very short periods but are nested within processes of very long duration. This idea gained a strong following among scholars following the work of French historian Fernand Braudel (1972). This type of flexibility in the timescale of investigation is essential to making real breakthroughs in understanding human-environmental relations.

Those concerned with today's environmental problems have not focused on experiences in the past because of a belief that the crisis is a product of modern technology and a world brimming with billions of people. Both of these factors are crucial to the problems we face today. There is little question that environmental problems were more regional or local in the past than the global threats we perceive today. As real as this viewpoint is, it underestimates the impact environmental crises had on people in antiquity. The case studies presented in this volume reveal what a disaster it was for those who experienced it. Having to abandon one's home and village where generations of one's ancestors had lived is a calamity that few of us have to face today because of environmental problems. In terms of human decision-making, the past has a great deal to tell us about how people confront the threat of environmental degradation.

Archaeology, with its insight into tens of thousands of years of human activities in all parts of the globe, is a tantalizing source of information on human-environmental relations. The archaeological record encodes hundreds of situations in which societies were able to develop long-term sustainable relationships with their environments, and thousands of situations in which the relationships were short-lived and mutually destructive. The archaeological record is "strewn with the wrecks" of communities that obviously had not learned to cope with their environment in a sustainable

Figure 1.1
Salinization has undermined the productive potential of this region in southern Iraq, as it did to many regions in the past.

manner or had found a sustainable path, but veered from it only to face self-destruction. Today, one only has to look at the impoverished surroundings of once-great civilizations such as Mesopotamia, the Indus Valley, or various locations in the American Southwest to recognize that archaeology has a great deal to contribute to an understanding of this most urgent issue (fig. 1.1).

Human-environmental interaction is not a new subject for archaeologists; it has always been a central domain of inquiry for the discipline. Until quite recently, however, the focus has been on how people adapted to their environment or how climatically induced changes in the environment affected regional settlement systems. There is much to be learned from the countless archaeological case studies of people who, through a seemingly rational set of decisions, seriously degraded their environments, thereby threatening their continued survival (see also Crumley 1994b; Baleé 1998b).

Examples of human impacts on the environment can be found scattered throughout the archaeological literature; however, it was only about 20 years ago that these accounts began to coalesce. The increasing social concern with our environment combined with a growing archaeological interest in environmental information led researchers to recognize the significant impacts people had during prehistory, such as the massive extinction of birds by the Polynesian colonizers of the Pacific Islands, the deforestation of the Maya lowlands, the salinization of farmland in southern Mesopotamia, and the severe soil erosion in Ancient Greece. In recent years, many other case studies have been reported by archaeologists from the American Southwest, Mexico, Europe, and the Near East. We can now acknowledge this domain of study as having become a central research focus of contemporary archaeology.

Human impact on the environment is an ideal topic for archaeological inquiry because answers to key questions in this area require exactly the kinds of data that we have available and are good at deciphering. Temporal sequences, demographic patterns, paleoenvironmental reconstructions, and subsistence strategies — the bread and butter information of modern interdisciplinary archaeology — are at the heart of understanding human impacts on the environment (Butzer 1982). Putting all of this together requires the researcher to have a broad scope of understanding and the ability to combine the efforts of many specialists — precisely what characterizes some of the greatest contributions of archaeology. In many ways, we stand at a threshold analogous to archaeology's assault on the origins of agriculture a generation ago, one of the most exciting intellectual challenges ever addressed by our discipline. The subject discussed in this volume is even more compelling. It's a topic that has direct relevance to the survival of modern society, and there are endless archaeological case studies from which to learn. Indeed, understanding the diversity of human environmental impacts, both sustainable and destructive, has the potential to become the hallmark of our discipline. No domain of inquiry is more appropriate for the archaeologist nor more pressing for contemporary society.

This is not an inquiry in which environmental and cultural processes can be examined independently, nor would blaming human environmental impact on some single factor like increasing population, a fuel-hungry technology, or misguided leaders provide sufficient insight. More likely, understanding this complex issue lies in a recognition of how productive strategies, social institutions, and natural environments have *coevolved,* each helping to shape the characteristics of the others (fig. 1.2; van der Leeuw 1998b). The dominant question focuses on the manner in which humans have developed productive strategies to extract sufficient food, commodities, and other resources from the natural environment. What has made humans distinct from other animals is that their productive strategies and organization have been established through social institutions that help regulate and direct human behavior. These institutions are based on the perceived benefits of cooperative action and on ideas shared by their members. Hence, perception is a fundamental aspect of human-environmental relations. The way we perceive the world around us is not uniform for all people at all times, but rather each

Figure 1.2
The context of human-environmental interactions.

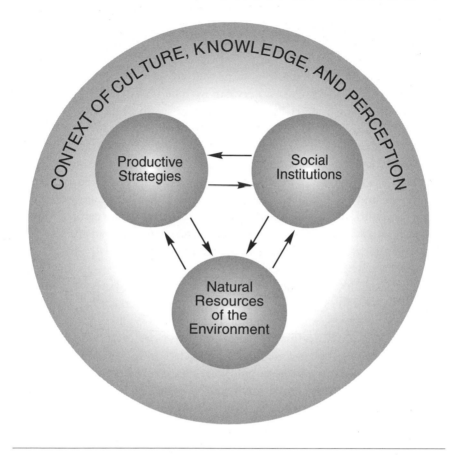

of us sees it in his or her own way. We create a *cognized environment* that is very real to us and is the basis upon which we make decisions. Human-environmental relations cannot be modeled in a strictly mechanistic way on some maximization theory; one must account for the "human" factor. Productive strategies, social institutions, and virtually every human interaction with the environment have been conditioned by the existence of that very uniquely human phenomenon — culture.

The power and poignancy of case studies from the past are made clear by a brief look at the archaeological evidence recently recovered from Easter Island and what it tells us about a society that has captured the popular imagination by its lingering mystery (Diamond 1995; Ponting 1991). The basis of this mystery is the seeming contradiction presented by the enormous stone statutes (moai), which imply a sophisticated prehistoric culture, and the barren, isolated island that supported its inhabitants at the time of European contact in the lowest poverty. The popular knowledge of Easter Island can be traced largely to the book *Kon-Tiki* by Norwegian Thor Heyerdahl, which recounts his voyage from South America to the island some 2000 miles away (1950); and to the more surrealistic account of Swiss writer Erich von Daniken who suggested that the stone statues were evidence of visits by extraterrestrials (1968). The mystery can even be traced back much further, to initial European contact by Dutch explorer Jacob Roggeveen on Easter day in 1722 and a subsequent visit by Captain James Cook 50 years later.

Their accounts recorded an island that was barren grassland without a single tree or bush over ten feet high. There were no sizable native animals and the roughly 2000 inhabitants kept only domestic chickens, grew root crops, and lived in abject poverty. Although their language made these people recognizable as Polynesians, it was clear that by the eighteenth century they had lost the superior knowledge of seafaring that had allowed their ancestors to traverse vast stretches of ocean to reach Easter Island.

Even Roggeveen recognized the basic contradiction — how could the prehistoric inhabitants of this island carve, transport, and erect hundreds of gigantic stone statues without metal tools, without the existence of substantial timber for moving and levering these enormous weights, and without the organizational sophistication to galvanize huge work forces? Even to a lay person the statues implied a very different society from the one encountered by the early explorers. A large population, an advanced prehistoric technology, and a very effective social organization would have been necessary to support the type of activities documented by the existence of the stone statues and the even larger stone platforms on which they were set. What happened to these people, and what happened to the resources that would have been required to support them?

A variety of archaeological discoveries, combined with the ethnohistorical accounts, have allowed us to reconstruct the story of this surprisingly accomplished yet ultimately tragic society. Radiocarbon dates from excavations indicate that around A.D. 400, Polynesian settlers reached Easter Island or, as they called it, Rapanui — an extremely isolated island of 64 square miles area and volcanic origin. One could expect that its soils were sufficiently fertile and its subtropical climate appropriate for an abundant vegetative cover. Palynological research by John Flenley and Sarah King (1984) revealed that the island the Polynesians discovered was in fact richly vegetated with a large palm, *Jubaea,* and a woody tree, *Sophora.* The palm is closely related to the Chilean wine palm, which grows up to 82 feet tall and 6 feet in diameter (Diamond 1995:67), and would have provided an excellent source of timber for constructing buildings, transporting the statues, and serving as levers to erect the statues. They may also have been used to construct seagoing canoes, and their nuts were probably a source of food.

Within a few hundred years of the arrival of people on the island, there is evidence that significant deforestation had occurred, with grasses comprising a greater proportion of the pollen record. Although the settlers had disturbed the natural setting, they had done it in a way that allowed them to thrive for almost a millennium. Nevertheless, their excesses eventually led to dire consequences. Soon after A.D. 1400 the palm became extinct on the island and the other woody species continued to decline to a point where they were virtually absent. In this same period it is likely that the fertility of the island's soils also diminished both from lack of forest nutrients and through erosion of the now exposed soils.

Major sources of food for the settlers were revealed through the zooarchaeological research of David Steadman (1995) and others. Not having any large land mammals and only bringing domestic chickens and, inadvertently, rats with them, the Polynesians turned to the sea and the air for their meat. Unlike settlers on other Polynesian islands where fish from nearby reefs provided the majority of marine food, the Easter Islanders relied more on deep-sea porpoises, which would have required fishing from seaworthy canoes (Diamond 1995:67). Steadman's research shows that before human contact Easter Island was home to a vast array of seabirds. Bones found at the site of Ahu Naunau (A.D. 1050–1300) reveal that even during the early Polynesian occupation, there were 30 species of seabirds, only one of which still nests on Easter Island. Easter Island probably had been the richest seabird-breeding site in Polynesia and perhaps in the entire Pacific. Steadman also found remains of six indigenous land birds, all of which disappeared before European contact. The virtually complete destruction of this rich avifauna for food by the Polynesian settlers was probably aided by the predation of the rats that they had unintentionally introduced onto the island. The impact of a relatively few centuries of human occupation on the vegetation, soils, birds, and invertebrates is one of the most dramatic examples of environmental degradation in the prehistoric record.

What is the story that can be reconstructed with the aid of the recent archaeological discoveries (Bahn and Flenley 1992; Diamond 1995)? Clearly the Polynesian settlers who arrived at Easter Island in about A.D. 400 found an island rich in plant and animal resources. They cleared some of the trees in this parklike environment so they could plant their root crops and build houses. With relatively fertile soil, a rich avifauna, and marine mammals, the settlers prospered and multiplied. Whether only a single party of Polynesians ever reached the island, or their numbers periodically were replenished from outside, the result was a rapidly growing population that by its peak, in about A.D. 1400, numbered 7000 to 10,000 people. During this period they began building large stone platforms, carving huge stone statues (moai), and erecting the statues on the platforms along the coastline. This practice is clearly derived from Polynesian rituals on other islands, but reached new heights on Easter Island. Probably through the competitive emulation of one leader trying to outdo the next, the number and size of these massive works increased until 200 statues had been erected and 700 more were in some stage of preparation. And then in about A.D. 1500 all work on the statues stopped. Decades before, the last of the giant palm trees had been cut down, and perhaps their supply, so necessary for transporting and erecting the statues, had finally run out. At the same time, the consumption of porpoises had ceased, probably because there were no longer trees for the construction of the seagoing canoes that were essential to hunting these sea mammals. Along with the disappearance of the palm, the other tree species virtually ceased to exist, and the soils were exposed to greater wind and water erosion, undermining the horticulture being practiced. The native bird populations had also been radically diminished by then and there is evidence that even the local shellfish were overexploited, so that small sea snails were being eaten instead of the larger cowries that typified the earlier prehistoric levels.

With the diminution of the formerly basic food sources, the inhabitants of the island increased their reliance on their chickens and resorted to what would be considered "famine" foods, such as rats. Numerous human bones found in the late prehistoric levels of these trash middens indicate the strong possibility that cannibalism was also being practiced. As sources of food diminish, so must the ability to support a social elite and to perform rituals that demand huge investments of labor and resources, such as creating the moai. Ethnohistorical accounts indicate that when the former social order broke down, a warrior class emerged and intra-island warfare increased. People abandoned their villages and began to live in caves, and the overall population of the island plummeted to a fraction of its peak numbers. Around A.D. 1700, it is believed that rival groups began to topple each other's standing statues, and the last moai was torn down in 1864. Throughout all of this breakdown, the extreme isolation of Easter Island and the inability of the prehistoric people to navigate long sea voyages without adequate timber and probably requisite seafaring knowledge meant that there was no escape from their situation. The most nagging question is how could these people not have foreseen what was happening and changed their course of action. The once prosperous and noble people of Easter Island were protagonists in one of the most total environmental and social breakdowns recorded in history, yet they appear to have been unable to reverse their fall. The poignancy of this case study in self-destruction is most powerful to those who see this as a model of what is happening in the modern world and a harbinger of a dire future for another isolated island — the "spaceship Earth."

It would be imprudent to jump to conclusions about all human-environmental interactions based on a single experience. The value of archaeology is that it makes available to us not just one, but hundreds of examples of how people have worked with their surroundings. The heart of this book is a series of brief archaeological case studies selected from various parts of the world, that deal with cultural and environmental situations as diverse as the human past itself. These case studies are organized into four chapters (4 through 7) reflecting four major domains of environmental impacts: habitat transformations and animal extinctions, agriculture practices, urban growth, and the forces that accompany complex society. The case studies used in each of these chapters document, in different ways, how archaeological research can provide unique insights into the nature of human stewardship of the earth.

The organizing theme throughout this volume is that humans as individuals, communities, and entire societies are continually making decisions on land use that profoundly affect the condition of the surrounding environment and therefore determine their own future. This theme will be repeatedly treated in subsequent chapters, but figure 1.3 is presented here to provide an overview of the interacting elements of this process. Changes in land use take many forms and are at the center of various human impacts on the environment. The forces that drive this process emanate from a variety of sources, but it is easiest to conceive of them as either from the human environment, such as demand for food and commodities, or from the natural environment, such as climatic change or natural disasters. The decision-makers work within their own context of knowledge of the environment and potential productive strategies in order to determine changes in the land-use system that both meet the demands and are socially appropriate. These changes in land use will have an immediate impact on the land cover and soil conditions. Over time this land-use change will result in more fundamental changes in the landscape and the biogeochemical processes that support it. As this process goes through an initial cycle, the results will lead to further human responses based on a variety of inputs to either expand the scope of the change, intensify it, or abandon it altogether. The objective of presenting case studies from the past is to investigate the long-term implications of how humans have changed their land-use patterns in reaction to various driving

Figure 1.3
Framework for interpreting human transformations of the natural environment.

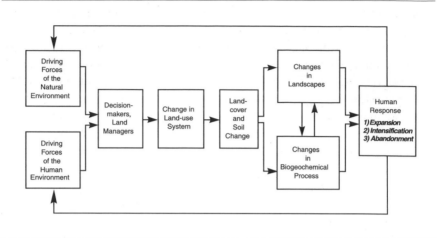

forces. Results of the process modeled in figure 1.3 can be immediate, they may become obvious in a few years, or their true implications may not be apparent for centuries.

The information archaeological case studies contribute to an improved understanding of cultural history is clear and the utility of models to help integrate this information is obvious, yet there are grander objectives behind presenting them in this volume. Taken together, they provide a platform from which to address some very basic questions about human nature and our relationship to other people and to our surroundings. Is there something inherent in the human condition that first allowed us to rise above other species and that now drives us to unreasonably exploit the very environment that sustains us? Or is it a question of fine-tuning: is sustainability really our trajectory, but now and then we fall slightly out of synch and need an adjustment? Or is the environmental crisis not really a crisis at all when seen from a long-term perspective, but a natural process in life's pathway?

While providing a general context of information for the reader to evaluate these fundamental, almost philosophical, issues, this volume will also attempt to provide new insights into a series of more specific concerns about the past and our attempts to understand their implications.

First, light will be shed on a widespread and important misconception that is found regularly in the public press and at least implicitly in the writings of some colleagues: that a natural landscape, untouched by human hands, exists; and that societies before European contact lived in a utopian paradise guided by an unselfish conservationist ethic (Baleé 1998a). This European premise that an Eden-like nature existed was based largely on the belief that native peoples, particularly in the Americas, did not share in the biblical fall from grace (Pyne 1998:98). Discussion of these notions opens a larger, philosophical issue — Is there a best, perfect condition for the world? If there can be a perfect world, did it exist in pre-human antiquity until humans debased it or, through continual progress, are humans in fact building this perfect world?

Second, many of the studies in the following chapters demonstrate that human impacts in antiquity, not just climatic changes, have led to significant environmental alterations. The archaeological literature is replete with discussions of settlement and regional abandonment that are attributed to climatic changes that undermined the productive suitability of an area. Without denying the significance of climatic change, it is imperative to understand the role humans have played in altering the environment.

Third, many contemporary environmental studies, particularly in academic settings, focus on the interaction of organisms and their physical surroundings, purposefully avoiding human involvement. This is largely because the researchers do not have the time depth or other experimental controls that would allow meaningful interpretations that include the complexity of human interaction. Archaeological information offers the exciting potential of numerous case studies of the full suite of human-biological-physical interactions over sufficient time depth to allow meaningful conclusions through the experimental approach of controlled observation.

Fourth, this volume provides an essential reference point for further study by documenting the human activities and decisions that led to sustainable situations or to environmental degradation at various points in the past. Much of this is tied to the introduction of agriculture in its multitudinous manifestations. Land clearing, stock grazing, and plant cultivation all had direct and indirect impacts that must be understood in their ecological contexts. At the beginning of each chapter, background information is provided for examining some of the key components of human-environmental interactions and for understanding the contexts within which crucial actions were made.

Fifth, human-environmental interactions and the decisions that conditioned these interactions are examined, to better understand why people frequently adopted strategies that may have made sense in the short term, but had dire long-term consequences. If my reading of the archaeological record is correct, this seemingly self-destructive situation occurs repeatedly — individuals, groups, and entire societies make decisions that initially are productive and logical, but over time have negative and sometimes disastrous environmental implications. What are the cultural filters and institutional frameworks that again and again appear to have inhibited otherwise highly successful societies and people of great creativity and intelligence from accurately perceiving the problems that beset them and acting to remedy them in a timely fashion?

Before embarking on a review of the archaeological evidence, it is important that the reader have a context within which to situate this information. Society's attitude toward the environment and the analytical perspectives used by researchers have profound impacts on the way information is collected and interpreted. Chapter 2 examines attitudes toward the environment from both historical and cross-cultural perspectives. It is important for the reader to recognize what attitudes were prevalent when research was conducted, because they may influence the objectives of the investigation and the nature of interpretation. More important, attitudes also condition one's personal view on the material and one's judgment of what is a negative or positive impact of human actions. Chapter 3 presents a brief and general overview of terms, concepts, and models that ecologists, archaeologists, and environmentalists use to investigate and understand the material we will be dealing with. Some of the processes key to understanding the operation of ecosystems are introduced. These may provide the readers with models for their own interpretation of the archaeological case studies presented.

2
Attitudes toward the Environment

From the earliest times and in all cultures around the world people have developed attitudes toward their surroundings—the world they live in. These attitudes certainly change over time and at any one time not all members of a society may share a common vision. Attitudes are a difficult domain to discuss, particularly those of the past, because our database is largely from written texts that might have a unique perspective and not be representative of the greater society. Nevertheless, it is possible to speak about normative views that were held by many and influenced the behavior of the society at large. Because attitudes shape all of our thinking—past and present—it is imperative that we consider this issue and its implications with whatever information is available.

This examination borders on philosophy or even religion and hence I will attempt not to champion any particular perspective as the correct one, but rather only to emphasize the importance of attitudes in shaping action in the past as well as in the present. My objective is to put forward a variety of ideas for consideration so that readers can build their own contexts within which to examine the evidence of the past and consider its meaning. An understanding of one's own perspective allows one to work with the insights that the past provides in order to draw conclusions about important aspects of the human career and choices that we now face.

To provide structure to this potentially ethereal discussion of attitudes, I first look at the historical development of attitudes towards the environment among Western Civilizations, then I give consideration to attitudes prevalent in non-Western societies, and I conclude with an examination of contemporary views on the environment. While proceeding through this discussion within a temporal and geographic framework, I will also focus the discussion on the evolution of a limited number of central ideas:

[first, whether the world was created in a "perfect" form; second, to what extent have the characteristics of the environment shaped humans and their cultures; and third, to what extent have we reshaped the world from its "pristine" condition (Simmons 1989:3).]

The first idea, that we live in an exquisitely well-designed world, one that was especially well suited for the human species, is a very old and pervasive notion. This idea is often expressed in religious writings where the purpose of the creation cannot be easily explained rationally, but is best considered as divinely sanctioned. Virtually all cultures have some version of a creation myth and in it the world and its inhabitants are carefully designed for each other. The designed world concept comes not only from religious writings, but also has some basis in the fundamental assumptions of some scientific disciplines. The holistic framework employed by many life scientists when they discuss ecology or evolution has an underlying theme of the unity and balance of the world. To the scientist the utility of this assumption is borne out by empirical examination, although it is constantly changing as new information is collected. Despite the transitory details, there is a general scientific recognition that our environment is highly evolved and specialized and that its present condition is extremely well suited to the survival of humans. It is almost inconceivable for us to have derived our sustenance from organisms of the distant past or survived without the complex populations of microorganisms that break down organic wastes. The seemingly orderly cycling of material and energy by plants, animals, and physical processes forces even the most skeptical scientist to occasionally consider the "divine" plan of nature.

The second idea, the influence of the environment on humans and their cultures, has a very strong basis in Western intellectual scholarship. As is discussed below, scientists and lay people alike have used this idea as a means of explaining the staggering array of human cultures and biological differences. Thomas Malthus (1878) saw the environment as setting limits on human population growth, while Ellsworth Huntington (1934) expanded this concept to a fuller environmental determinism, in which the characteristics of the environment directed which pathway local social development would follow. This viewpoint was given an operational mechanism by Arnold Toynbee (1934), who wrote a history of the world in which cultural change could be best understood as a series of human responses to environmental challenges.

The third idea, humans as modifiers of the environment, sees nature as a set of resources to be used to satisfy human demands. From this viewpoint the creation of the world was incomplete, and humans are to finish the task by developing nature's potential for human sustenance and other human-defined goals. This perspective is very consistent with modern industrialism and economic development theories.

Western Attitudes toward the Environment

With these three ideas in mind, let us turn to the seminal document of early Western thinking: the Old Testament and, in particular, its story of creation. The Bible provides a profoundly symbolic account of the act of creation, defining relations between humans and their surroundings, and thereby granting humankind a privileged status in the hierarchy of life (Hillel 1991:4–16). As is often the case in the Old Testament, there is more than one account of the same event (two in this case), and when the early versions of the Bible were codified, it was deemed appropriate to include both. Even 3000 years ago, there was some ambiguity as to what our relationship to the environment should be.

In the first account, God created man in his own image and "let him rule over the fish of the sea, fowl of the air, and over the cattle and over all the earth . . . and God blessed man and woman and said unto them: be fruitful, and multiply, and fill the earth and conquer it and rule over it . . . here, I have given you every herb yielding seed and every tree with fruit. . . . to you it shall be for food." In this version God is seen as creating humans with the intention that they should dominate the earth and use everything in it for their own purposes.

In the generally accepted version of the Bible, there then follows a second account of roughly the same event. In this act of creation, "God formed man out of the soil of the earth and blew breath of life into him . . . and God planted a garden in Eden and placed man therein and God took man and put him in the garden of Eden to serve and preserve it" (fig. 2.1). In this passage, humans are clearly given the responsibility to nurture and protect God's creation; that is, to be stewards of the environment (ibid.:12). Thus, in what is probably the most important source of Western ethics and law (let alone religion), there are two very different depictions of the human role: first, the anthropocentric — man above nature — and second, that man is made of soil — not set above nature. Moreover, in this second telling, the power of humans is constrained by duty and responsibility. The earth is not their property, rather they are its custodians, entrusted with the stewardship of the garden.

Interestingly, in the Bible, humans quickly abused their responsibility and were exiled from the garden and condemned to a life of toil. To the extent that they were to be stewards to nature, our progenitors failed, yet in

Figure 2.1
Adam and Eve in the Garden of Eden, from a fifteenth-century manuscript. Courtesy of the Bodleian Library, University of Oxford, MS. Douce 336, fol. 6r.

the Bible they were eventually forgiven. The overriding message is that as long as humans maintain their spiritual purity, they should be successful, multiply, and take advantage of the earth's resources.

In balance, the Judeo-Christian tradition is strongly anthropocentric. The plants and animals, the earth and the seas are all planned by God for the benefit of humans, and no item in the physical creation had any purpose except to serve human needs (White 1967:1205). From that time forward individuals have claimed that it is God's will that they multiply freely and exploit nature for society's self-determined goals. The dualism of humans and nature is a consistent theme in later religious teachings as is human dominance over nature.

The growth of Christianity in the West, where it strongly followed the doctrine of the duality of humans and nature, replaced a pagan world defined by Greeks, Romans, and others. The local religious traditions of these great civilizations had bestowed upon places in the environment a special significance. Every tree, hill, and spring had its own guardian spirit, spirits that were accessible to common people and took the form of centaurs, fauns, and mermaids. Before taking an action that would affect a natural element, one had to placate the spirit. By destroying this pagan animism, Christianity made it possible to exploit nature in a mood of indifference to the natural objects (White 1967:1205). Nevertheless, religiously based ideas of "right from wrong" and "the sanctity of all living creatures" maintain a strong currency in contemporary society. In a recent survey of Americans from various walks of life, a strong majority of people felt that all creatures have a "right to exist" and more implicitly that there is a divinely created order that humans should not disturb (Kempton, Boster, and Hartley 1995:87–94).

Several lines of thinking relevant to the environment can be traced from Judeo-Christian and pagan origins to Greek and Roman literature and philosophy, important sources of later Western ideas (Glacken 1956). Primary among these is the often repeated concept of the "lost golden age" when the earth was more bountiful, the soils of Greece were more fertile, and life was better. This notion includes a pregolden age, when the "savage" world was tamed by people who cut the forests and planted the fields. In the golden age, people were more orderly and less intrusive than during the Classical and Hellenistic periods of Greek history when these ideas were being written down.

A second Greek concept derived from an interest in the "cycles" of nature and humans, and the "design" of nature in which all things had their proper place. This interest led easily to a dominant theme of Greek philosophy that "man is the measure of all things." As Cicero said in *Nature of the Gods*, "man, as the highest being in the scale, changes nature by using his

19

hands, with which, guided by the intellect, he has created the art of agriculture and the techniques of fishing, animal domestication, mining, clearing and navigation ... we are the absolute masters of what the earth produces ... we endeavor, by our various operation in this world, to make as it were, another Nature."

The Greeks, and the Romans after them, had a clear grasp of the notion that long-term farming often led to impoverishment. The early years in which the vast tracts of land were brought under intensive agriculture were clearly more productive than after generations of use. They also were quite sophisticated about techniques to increase agricultural production and to conserve soil fertility. Fallow periods, manuring, and terracing steep slopes were all well known to them. In fact, through investments in these techniques, especially terracing, during the Roman period, the Holy Land reached its highest population until the second half of the twentieth century.

The massive alteration of the landscape by Roman agrarian techniques lessened with the fall of its Empire and the political fragmentation of Europe and the Mediterranean. In many regions overall settled population decreased as the scale of farming diminished and efforts at major land transforming projects became almost nonexistent. Ethically, most of Europe turned to the Church as the center of life, and attitudes toward virtually everything were conditioned by Christian beliefs. At least among the intellectuals, nature was seen as the divine creation of God, and hence, its study might reveal further proofs of the wisdom of God. This attitude assumed various manifestations by late medieval times. Some people sought to show how perfect the world was; in particular, that the distribution of living things was too complex to have occurred by chance alone. Others emphasized that all forms of life had their proper place in this world order, with humans at the pinnacle and with a concomitant responsibility to be caretaker. Those who accepted the caretaker role over the divine aspects of nature promoted the setting aside of sacred groves, a practice that receives little comment in more critical reviews of Christian attitudes. Others accepted their ordained role to improve upon the primeval art of nature through landscaping, the epitome being the formal gardens of European estates.

For the empirically inclined of late Medieval and early Renaissance times, science meant studying nature to unravel the magnificence of the divine creation. To understand how nature operates was seen as one means of coming closer to understanding the workings of God's mind. Major scientists such as Galileo and Newton considered themselves theologians more than scientists, with their major goal to "think God's thoughts after him" (White 1967:1206). This marriage of science and religion was not altogether successful, as witnessed by the sad fate of Galileo, whose discoveries inadvertently led him to be considered a heretic by some of the more conservative elements in the Church.

Eventually, intellectuals such as Sir Francis Bacon sought to separate scientific from religious inquiry. He saw humans living in a world — which they could change and improve — where the order and beauty of nature could be seen everywhere, but much of it was actually at the hand of humans, such as farmed fields, vast orchards, and created landscapes. The Renaissance redirected people from viewing the world through God, to viewing the natural world directly. Thus, people began to understand the rationality of the natural world and were better able to utilize it for their own ends. As people developed insights into the operation of the world, technology became a dominant theme in Western society, and progress, which included increasingly harnessing natural resources for human good, became our goal.

The eighteenth and nineteenth centuries were spectacular years for the advancement of natural history disciplines. Europeans were exploring the natural world in all of its geographical variation and detail. Syntheses such as those of Charles Lyell and Charles Darwin put a rational order to this immense diversity. Notwithstanding Copernicus's discovery, and the burgeoning of natural historic inquiry, the dominant thinking of Western civilization during the nineteenth century was that humans were above nature, and there was a faith in perpetual progress. People still felt that the cosmos rotated around their little globe, and despite Darwin, that they were not, in their hearts, part of the natural scene. To use the simplest terms, most people had adopted a *utilitarian* view of nature, in which nature provided resources that were to be used to best advantage by humans. Nature was analogous to a machine, a complex operation of physical forces without value of its own (Westoff 1983:15).

It would be too facile and cynical to suggest that all Western civilization evolved in a tradition that viewed nature in a strictly utilitarian manner. Religious ideas, philosophical discourse, scientific paradigms, and lay perspectives have revealed multiple and often conflicting attitudes toward the proper relation of humans and their environment. The seeds of modern attitudes toward the environment are found in these diverse ideas and their apparent contradictions. Acknowledging that utilitarianism was the dominant trend in historical thinking, it is still useful to highlight the premodern origin of at least three *conservationist* ideas (Westoff 1983:16). The first is *man's unity with nature*, an idea often associated with Eastern religions or indigenous peoples, but one that also had a strong following in Western society. We can look back as far as the Middle Ages when Saint Francis of Assisi suggested that humans were not paramount and that there should be a democracy of all God's creatures, all of whom had souls (White 1967:1206–

1207). One can also trace to Darwin and others a strong nineteenth century scientific endorsement of humans being solely a strand in a web, a part of a far more inclusive ecosystem that considered all living organisms to be just as *highly evolved* as humans. The idea of man's unity with nature can be seen in many of America's great early writers, but is probably nowhere more evident than in Thoreau, who valued and respected nature to the point where it was virtually a religion.

The second conservationist tradition prevalent in Western thinking and action was *stewardship*, an idea as old and important as the Bible. As we discussed above, in the Book of Genesis the second account of creation sees God creating animals to be companions of man and instructing him to manage and protect the Garden of Eden and all of the creatures in it. Stewardship clearly flies in the face of limitless exploitation, but it did have early adherents in the West, as well as elsewhere. Many ethical ideas held in ancient times considered nature not as one's private property, but either as something communally held or, for some aspects of nature, as not held at all by humans (Black 1970:46). As we will see later in this chapter, the notion of stewardship becomes the key to early American conservationists such as John Muir and George Marsh.

The third conservationist tradition, *human cooperation with nature*, certainly emanates from the stewardship notion, but can lead to diverse attitudes toward the use of nature. These include wanting to bring nature to perfection, returning it to a former state, enhancing its ecological diversity, and transforming it to a greater level of productivity for exploitation. These attitudes embody a respect for nature, but also an acceptance of the notion that human presence involves intervention. People can interpret this in radically different manners, but the basic premise of this notion is that people want their surroundings to be of maximum benefit. To some this would involve agrarian transformations, to others it might involve designation of a sacred grove, while to yet others it might mean reforestation. The key here is what condition was perceived as yielding the maximum benefit. Although it receives less attention in environmental literature, I believe this attitude of cooperation with nature is in fact the dominant theme in Western and probably most other societies. That we are neither an unfettered master nor an equal participant in the natural order is a perspective we will return to frequently in this volume.

An interesting exemplification of the range of attitudes of cooperation that exist can be seen in the world's gardens (Westoff 1983:19). A garden closely reflects the owner's vision of the potentials of the environment and the social values associated with it. The seventeenth century French nobility's attitude was to impose a formal geometric order on their gardens, which had straight lines, artificially shaped plants, and a sense of spatial balance and precision. In the eighteenth and nineteenth century English landscape gardens, one took natural features and plants and worked with them, improving their composition, but still retaining an overall vision of their natural setting. A strongly contrasting attitude toward nature can be seen in the Zen gardens of Japan where simplicity is treasured and the nonessential elements, such as wild plants, are eliminated. And then there is the Americans' avocational vegetable garden, which likely does not have as old a lineage as the others, but clearly represents an important attitude toward what the environment ought to be, even when one's lifestyle has long since ceased to include food production.

Non-Western Attitudes toward the Environment

Many critics in modern Western society are anxious to contrast the aggressive, exploitative attitude toward nature of their own society with the harmonious relationships reported for other times and other places. A survey of non-Western religious and philosophical thought would surely reveal many societies where harmony with nature is a priority, where natural entities are sacred and protected, and where living an austere life without transgressing on nature is respected. Often in these societies a oneness with nature is emphasized or even that past or future human spirits are embodied in specific plants or animals and hence must be respected.

China is often presented by critics of the West as having an alternate way of going about things. Chinese ethical thought that derives from Buddhist and Taoist traditions sees humans as part of nature and living in harmony with it. However, closer inspection reveals that in China, as in other countries, the publicly espoused ethical traditions seldom cover more than a fraction of the total range of attitudes and practices of its citizens pertaining to the environment (Tuan 1970:244). There are ancient literary references to an old tradition of forest care in China, but it is clear that the concern arose in response to damage that had already occurred due to human action. In the play of competing forces that govern the world, aesthetic and religious ideals are tremendously important, but so are a whole suite of pragmatic considerations that may ultimately override them.

China's religious traditions emphasized a quiescent and adaptive approach toward nature and other life forms. Harmonizing with one's surroundings was recommended as the proper path. Animistic beliefs and Taoist nature philosophy are at the foundation of the Chinese adaptive attitude toward the environment, and they alone might have produced a sequestered utopia. With her tranquil gardens and temple grounds, however, China also was a civilization with a growing population, a vast bureaucracy, and militaristic empires. Male dominance was fundamental and territorial conquest and engineering feats were revered. It should not be surprising that despite philosophical support for preserving forests and sanctifying the land, the demands of growing cities, industries, and the religious elite and their temples themselves led to the despoiling of the land. We have written evidence that by 1000 years ago the cities of the North required clearing of vast lands for farming, huge amounts of lumber for building, and fuel for industry and the domestic hearths. The archaeological evidence is only now being collected, but it is likely that we will find substantial evidence of deforestation and soil erosion in the northern provinces as early as the Anyang Dynasty some 3500 years ago. Hence, we know that well before Western influence affected China, at least the heartland of her civilization in the north suffered from deforestation in the highlands and the accompanying soil erosion. The conflict between social attitudes and the pragmatic consideration of fuel, food, and growth is as old as civilization and a theme we will frequently return to in this book.

(Rather than thinking of the dichotomy of attitudes as being Western/non-Western, perhaps we should conceptualize it as large-scale versus small-scale societies / If we look at the many examples of small-scale societies studied by anthropologists, ranging from the Australian aborigines, to the island Polynesians, to the American Indian societies, we will repeatedly find humans seen as a part of nature on a par with the animals. The dominant theme is *mutuality*; that is, existing under a moral order that binds together humans, nature, and sometimes even the gods into one family (Spoehr 1956:97). Nature offered provisions to humans, but their extraction was to be judicious and their treatment was to be respectful. In small-scale societies, the concept of ownership of property or the production of a surplus were poorly developed or only seen as acting at a community-wide level.

I would argue strongly that these ideas and conditions were not limited to non-Western societies, but also were prevalent in the small-scale predecessors of Western civilization. Clearly, it is easier to adhere to the notion of peace with nature when populations are low and settlements widely scattered and able to move about frequently. Yet, even with these altruistic intentions and the modest demands of small-scale societies, I do not believe that harmony was always their means of operation. Just as we know of periodic and serious social rifts in small-scale societies, past evidence also reveals cases of environmental degradation. Were impacts of these cases serious and enduring, or are we looking at exceptions in an otherwise harmonious way of life? Part of the aim of this volume will be to examine the archaeological record for new evidence to provide an answer to these questions.

Contemporary Views toward the Environment

Many of the ethical notions we associate most closely with small-scale and non-Western societies' attitudes have become a part of the overall attitude held by many individuals in the modern world. They are integral parts of the attitudes that gave birth to national conservation movements in the nineteenth century and to our own modern environmental movement. However, the overriding attitude toward the environment that emerged in early modern times in the West and has been adopted by most, if not all, countries around the world is one of *use of the environment for the maximum benefit of humankind.* The most obvious consequence of this attitude has been economic exploitation for agriculture, industry, and urban space. The prevailing attitude of the nineteenth and twentieth centuries was of the endless bounty of nature and the ability of humans through ingenuity and technology to overcome any problems that might arise from their actions.

Yet, even at the times of great emphasis in America on industrialization and expansionism, such as the mid-nineteenth century, there have been powerful advocates of a greater concern for the environmental implications of our action. George Perkins Marsh was just such an individual and is considered by many to be the father of the modern environmental movement (fig. 2.2). George Marsh was raised in early nineteenth century New England and was a keen observer of the changes that people had brought about in the forested hills and valleys of the countryside (Thomas 1956:xxxviii). Marsh maintained this interest in human modification of the earth's surface throughout his illustrious career as a lawyer, member of the U.S. Congress, and minister to Turkey and Italy. His seminal contribution was the compilation of his observations in America and abroad in a book, *Man and Nature,* published in 1864. Marsh put forth his idea that humans were a dynamic force and were often irrational in their treatment of the environment. They endangered themselves by this behavior, because it threatened to destroy their base of subsistence. One of Marsh's main objectives was to show that, far from being impotent and without choice, humans were free agents working independently of nature. It was not the earth that made humans, but humans who made the earth.

Marsh was a practical man and interested in solutions. He advocated moderation in exploitative activities and the development of a new

Figure 2.2
Portrait of George Perkins Marsh, by Mathew Brady. Courtesy of the Library of Congress, LC-BH8201-4981.

morality with respect to the use of the earth's resources. To him one solution was to set aside a certain portion of the land to remain forever in forest. Perhaps even more prescient was his proposal that before land-transforming activities be undertaken, it was important to ascertain the probable effects of the action. *Man and Nature* was widely read at the time and continued to be influential in certain circles, but in the society at large, Marsh was not able to change the dominant, exploitative, American attitude toward the environment. *Man and Nature* was the first great work of synthesis that examined in detail how humans had altered the face of the earth. In its own way it helped define the future agenda of environmentalism, but another century passed before many of his pleas were taken up in earnest.

One symbol of the reemergence of interest in Marsh's ideas was the convening of an international symposium in 1954 that gave rise to the preeminent environmental book, *Man's Role in Changing the Face of the Earth* (Thomas 1956). The two volumes of this book comprise contributions from dozens of scholars representing many disciplines who were asked to evaluate the global situation in their specialty. Its chapters laid the foundation for virtually every thrust in environmental studies and the modern environmental movement. Its table of contents reads like a list of the issues that now confront us.

Carl Sauer, one of the organizers of the *Man's Role in Changing the Face of the Earth* symposium and considered by many to be the father of modern American geography, carried many of Marsh's ideas into the midtwentieth century. He believed that "every human population, at all times, has needed to evaluate the economic potential of its inhabited area, to organize its life about its natural environment in terms of the skills available to it and the values which it accepts" (1956:49). A basic proposition of Sauer's was that "built into the biologic nature of man were qualities tending to maximize geographic expansiveness, vigorous reproduction, and the bent toward social development" (ibid.:49).

Conceptually, many of the preceding controversies can be reduced to a duality of perspectives—nature versus culture. The key question that has confounded philosophers and scientists alike is whether we, as humans with our culture, are a part of nature or whether nature, as sensed through human perception, is a construct of human culture. I do not intend to offer an answer to that question; in fact, I am not sure there is a single acceptable answer. Nevertheless, where one lies along this continuum of views, from the dominance of nature to that of culture, will condition one's interpretation of the world about us and how it should be managed. In order to move forward with the presentations in this volume without accepting either extreme position, I have chosen to focus on the intersection of these two domains: culture-nature interactions. At the same time I find it necessary to acknowledge at least a minimal level of credence to both positions. That is, first, nature exists as a functioning entity independent of its human perception; and second, nature takes on meaning only through the act of human perception. The second position implies that humans may operate in a manner significantly different from all other living creatures, particularly when it comes to decision-making concerning their relationship to the environment.

Even by the middle of the twentieth century, most scholars, and certainly the lay public, were still regarding nature and culture as separate entities or opposing forces, rather than as interlocking components of a single system. Yet, at least for the academic community, human-environmental relations were becoming a central focus of study. For the public, humans were still seen as acting in response to nature or even as having their futures determined by changes in the environment. The former viewpoint was particularly useful to those who sought a perpetually expanding economy and believed that the application of science and technology could meet all emergencies.

It was not until well into the second half of the twentieth century that the public also embraced environmental studies as crucially important and that environmental scholars began to perceive of humans as integral elements in a total natural system. This approach, often termed _human ecology,_ was championed by anthropologists as well as geographers (Steward 1955; Sears 1956; Bennett 1976; Netting 1977; Moran 1990). There were some differences among these scholars: some saw humans as part of a grander natural system, while others conceived of nature as part of a larger human system. Although their emphases were different, the overall thrust of their studies, that people were active participants in the natural system, was shared by all. The concept of _human adaptation_ — that is, what people want and how they go about getting it and what effects this has on themselves and on nature — became central for anthropologists. These studies usually focused on subsistence pursuits, settlement mobility, and social organization that each functioned to promote the success of the community.

It was a logical next step for archaeologists who pursued human ecology to adopt a diachronic, or historical perspective, an approach that some referred to as _historical ecology._ This term was probably first used to signify interdisciplinary research of biologists and archaeologists (Rice 1996), but in recent years it is becoming associated with a multidisciplinary perspective that focuses on the landscape (Crumley 1994b; Baleé 1998b). Historical ecology's central subject is long-term regional processes, but it acknowledges that processes operate at varying temporal and spatial scales (see also Braudel 1972; Adams 1977, 1978). The approach draws heavily on the spatial analysis of geography and the historical contextualism of anthropology to provide what promises to be an exciting way to look at the past.

Many contemporary anthropologists follow the lead of John Bennett, who originally conceptualized the history of human-environmental relationships as a growing absorption of the physical environment into the cognitively defined world of human events and actions. Hence, humans are constantly engaged in seizing natural phenomena, converting them into cultural objects, and reinterpreting them with cultural ideas (1976:4). There is little question that prehistoric societies developed their own system for understanding the operation of the environment, as do indigenous peoples today. Anthropologists refer to this as ethnoscience or folk science and often find that indigenous people have a very detailed knowledge of the world about them (Posey 1998). While the empirical, observational knowledge of these people was usually quite precise, the causal and explanatory statements were more based on cultural belief systems than they were on what we now accept as scientific principles. Although few would contest the advances in our scientific understanding of the operation of the environment, it is important to recognize that popular interpretations of ecology even today are not completely congruent with scientific principles and were surely more strongly influenced by cultural norms in the past.

Looking at contemporary models of nature provides insight into our own ways of interpreting data and making decisions, possibly revealing some attitudes that might have guided peoples in the past as well. Recent survey research indicates that Americans hold a series of cultural models related to the environment that are not entirely consistent with modern science. Anthropologists Kempton, Boster, and Hartley have identified three models that were widespread among the people they interviewed (1995:39–62). The first implies that humans are part of the environment, we depend on it, and this planet is limited in size. Because of its limited size, things we do to it will come back to haunt us and perhaps endanger our health. The second type of model portrays the interdependency of species and conditions, wherein changing one might cause damage to others. Kempton, Boster, and Hartley argue that this belief in the "balance of nature" is widely held and surprisingly consistent with modern ecological principles. The third widely held model suggests that nature has become separated from the main currents of modern society and is no longer appropriately valued by it.

Culturally derived systems of knowledge of the environment can be translated into very specific understandings that often lead to ill-founded actions. For example, culturally constructed understandings of global warming, greenhouse gases, and air pollution have led to potentially dangerous ideas held by contemporary Americans. Some of the popularly held notions that are not scientifically sound and that may lead to further problems if acted upon are as follows (ibid.:63–77): (1) pollution consists only of artificial chemicals, not natural substances; (2) pollution is fixed by installing additional filtering equipment; (3) global warming results from ozone depletion; and (4) global warming is caused by air pollution. These misunderstandings arose in a society where there are many outlets with easily understood science available. Imagine how much easier it was for popular, folk models of the environment to be misconstrued in the past.

The anthropological insight, that humans put interpretations and values on aspects of the environment by bringing them into their frame of reference, does not deny the equality of humans and other elements in the natural world, but it clearly gives humans a primacy in defining the world and what is happening to it. This book employs a *human-centered perspective,* because even if all participants in the natural system have equal value and act on their own behalf, we as humans must act on the world around us using our own attitudes, knowledge, and values to understand the situation and devise solutions to current problems. This is what makes it important for us to consider the evolution of human attitudes toward the environment as we have done in this chapter and to consider contemporary views held by the lay public, as I will continue to do below.

Much that is still in popular thought about the environment took shape during what some have called the environmental crusade of the late 1960s (Mikesell 1974). This crusade was part of a bigger social movement that included other issues such as civil rights, antiwar, gender equality, and overall distrust of the establishment. Each of these issues progressed on its own merits, but each also took on momentum by being part of the larger social upheaval. For the environment, the culminating event was the first Earth Day in April of 1970. There was a very immediate quality about the environmental crusade: people had never faced problems before that were a result of the mistakes of modern urban and industrial society. The problems were not looked at as having developed over time, as we now know they did, but as having sprung full blown into world-class calamities.

This environmental movement gave rise to several widely accepted attitudes that shaped many people's thinking on all environmental issues and continue to condition the perspectives of many (Mikesell 1974). First, the *doomsday theme* anticipated that the environmental disasters were of such vast scope that the very survival of the human species was threatened. Something had to be done immediately to avert this *crisis.* Second, Americans in particular and urban-industrial society in general were responsible for this planetary crisis and hence were *guilty.* Third, society was *wasteful* and our natural resources were being depleted at an alarming rate. This led to the logical emphasis on recycling, a very powerful proposal because it was some-thing that could be done by individuals, in the home. The fourth attitude that affected many people's thinking was the idea of *spaceship Earth*; that is, we live in a fragile system where the atmosphere and other elements of the biosphere are limited and closely interdependent.

Some solutions were proposed, most of which required radical changes, and some of which have actually taken hold in limited areas. The most fundamental demand was for people, especially Americans, to change their lifestyles by reexamining their endless need for material goods. The American Indian, "who used only according to his needs," was offered as an ideal, and Americans were admonished to reconsider whether a "simpler" life would be preferable to the demands of current standards of living. In-stead of changing our standard of living to conserve, however, we found conservationist measures that accommodated our standards, such as curb-side recycling, low-flow toilets, and carpool lanes on freeways. Overall re-source conservation was aided by industries that saw their own economic benefit in this type of conservation and by the Oil Embargo of the mid-1970s that led to the sharp increase in the price of oil and other raw materials.

Growing numbers of people were also seen as a threat to the world and the *zero population growth* movement was born. It was not hard for many to see that a burgeoning population exacerbated the problems of con-sumption and limited resources. Happily, the people of many countries have responded to this, and among segments of the population, overall growth has slowed significantly. (There are other factors involved in the slowing of popu-lation growth in certain areas and its acceleration in others that we will treat in more detail in Chapter 7.)

Earth Day 1970 and what followed set the basic environmental agenda that we still strive toward. Over time the immediacy and crusade aspect of the movement diminished, especially with the growing recogni-tion that environmental problems are exceedingly complex and some of them may never be solved. But the basic message of the movement is still strong. We must do whatever it takes to ensure the survival of our species on this planet. The environmental movement is no longer restricted to anti-establishment demonstrators, with various aspects of it having been taken up by politicians representing all shades of the political spectrum, as well as by the people who control business and industry. But the word envi-ronmentalism means very different things to each of them. Surveys tell us that foremost in the minds of most Americans are environmental actions that will preserve community health, through improvements in air and wa-ter quality and the control of hazardous materials (Kempton, Boster, and Hartley 1995:202–207). Next in importance comes an environment that is aesthetically pleasing and suitable for recreation and learning. And finally, it would be good to preserve the biodiversity of the world's living species for medical, aesthetic, and ethical reasons.

Recognizing the interaction between the continued functioning of ecosystems throughout the world and human decisions based to a great extent on economics, a group of scholars and policy makers have been developing a perspective they refer to as "ecological economics" (Costanza 1996; Costanza et. al. 1997; Prugh 1995). Their approach is to develop complex models of ecosystems that take into account the many human-environmental interactions. The shortcoming they see in most economic models used by business and government is that they do not take into account the "real costs" of environmental impacts, such as the replacement of raw materials extracted or the disposal of industrial wastes. The "ecological economists" assert that for the economy of the world to be sustainable, these costs must be accounted for. They also argue that the economic benefits of the operation of the system must be more equally distributed to all people. Whereas most policy makers view the economy (i.e., manufactured capital) as the dominant force to be considered, this new perspective has demonstrated that the ecosystem is a much larger player than most think in contributing to the economic productivity of the world (fig. 2.3).

Just as the environmental movement has attracted backers of all types, it has also prompted backlashes both inside and outside of the movement. The most obvious backlash is from those who see their economic objectives curtailed by the movement. Restrictions on real estate development, logging, mining, grazing, and virtually all forms of publicly sponsored development has angered those most affected. In the struggle of economic prosperity versus preserving aspects of the environment, people come down on both sides. Environmental regulations by government have also engendered a strong backlash from those who see them as the most egregious aspect of creeping government control and the loss of their personal freedoms. These people may not be suffering economic harm, but they bristle against the intrusion of government in their personal lives.

There is also a backlash here and abroad that can be attributed to the fact that environmental preservation and regulation may affect citizens of different countries (or different segments of one country) quite differently. We in America may ask Brazilians not to cut down the rain forest, but they are seeking grazing land for their cattle. We ask other countries to install expensive machinery to minimize industrial pollution when they are already not competitive in the world market. To some, the environment has become a means for the currently industrialized world to keep the under-developed countries in their place. And to some it has also become another

Figure 2.3
Alternate viewpoints on the relative importance of the economy and the ecosystem (adapted from Costanza et al. 1997).

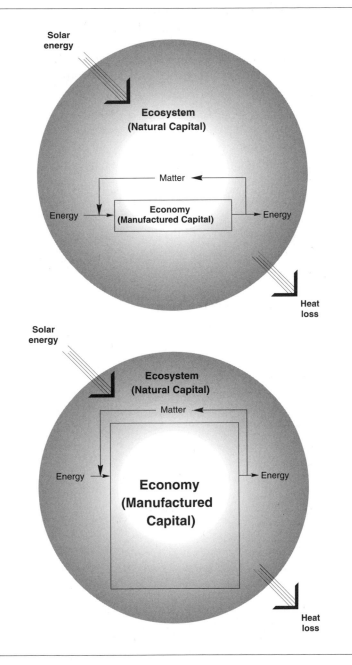

form of racism within our own country, with the ills of environmental degradation being born most heavily by already disadvantaged segments of our population.

This brings us to a very big issue that has no resolution but should be considered by every individual contemplating the condition of the environment and action to *preserve* it. What is an *ideal* environment, or even, what can be done to *improve* the environment are certainly not questions that would be answered the same way by all people. Our perception of the environment is conditioned by our attitude toward it, and our attitudes are influenced by many of the ideas discussed in this chapter and by many factors in an individual's own life. How important are long-term issues to us when they conflict with more immediate needs? What do we consider beauty, value, and meaning in the world around us? These are very personal issues and lead to attitudes as diverse as the people who hold them. Natural landscapes and pristine habitats are of immeasurable beauty to many of us, but what actually constitutes a *natural* landscape or a *pristine* habitat? What about the beauty in wheat fields or hills covered with grapevines or an endless highway? These issues have no simple answers, but they are at the very core of our environmental future. They are not new issues, and in some form they must have been faced repeatedly throughout human history. Hence we will revisit them many times in this volume.

3
Concepts That Organize
Our Thoughts

Just as we must recognize that attitudes shape the way we view a problem, we should also be aware that to understand and solve a problem, we must employ concepts to organize the complexity of the real world into manageable units. These concepts not only simplify and give names to the intricacies of nature, but also incorporate some of the basic means by which the world operates. This chapter defines concepts that allow us to better communicate about the environment and explains some of the basic operating principles of nature.

Who are the participants in this drama of human-environmental interactions that this volume is dedicated to elucidating? At the most basic level, one can divide the world into abiotic (nonliving) and biotic (living) components (fig. 3.1). Abiotic aspects are commonly called the physical environment and are made up of entities and forces such as soil, water, air, climate, topography, etc. In keeping with our objective of integrating human activities into our thinking, it is useful to add a second component to the physical environment — the "built environment." Biotic aspects of the world are its living organisms: plants and animals. Although we recognize people as members of the more general animal kingdom, it is useful once again to separate specifically human activities from the remainder of biotic elements.

The biotic components of the world comprise a dazzling array of organisms. At the broadest level, the *biosphere* encompasses all of the earth's living organisms and the physical environment with which they interact. At the smallest level, all biotic components are made up of cells, genes, and strands of DNA, but our interest begins at the basic level of integration, the *organism*. An organism is a coherent living entity that on its own or with the help of other similar entities is able to survive for varying lengths of time and to reproduce progeny of similar characteristics. A *population* comprises

Figure 3.1
Conceptual model relating aspects of the environment.

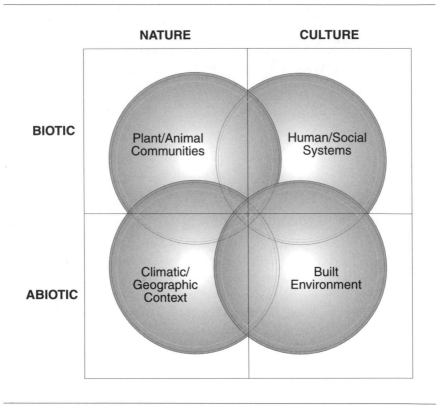

groups of individuals of one species, that is, one kind of organism. Since populations are composed of aggregates of the same species, they tend to exploit resources in a specific manner. This pattern of resource exploitation of a species is referred to as its *niche,* and although it often coincides with a physical space, the niche should be distinguished as a set of relationships rather than a particular habitat. In fact, the niche represents the relationship of the individual to all aspects of its environment, complete with the range of conditions and resource qualities within which the individual can survive. Hence, ecologists often think of the niche as the occupation of a population of organisms and the habitat as their current address (Butzer 1982:15).

All the populations of various species, both plant and animal, that occupy a given area are called a *community.* The biotic community of an area and the abiotic environment in which it lies are together considered an *ecosystem.* A famous ecologist, Eugene Odum, defined an ecosystem as all of the organisms in a given area interacting with the biotic and physical environment. An ecosystem is characterized by energy flows, food chains, biotic diversity, and cycling of materials (1963). Entities within the ecosystem that affect each other through one or more of these processes are said to have a *functional relationship*. The central issues addressed in this book involve the functional relationships among participants in particular ecosystems, especially the relationships involving human populations. Because of this, it is most useful to follow the lead of many scholars who refer to ecosystems in which humans play a substantial role as human or anthropogenic ecosystems. Specific, regionally bounded, anthropogenic ecosystems are the basic unit of discussion and analysis in this book. Yet, even a single ecosystem is extremely complex for a complete empirical study. The fact that the case studies presented are all in the past makes elucidation even more difficult. Hence, the ecosystem concept will be used as a paradigm to organize the facts about each case, but most descriptions and analyses will involve functional parts of the ecosystem, such as soil/vegetation dynamics, crops/livestock dynamics, or human population/settlement dynamics (fig. 3.2). The interplay of all of these components takes place in the context of a climate, a geography, a social system, and subsistence technology. In the following chapters, case studies will be used to describe these components as they occurred in the past, and an attempt will be made to delineate as many interrelationships as possible.

The variability across the earth's land masses can be classified into a limited number of major regions, each with distinctive plant and animal groupings. Ecologists have divided the world into zones or biomes in various ways, but seven categories are commonly used: tropical forest, temperate deciduous forest, temperate coniferous forest, grasslands, desert, tundra, and mountains. In one type of biome located in two widely separated regions (perhaps even continents), the component species of the communities may be quite different, but they occupy analogous niches and function within the biome in similar ways. For example, the bison of North American savanna biome (a type of grassland) might be considered as analogous to the wildebeest of the African savanna. In this volume I will draw on archaeological case studies from widely separated locations and time ranges, each with its own resources and strategies. However, because of the functional similarity of communities and populations within even widely separated ecosystems of the same biome, it will be possible to recognize similar situations and responses.

The human-environmental interactions in the case studies in the following chapters can be looked at in terms of how stability and change affect the overall system — more particularly, the human ecosystem of the region. A

Figure 3.2
Influences that affect the components of an ecosystem.

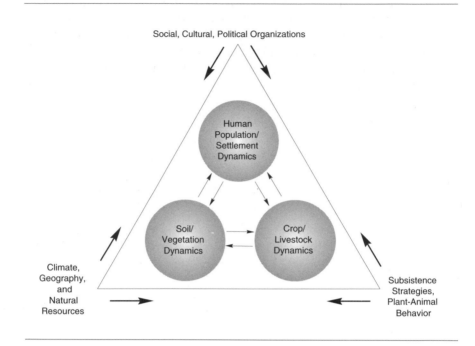

system is a group of elements that are bound together by a set of relations such that a change in one element will cause changes in all others. A human ecosystem comprises an assemblage of different species of organisms — including humans and their nonbiotic environment — all bound together by regular interactions.

These interactions are defined by the movement of energy, matter, and information, and are regulated by feedback relationships in which the outcome of each change affects subsequent inputs. Feedback relationships that act to dampen potential changes are referred to as negative feedback, whereas those that enhance changes are termed positive feedback. Change is always taking place in an ecosystem, but what is important is whether the change is of sufficient magnitude to permanently alter it. Crossing this type of limit, or *threshold*, distinguishes the repeated alternations that constitute cycles, such as those that reoccur on a seasonal pattern, from the cumulative changes that define a real transformation. Because its constituent elements are subject to change, an ecosystem continually changes through time.

Most natural and human systems, at any point in time, appear to be primarily governed by *negative feedback,* which allows the system's values to oscillate but keeps them within limits so that the basic nature of the system remains stable. Three very important characteristics of human ecosystems are their *predictability, resistance* and *resilience* (fig. 3.3). The key aspect of predictability is the extent to which the impact of forces acting on the system can be anticipated, and hence predicted, based on past experience. The resistance of a system is its ability to resist or accommodate external pressures without seriously transforming itself. The resilience of a system is its ability to return to close to its predisturbance state. All ecosystems are exposed to continual external and internal pressures, and the ability of the system to maintain stability will depend on its structural resistance, its resilience, and whether impacts to the system are predictable enough to be effectively assimilated.

Most of the activities within an ecosystem involve the exchange of material and energy (the ability to do work) between two entities or between one entity and the physical environment (fig. 3.4). Energy exists in many forms, but the three fundamental varieties for our consideration are *radiant, mechanical,* and *chemical.* The source of all radiant energy entering our biosphere is the sun, and this energy is captured and exchanged by both abiotic and biotic mechanisms. Mechanical energy comes from the external force of gravity of the moon and sun, and rotational forces of the spin of the earth. In addition, organisms can use the earth's gravitational pull by taking

Figure 3.3
Model of changing system state (after Nancy Grimm, personal communication).

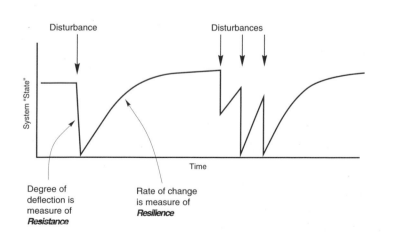

Figure 3.4
Exchanges among the components of the environment.

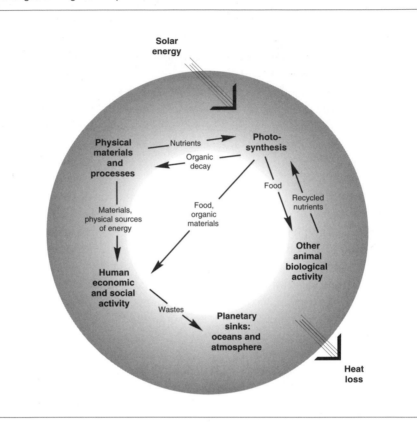

advantage of differing potentials or heights. Chemical energy derives from various chemical reactions that capture or emit energy, most often in the form of heat. Fire is probably the most commonly recognized form of extra somatic energy release. *Photosynthesis,* which takes place in plants, is the fundamental source of stored chemical energy in living organisms (in the form of sugars). Animals release this energy for their own use through *metabolism* of the plant-produced material or of other animal material that already ingested plant material.

There is a crucial relationship between the existence of life forms and the transfer of energy. According to the second law of thermodynamics, we live in a universe that with every interaction is tending toward greater disorder, yet life requires an enormous degree of orderliness. The creation and maintenance of life forms can only be achieved at a very high cost of energy consumed. The transfer of this chemical energy, usually as food, from one life form to another is fundamental to all our thinking about ecosystemic behavior and, more specifically, to all human-environmental interactions. In reality, it is a very complex process, but it can be thought of as a *food chain* with many links and simply represented as a *trophic pyramid of energy* (Ricklefs 1993:104; Little and Moren 1976:7). At the base of this pyramid are green plants, which are the primary producers, providing all food for higher level organisms (see fig. 3.5). Above the primary producers are consumers of various levels: herbivores, carnivores, and omnivores. Decomposers break down the remains of organisms at all levels into constituent compounds that can once again be used by primary producers.

At each successively higher level of the pyramid, much of the available chemical energy is lost on maintaining the lower level organisms and the basic inefficiency of biological energy transfers. Hence, less and less energy is produced as one progresses up the trophic pyramid, which usually translates to fewer and fewer organisms. Therefore, the primary production of plants must be enormous in order to support a large biomass of herbivores, and it takes many herbivores to support a few carnivores. The ratio of production on one trophic level to that on the level below it is defined as the *ecological efficiency* of that link in the food chain. Several variables must be specified to

Figure 3.5
Schematic diagram of a trophic pyramid.

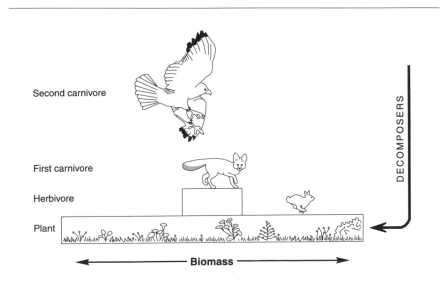

allow an accurate measurement of this ratio, but as a general guideline, it has been estimated that the conversion of food biomass into consumer's biomass involves an efficiency of about 10% (Diamond 1997:169).

The enormously important implication of this ratio for omnivores (such as humans), who are able to choose their source of food, is that eating primary producer plants is a more efficient use of available food resources than depending on herbivores, who themselves consume the plant material. Put simply, a vegetarian diet could potentially support significantly more people than a diet that consists of large quantities of meat from domestic animals. But the issue is far more complex than this statement or the simple diagram in figure 3.5. Plants, animals, and humans are not related in a simple linear pyramid flow, but by a series of complex and changing food chains that can be best represented by a multidimensional "web." Many creatures on intermediate levels of the pyramid are able to digest, and convert to useable energy sources, foods that those at the higher levels (especially humans) can not consume due to limitations of their digestive system and selective tastes. Therefore, the food chain humans depend upon does have inefficiencies due to our reliance on meat from animals that dissipate plant energy in supporting themselves, but at the same time, these animals extend our reach to sources of plant energy we would never be able to ingest ourselves. (Food chains will be discussed in greater detail in chapter 4.)

Human Decision-Making

Although it is convenient to use ecosystem concepts as formulated by biologists, it is essential to recognize that human-dominated ecosystems differ in fundamental ways from other biological systems: information, technology, economics, and social organization play inordinately greater roles (Butzer 1982:32). This difference takes the form of purposeful behavior and the ability to evaluate potential outcomes without actually attempting them.

The actual state, or condition, of a human ecosystem is the cumulative result of previous conditions being influenced by both *driving* and *mitigating forces*. Driving and mitigating forces are another way of conceptualizing the various elements and influences that affect an ecosystem (see fig. 3.2). Driving forces themselves are conditioned by a variety of influences, which can be separated into four categories: demographic, economic/technological, social/political, and environmental. These drivers do not work in isolation, but usually interact with each other and are limited by a series of mitigating forces. The human population of a system can grow through both fertility and immigration, but the increase in numbers is ultimately limited by resources needed to sustain itself, increased disease, higher social tension, and many other mitigating forces. By understanding the nature of driving and mitigating forces that affect a particular system, it is possible to model the factors that have led to the current condition or state of the system.

If all of these forces and the processes that influence them remained constant, our study would be more straightforward. But change, as well as stability, characterizes human and nonhuman systems. What is unique about human-dominated systems is that many of these changes give rise to a *stress* that is recognized and consciously acted upon. In the normal course of events, humans continually find themselves in situations where they can choose how to adjust to the effects of a stress. Hence, humans play an active role in shaping the future state of their ecosystem through rational processes of defining alternatives and choosing among them based on past experience or knowledge gained from others. Taking their lead from biological evolutionists, anthropologists have focused on the term *human adaptation* as the strategies adopted by people to enhance their chance of survival and reproduction. *Adaptability* is a term used to indicate the capacity of a cultural system or groups within it to adjust to stresses. *Stresses* can take many forms, each posing a different kind of threat to the system and prompting differing responses. Archaeologists have long recognized that *climatic stresses,* such as changing temperature, rainfall, or seasonal variations, can cause tremendous problems for human survival. In most of these cases the climatic change is seen as external and uncontrollable, and the human response is the dependent variable. There are, however, other types of stress that may be affected by external factors, such as climate, but are more actively influenced by human actions. These would include *nutritional stress, disease stress, demographic stress,* and *stress caused by competition from other human groups* (Little and Moren 1976:29–45).

Responses to stresses can take many forms, the most basic being a *genetic* change in the organisms themselves. This is a long-term response that does not relieve the pressure for numerous generations and simultaneously acts to decrease the potential flexibility of the organism by focusing on specific adaptations. Although genetic changes are constantly occurring in all populations, it is not apparent that this type of change has had significant impact on human populations as a result of the types of stresses described in this book nor over the time span discussed. The second basic category of response is *physiological,* which involves actual bodily changes in the organism. Physiological changes can often help organisms cope with stresses and mitigate the need for genetic changes to occur for an organism to survive and reproduce. These types of responses have been documented in human populations, but they have largely been superseded by the third type of response as described below.

The primary category of human responses to environmental and other stresses is *behavioral*. These are usually the result of a conscious decision and obviate the need for more fundamental responses. Although all animals may be able to respond through changes in behavior, the human ability to learn from past cases, to plan for the future, and to associate cause and effect make behavioral changes for humans a tremendously flexible and effective means of responding. The two basic arenas through which humans can respond are population control and resource management (Little and Moren 1976). *Population control* is often used to bring the number of people back below the readily available food supply. Changing reproductive strategies or activities that affect longevity could do this. It also could be done by spatial strategies such as aggregation, dispersion, or emigration. *Resource management* is a distinctly human adaptive behavior and probably represents the most common approach taken in response to environmental stresses. Among the basic kinds of behavioral responses people in the case studies display are new patterns of movement or area integration of settlements, environmental alteration, and altered technologies of resource production.

Two widely held notions about responses to resource shortages are incorrect. First, many people adhere to the assumption that the energetic efficiency of food production has improved in the course of cultural evolution. Yes, we produce more food globally than ever before and some groups are able to produce more per capita than before. What is not taken into account, however, is that this is done with tremendous inputs of energy indirectly into the process. Productive intensification has characterized much of human history and most of the case studies dealt with here, but it must be realized that intensification requires enormous inputs of labor and secondary products. The total energy input per unit of food yielded may in fact have increased (see discussion in chapter 7). In addition, food production often relies on processes that deplete natural resources that are slow to regenerate and hence incur an additional cost.

The second notion is that the most common stress placed on human subsistence systems is a shortfall in the availability of overall nutritional energy. Closer examination of actual situations reveals that not enough food is only one possible problem. More often it is a shortage in selected resources, such as protein, that represents the real stress, or the food that is available is deemed culturally undesirable. There are two aspects of this condition that helps one understand human behavior: first, stresses are usually focused on selected components of systems that are nearing limiting conditions; and second, stresses do not act evenly on all segments of a society; that is, some people feel the pressure more than others.

The kinds of human responses to environmental stresses most directly relevant to the studies in this volume are those concerned with productive strategies; although decisions on settlement location, institutional alternatives, and social life can also have important environmental impacts. A well-known model for understanding production strategy decisions is popularly called the "least-cost model" (Zipf 1949). The model's working principle is that people try to get jobs done with the least outlay of energy (i.e., labor, capital, and land). A common application of the least-cost model is in understanding the optimal location for a settlement in a region, given its technology (fig. 3.6; also see Chisholm 1968; Euler and Gumerman 1978). For archaeologists, this often has taken the form of catchment analysis (Higgs and Vita-Finzi 1972).

Some scholars who study decision-making argue that in actual situations, least cost is not the most common governing principle; rather, people "optimize" their situation according to their economic alternatives (Simon 1957). Although economists regularly utilize models that maximize or at least optimize production, most ethnographic observations suggest that preindustrial producers are conservative and are most concerned with reducing the risk to their families' survival. Thus, models for preventing economic disasters are probably more appropriate than those that assume a maximizing strategy. Two models that meet this criterion are the "mini-max" strategy, where if the worst case happens the value will be the best possible, and the "Bayesian" solution that maximizes the average payoffs (Cowgill 1993).

The decisions that impact the environment the most are those involved with the selection from among subsistence alternatives (Green 1980). Key among these are whether to gather or produce food, whether to raise crops or keep domestic animals, whether to rely on a range of food sources or a single source, and how intensively to extract resources from the landscape (see figs. 3.2 and 5.13). In making these decisions, the producer would rely on a store of knowledge that would be largely derived from personal or communal experience. Hence, decisions made by indigenous groups are usually conservative and result in modest or gradual restructuring of relationships within the productive ecosystem rather than radical shifts.

Agriculturists increase the production of useable plants on the landscape by managing ecological succession: clearing indigenous plants and replacing them with new domesticated species. In general, increased productivity is maintained by keeping the system at an early stage of plant community succession; by encouraging fast-growing, short-lived species and eliminating slower growing competitors for sunlight, water, and nutrients. How

Figure 3.6
"Least-cost" model for the more intensive use of land closer to the settlement, as proposed by von Thünen (1966).

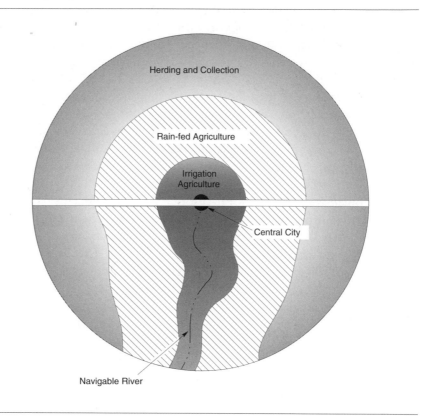

intensively the agriculturist will restructure the landscape is based on a complex series of decisions related to labor input, resource productivity, and the nature of the landscape (Boserup 1965). Contemporary ethnographic research indicates that traditional farmers make these decisions in an ordered, two-staged fashion (Gladwin 1980). When confronted with a large number of alternatives, the decision-maker first narrows the set to a feasible subset that satisfies certain minimal conditions. In the selection of appropriate crops, this might involve their desirability, adequate soil and water, the farmer's knowledge, and the labor requirements. Having identified a limited number of reasonable alternatives, the farmer makes the final decision based on a ranking of the alternatives. Criteria for ranking might involve the susceptibility to failure of certain crops, their ability to be stored, or their value as trade goods or in ceremonies.

In contrast to the gradual changes prompted by a community remaining in the same region, a group moving into a new region will likely attempt to recreate the productive strategies with which its members are acquainted. The producers' decision-making ability is seriously constrained by their lack of knowledge of how alternative strategies will operate in the new environment. This may lead to drastic changes in the ecosystem, including localized depletion of species and possible extinctions.

As many agrarian societies began to develop complex social systems, new forces reshaped the decision-making process, seriously threatening human-land relationships. In a complex society, many decisions are not made by those who actually produce the food and goods, but by individuals and groups who may not be under the same constraints as the producers and may view risks and rewards quite differently. Not only may people at the top of the decision-making hierarchy have different viewpoints, but they also may not have good access to information on the productive situation.

People in positions of control in a complex society often fashion institutional structures and belief systems that encourage producers to make decisions that appear illogical to people outside that society. These institutions and the ideologies that legitimize them are essential to the maintenance of complex societies. For social hierarchies to be supported, ideologies must be designed to influence those producing goods to generate a surplus that can be used to maintain those who are not involved with producing goods. Complex societies could not exist without this general process whereby agrarian producers create goods beyond their biological needs — to be accumulated and transferred to others through peaceful exchange or violent theft. In addition to supporting nonproducing individuals such as soldiers, scribes, and elite, some of the excess goods can be transformed into valuable goods whose flow can be restricted to members of the elite.

Goods with a long "life," such as domestic animals and stored agricultural produce, also are fundamental to the maintenance of a complex society: they provide a further economic basis for a military, bureaucracy, or cadre of elite. Beyond being a form of wealth in themselves, they also can be stored until there is sufficient quantity to be converted into elaborate prestige goods or monumental constructions. It is in the interest of those who benefit from a complex social hierarchy to encourage increasing production and collection of agricultural surpluses, regardless of the long-term environmental consequences.

To better understand the role of decision-making in human-environmental interactions, it is useful to discuss some of the major cycles of environmental degradation in which human action has played a significant role. Nature is in many ways quite resilient, and hence it is very unlikely that any single decision or action has resulted in long-term or massive environmental degradation. The archaeological record documents numerous societies that for long periods of time conducted their activities in such a manner that their subsistence activities did not upset the local ecosystem.

To understand how human groups could make decisions that appear not to have served their purpose of long-term survival, it is useful to think of their decision-making in terms of cybernetic processes (Rappaport 1978). Adaptation for an organism or an entire system includes both processes through which the living system maintains itself in a fluctuating environment and the processes by which it transforms itself in response to directional environmental change. Systems at all levels attempt to maintain their *truth-value*, i.e., their key identifying features, in the face of changing environmental conditions. Truth-value in a human system may vary from case to case and may not be the equivalent of a biologically defined gene pool or population, such as being defined by ethnicity or membership in a state or language group.

Human systems are made up of subsystems that, although they are interdependent, may each have their own objectives. This interdependence is referred to as *coherence* — the extent to which a change in one system component affects changes in others. No living system can be totally incoherent or totally coherent. As a rule, organisms are more coherent than social systems, and social systems are more coherent than ecosystems. The more inclusive the system, and the greater the degree of relative autonomy inhering in its subsystems, the less coherence it will exhibit (Rappaport 1978:53). In viewing the change of a human ecosystem over time, there often appears to be increasing differentiation into special purpose subsystems. The basis of orderliness, or coherence, in ecosystems of increasing species diversity seems to shift from a reliance on the resilience of individual organisms to a reliance on the resilience of the linkages that hold the components of the system together, often achieved through greater centralization of regulatory operation.

As we will see in the following case studies, human systems do not always act in an adaptive manner to maintain themselves in face of stresses. Roy Rappaport has introduced the term *maladaptation* for factors internal to social systems that interfere with successful responses by a system. Maladaptation reduces the survival chances of a system not by subjecting the system to stress, but by inhibiting the effectiveness of its response to stress. These difficulties appear to become worse as societies become larger. They include poor detection of deviation of variables from crucial ranges, breaks in feedback loops, excessive delay of information transmissions, distortion of information in transit, and failure of higher order regulators to understand the information they have received (Rappaport 1978:58). Because of these failings, social evolutionary changes that perpetuate economic or political institutions may be maintained at the expense of the biological well being of the majority of the people in the system.

If one accepts both conclusions — that large-scale civilizations are maladaptive and that at the same time these civilizations appear to be the inevitable product of the evolution of small-scale societies — then we must ask ourselves the ponderous question of whether the evolution of culture and the entire human experience is in fact maladaptive. If rational logic and purposeful behavior are the salient characteristics of human society, how can they have again and again developed in a direction that appears to defy logic? These are questions that we will return to in the final chapter of this book after having presented information on adaptive and maladaptive behaviors from around the globe.

Coevolutionary Perspective

When trying to integrate information on changing social strategies for survival and their impact on the operation of biological support systems, it is necessary to bridge the social and life sciences and to do so in a paradigm that illuminates system interactions as well as system transformation. One potentially productive approach is to think of social change as a coevolutionary process. The term coevolution was first coined by biologists Paul Ehrlich and Peter Raven to help explain community evolution (1964). For them, it meant the examination of patterns of interactions between two major groups of organisms with a close ecological relationship, such as plants and herbivores (ibid.:586). They found in their study of butterflies and the plants that they fed on, that the reciprocal selective pressures of this feeding relationship were central in generating community diversity. This happens because the fitness of genetic traits within each species is largely governed by the dominant genetic traits of the other. Entities and relationships in an ecological community are constantly changing, yet they constantly reflect each other (Norgaard 1994:26).

Some anthropologists have adopted this approach to attempt to bridge biological studies of human genetics and the social organization that guides marriage and descent (Durham 1991). For this book the most relevant attempt to employ a coevolutionary perspective has been that of David Rindos (1984). He postulates that changes in human-environmental systems are not the product of intentional decision-making, but rather a process of symbiotic community evolution. In considering the origins of agriculture, Rindos strongly argues that humans, like other organisms in nature, are unconscious agents selecting only for immediate benefit: the best, most useful, most desirable, most vigorous — whether it be a plant, an animal, or a way of securing food. The idea that "we as a culture, a nation, or a species are in conscious control of our environment and thus of our destiny is one part truth, one part rhetoric, and two parts wishful thinking," according to Rindos (1984:4–6). He identifies three mistaken assumptions about the introduction of agriculture: (1) ultimate benefits were observable in early stages; (2) society would act on these benefits, if known; and (3) the event can be removed from its context of being a gradual process.

In place of these assumptions, Rindos suggests that humans and their culture have evolved in an analogous fashion to the plants and animals we have domesticated. Using the term coevolution, put forth by Ehrlich and Raven, Rindos suggests that the changes in the domesticated plants and animals had a profound effect on the changes in human culture that were part of the agricultural revolution. Available plants, animals, soils, technology, and social systems are all interacting components of the agricultural system.

Early agriculture came about through a gradual process that was consistent with the genetic abilities of all of the players, and it was through generations of unintentional selection that the current system evolved. It was our proclivity toward extractive efficiencies that led us to make various decisions, such as control of animal breeding or crop seed selection, but we were encouraged to go in these directions by the nature of the resources. Moreover, given the decisions we did make, such as to depend on planted crops like wheat, it was then necessary to change our pattern of settlement movement to insure that we would be able to plant, cultivate, and harvest the wheat at the appropriate times. To what extent have we and our culture been shaped by the resources we rely on and the character of the world around us? Has it been a long-term symbiotic process in which both human culture and the environment have been equal players, resulting in a world that is well suited for both? This is a serious question that must be considered from a variety of perspectives. I will return to it in the final chapter with more evidence to bring to bear.

When selecting topics and case studies to examine in this book, of special interest were the times and places where human actions have tipped the balance, setting in motion progressive, positive feedback cycles that resulted in lasting environmental impacts. The archaeological record shows that many societies found it possible to live in a particular setting for only a relatively short period of time, and even the most long-lived communities ultimately tipped the scale and were forced to leave what had formerly been a suitable setting. Factors other than human-induced degradation of the environment — such as climate change, warfare, disease, or changing patterns of commerce — were certainly the impetus for many of these abandonments, but close scrutiny of archaeological evidence from all parts of the globe indicates that human-caused degradation may be a more pervasive cause of forced mobility and settlement abandonment than previously suspected.

It is possible to identify several fundamental cycles of environmental degradation in which humans play a substantial role. As with most aspects of the natural world, these cycles overlap, sharing both the actors and the forces involved. It is impossible to identify any set of activities that works independently of all other sets or to attribute a particular case study of degradation to a single cause. Even in the face of this complex web of interdependence, it is useful to focus our examination on a limited set of interrelated elements, while recognizing that the boundaries drawn are artificial. The information and archaeological case studies in the following chapters illustrate four basic processes: (1) habitat destruction and animal extinctions; (2) agriculture and human-induced removal of ground cover; (3) expanding settlement systems; and (4) the growth of administrative hierarchies. Reviewing the case studies in this volume, as well as those in the general literature, I have found that these four processes are among the most pervasive in the past and repeatedly have demonstrated their potential for great harm, then as well as today.

4
Animal Exploitation

The Prehistoric Loss of
Habitat and Biodiversity

Animal-Related Systems

Animals are of tremendous importance to us, both because they are a major source of food and labor and because we are specialized animals ourselves. Although the fundamental differences that have emerged between humans and other animals may hold some of the answers to the basic questions posed in this book, our concern in this chapter is with the various activities through which humans have exploited animals to their benefit. This can be simply conceived of as a food web, with humans at various levels including the top, as the highest level consumer. Plants, as always, are at the bottom, as the primary producers. A food web depicts the passage of energy and materials from one species to another. Focusing on the last 10,000 years, since the introduction of agriculture, one can subdivide this web into domestic and wild plants as well as domestic and wild animals, which themselves can be divided into herbivores and carnivores.

The most important animal food source for humans has been herbivores, at first wild, but now largely domestic stock. These creatures graze on wild plants and, for the past few millennia, domestic plants grown by us to be used as animal feed. Secondary and tertiary level carnivores specialize in the consumption of lower level animals, often the herbivores that are also of use to humans. Carnivores have rarely been a substantial source of food for humans, perhaps due to their dispersed range or to some more basic avoidance of this type of food source. After all, we were among their prey at one time, and they remain a threat to us in some circumstances. Still, wild carnivores are a source of recreation for humans (hunting, zoos, circuses), while other carnivores have been domesticated (e.g., dogs and cats) and have served humans in a variety of utilitarian and recreational activities. Wild herbivores (also species of birds and fish, both herbivore and carnivore) have served humans as sources of food, although in decreasing proportion in recent millennia, and continue to serve in recreational capacities. Domesticated herbivores, as well as poultry, farmed fish, and selected other animals, have come to comprise the major source of animal protein for humans. Some of these herbivores became useful as beasts of burden (cattle, horses, camels, donkeys, etc.) and as providers of secondary products such as milk and hair.

Thus, the animal members of our food web are more than just a source of food for us (albeit an essential one for their proteins and fats). Relationships in this web also indicate competition, mutualism between species, and allocation of our limited available labor. Our reliance on this food web has engendered a series of relationships that has led to the evolution of humans and their culture into what we know them as today.

Animals have several key characteristics that have conditioned our relationships with them. First, animals consume energy from the primary producers (plants) and primary predators making it more readily accessible to us. Some of this plant energy is inaccessible to our digestive system, but herbivores have developed specialized digestive tracts that can convert a wide range of plant material into nutrients. Goats in particular are efficient because not only are they able to digest a wide variety of plant material, but their stomachs are large relative to their weight. Because these animals are highly mobile, they also can consume energy from sources that are too dispersed to be of value to us (fig. 4.1). Goats are also able to bend plants down or climb small trees to expand the food available to them. Their ability to store food as fat and muscle between eating allows them to rely on seasonally ripening food sources as well as those in widely separated localities. They are also able to concentrate and produce nutrients that are rare in plants yet are essential for humans, such as proteins, fats, and calcium. A further advantage of goats over other herbivores is that they are willing to consume food sources, such as oily and woody plants, that people may consider undesirable, and can convert them into desirable food. Basically, goats centralize energy from widely dispersed and inaccessible sources into a form that can be more easily procured and consumed by humans. It should be noted, however, that these animals themselves consume the vast majority of this energy, hence only a small proportion of the original energy is available to us.

Herbivores had several characteristics that influenced humans to alter their activities in response to the potential provided by the animals. The slaughter of an herbivore offers more than meat alone, including such valuable items as hide, bone, antlers, oil, and ligaments. The possibility of using animal products without killing the animals was equally influential on human behavior. Milk and wool are the two most apparent products, with animal dung eventually becoming important as fertilizer in the fields and fuel for the domestic hearth. Some herbivores were well suited to serve as beasts

Figure 4.1
Goats consume both leaves and twigs on these oak trees. Note the goat foraging in the tree in the foreground.

of burden for carrying goods, pulling carts, and being mounts for people. Another important characteristic of herbivores was that they usually traveled in large groups, or herds, which could be most efficiently harvested by organized hunting and provided such a concentration of food that large groups of humans could rely upon them. This favored the growth of human groups that relied on these animals.

Another animal characteristic provided a further basis for the growth in human group size: herbivores stored the food energy they consumed as fat and meat that stayed fresh while the animals were alive. Thus, in a way, animals banked this food for people by consuming plant food when it was abundant and keeping it available for lean seasons. Not only could this food source be kept for times of shortage, but once it was domesticated, it could be moved around so that it was available in areas where humans were conducting other activities, but needed food.

Even before animal domestication, the exploitation of animals by virtually all human groups had profound effects on the biological and cultural evolution of humans. The fabrication of increasingly effective hunting implements was a major stimulus to the growing effectiveness of the human brain and the physical dexterity it controlled. The planning of hunting activities may have been a stimulus to rational and conceptual thought patterns in humans. Hunting encouraged food sharing, which favored increased group size and enhanced social organization. The seasonally determined periods of concentrated hunting activity brought disparate groups together for the hunt, providing an expanded human gene pool for potential mates and providing an opportunity for supplemental activities to be conducted that may have led to other food sources and cultural developments.

Many early hunters practiced some forms of conservation, such as selective killing of young males, that were precursors to herding and domestication. Reliance on animal food sources was an important aspect of becoming human and continued to be a strong factor in guiding general cultural developments.

Our relationship with animals has resulted in three general impacts: domestication, dispersal, and extinction. Domestication is probably the most profound way humans have influenced nature, and I will argue later that it has also profoundly influenced the course of human social development. All of this has happened in the last 10,000 years or less. Although often used interchangeably, domestication refers to the specific relations we established with plants and animals, while the term agriculture includes the general aspects of a lifeway dependent on domesticates. The changes agriculture brought about permeated virtually every aspect of human life and fundamentally affected human-environmental interactions (Redman 1978). Agricul-

Figure 4.2
Changing relationships of humans and animals.

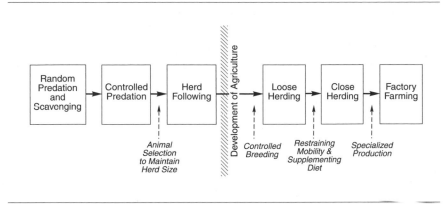

ture, quite simply, can be seen as a human attempt to transform the natural landscape and its inhabitants to better serve the needs of people. To begin with, advanced agriculturists required far less land than their hunter-gatherer predecessors, so they could live more closely together in villages and ultimately cities. Second, agriculturists usually acted to simplify the local ecosystem by planting single species or, at most, a very limited number of species where a broader diversity had once existed. This also was paralleled by the focus on a limited number of domestic animals instead of on the broader spectrum of hunted species.

The relationship between humans and animals that were potential food sources can be considered to have passed through a series of stages, each tying people and animals more closely together. This was a gradual process that took millennia and progressed at different rates in each region of the world. Jarman has proposed six general stages that human exploitation of animals has passed through since earliest times (1977; fig. 4.2). The first three — random predation, controlled predation, and herd following — can all be considered pre-agricultural, but they also reflect an increasing effort on the part of people to extract maximum food without disturbing the success of the animals. The following three stages — loose herding, close herding, and factory farming — reflect a domestic relationship with increasing control of the behavior of the animals, especially their breeding.

With the control of breeding came enormous changes in the animal stock itself, favoring characteristics more useful to humans. Humans have substantially changed the morphology and behavior of domestic animals by enhancing some characteristics and repressing others. For example, in the first stages of the domestication of several species it was deemed favorable to select for more docile individuals, which often meant smaller animals. Evidence of early domesticates is almost always of individuals smaller than their wild progenitors. However, once domestication was firmly under human control, it became important to increase meat yield or strength, so human selection began to favor larger individuals. To supplement the range of selection, wild individuals of the species were often purposely bred into the domestic population.

Domestication resulted in human control of animal reproduction so that some species could be multiplied in number and their traits selected for through breeding. Species that competed with the food animals or preyed on them have been purposely suppressed by humans, thus relieving the need for defensive characteristics to be maintained in the food species. This combined with controlled reproductive circumstances has meant that many domestic species can no longer survive in the wild: they are dependent for their very survival on continued human intervention. Through selective breeding, humans have transformed these species' value to human success by enhancing their ability to produce a continuing flow of secondary products like milk and wool, to store more food on the hoof for lean times, and to develop harnessable motive power that can substitute for human labor through service as beasts of burden (fig. 4.3).

The importance of the coevolution of domestic animals and Old World civilizations should not be underestimated. The existence of domestic animals, both similar to us biologically, but also subservient in so many ways, may have helped to color our overall attitude toward nature and nonhuman members of it. The most fundamental difference in the developmental trajectories of Old World and New World civilizations is the abundance of domestic food and draft animals in the Old World (Redman 1978). If the situation had been reversed, it may have affected who conquered whom. Jared Diamond has examined this issue in his recent book *Guns, Germs, and Steel: The Fates of Human Societies* (1997). He thinks that the differing geographic arrangement of the continents and the availability of species that could be domesticated was more important to who became dominant than differences among the human races or their cultures. Eurasia's basic advantages were environmental: many potentially productive wild plants and animals, a large landmass to support more people, and an east-west orientation that was environmentally efficient for transportation of ideas and resources (ibid.:405–408). The single most important difference may have been Eurasia's 13 species of domestic large mammals versus the New World's one. As sources of protein, wool, hides, land transport, mechanisms of warfare, and

Figure 4.3
Domesticated cattle are crucial to the success of this traditional farmer in southeastern Turkey.

sources of industrial energy, domestic animals changed the course of Old World history (ibid.:354–359).

In addition to domestication, a second fundamental impact that humans have had on animal species is dispersal: the expansion of geographic range. Animals, due to their particular physiological condition and adaptation, are limited to a specified range of climates, landforms, and available resources. Other topographic factors, such as mountains, deserts, and oceans, have influenced the movement, and hence, the ultimate distribution of animals. These barriers impede the spread of a species from where it originally developed to other suitable regions. The dispersal of animal species is a process that has been operating since the beginning of time. When the environmental gradient is gradual, animals have been able to adapt slowly to the changes, some of these eventually being reflected in genetic modifications in the animals themselves. When the environmental gradient is abrupt, it has served as an effective barrier to movement. Sometimes dispersals have been facilitated by global or regional climate change, the most dramatic recent events being the surfacing of submerged land bridges during the Ice Age or the expansion of temperate conditions at the end of that Ice Age. At any point in time, in all regions of the world, there have been expansions and contractions of the range of many species, but looked at overall there is a balance that is slow to change. In fact, the short-term direction of evolutionary change is to favor highly specialized animals that are closely adapted to their specific environment.

However, it should be noted that the human is probably the most successful animal at expanding its initial range. Although there is no consensus about the actual birthplace of humans, it is widely agreed that it was a very restricted area, most likely in east Africa. There may have been more than one radiation from that general region, with earlier humanlike creatures being replaced by new, more modern humans about 50,000 years ago (Clark and Willermet 1997). Whether we claim descent from humans that spread throughout Eurasia/Africa by 500,000 years ago or 50,000 years ago, the point for us is clear: humans started from one small area and have dispersed to all of the continents of the world except Antarctica (and some might say we inhabit that as well). Hence, dispersal is a process with which humans are very much at ease. It might even be argued that the movement into new environmental settings and ecological niches is very much a part of being human or at least valued by humans.

Therefore, it is no surprise that from early on humans have been interfering with the geographic ranges of many species of animals. Much of this is done intentionally, but we have also inadvertently disrupted local balances and accidentally transported some species over great distances. We have transported species of plants and animals over short and very long distances for a variety of reasons. Such introductions of nonnative species are often very disruptive of the invaded ecosystems. Our ability to transport things long distances and our proclivity for this type of movement have been a part of the human existence for a long time, but these elements have multiplied in recent centuries.

Numerous factors have motivated people to transport species to new localities. The most obvious is bringing them along as a source of food, both for the immediate situation and to raise as a source of future food. Other reasons include sport, sentimental attachment, or as a means of controlling pests in a newly settled region. The examples of plants and animals being brought by colonists to new lands and by traders to settled areas are too numerous to recount. In fact, this is such a widespread and powerful inclination that the term *transported landscapes* has been introduced to refer to this activity (Kirch 1982). People want a reliable source of food, and it is natural for them to try to duplicate what they know best. But transported landscapes go beyond food sources. People also transport plant species to recreate surroundings they feel comfortable with, such as lawns and shade trees even in the desert.

In the course of moving between localities, humans have often carried organisms along inadvertently. Initially, this process was probably limited to small organisms that were on the animals being purposely transported, in the soil of the plants being carried, or in the ballast of the ships. But with wheeled vehicles and, ultimately, oceangoing vessels, this accidental transport grew rapidly in scale. Unwanted small animals like rodents were frequent passengers with food supplies, as were weeds. This is not strictly a problem of the twentieth century; it clearly was a problem when the European explorers began crossing the ocean in the late fifteenth century and when the Polynesians crossed the Pacific over 1000 years before that. Certain species were more likely to be transported, including insects, rodents, disease vectors, and seeds, because either the host media were widely available (such as humans or soil) or the organisms could easily hide within the ships (like rodents). Other characteristics that aided in the successful establishment of these invaders were the adaptability of the species itself, whether the host environment had been isolated and had unfilled niches, and whether the new environment was similar to that of the homeland. As we will discuss below, certain kinds of environments were more susceptible to being changed by invaders.

The third basic human impact on animals is the impoverishment of animal species, which leads to a contraction of their range or even to their extinction. This is the extreme result of human intervention and is of central importance to our thinking about long-term human impacts on the environment. The most direct causes of impoverishments and extinctions have been the killing of animals for food, the use of animal parts such as feathers and skins for domestic purposes, and the trade of animals as commodities. Some species are overhunted by humans because they prey on domestic stock, they are seen as a danger to humans, they are in competition with domestic species, or they threaten agricultural fields.

Interestingly, indirect causes have probably been as important in the extinction of many species as the more obvious direct killing. Primary among the indirect causes is habitat transformation caused by humans. Many scholars now believe that in an effort to enhance grazing land for wild herds and to hunt them in an organized manner, humans have used range fires from before the earliest attempts at agriculture some 10,000 years ago. This may be the earliest method of environmental transformation practiced by humans, and it may have been done on a large scale and with sufficient frequency to permanently alter the landscape and the suitability of the habitats for many species.

With the development of agriculture, humans began clearing large tracts of natural vegetation to make room for their cultivated plants. This type of land clearance or deforestation was most intense in the immediate vicinity of agricultural villages, but as we will see in the next chapter, this often spread across the countryside until it became a regional problem. Habitat destruction, or at least transformation, has been associated with human-caused pollution as well. Air and water pollution are problems that have become very serious in the last century; the commonly held view is that these were not problems before the Industrial Revolution of the nineteenth century. Although acknowledging that the worst conditions have only emerged in recent decades, archaeologists have found evidence of mercury pollution in water during pre-Columbian times (Ford 1973) and serious lead pollution in the air two millennia ago (Hong et al. 1994).

Another indirect cause of impoverishments would be the introduction of new competitors or predators to a region. Some of this was inadvertent, like rodents or weeds, while at other times humans purposefully introduced species that had many unexpected negative effects. A recent case of this is the African "killer" bees that were purposefully brought to Brazil in 1957 and since then have methodically spread on their own until entering North America 30 years later.

Factors Favoring Extinction

There are several general characteristics of animals and their environmental settings that strongly influence which species are more likely to go extinct and under what conditions. Interestingly, extinctions did befall some beasts in some places at some times, but not other beasts in the same places nor similar beasts at other places or times. To get an accurate perspective on this process, one must look at long time spans and broad geographic areas. History is replete with local disappearances of various species on small islands or in tiny study areas that were recolonized after a period of time. The local impoverishments are of importance to those who lived in the area, but they are not the same as extinctions that are global, complete, and hence, a permanent loss to the world's biodiversity.

Jared Diamond, an animal ethologist specializing in birds, points to several general conclusions about the nature of extinctions. First, there is an inverse relation between extinction rates and population size. Those species inhabiting a vast area in large numbers are less likely to go extinct. Hence, species occupying continental land masses with wide-ranging habitats are most secure from extinctions. The converse is also true; those species that inhabit small isolated areas are more susceptible to extinction. Therefore, species inhabiting islands in the ocean, disconnected mountaintops, or other environmentally dissected landscapes are most vulnerable to extinctions. Second, for species with similar population size, the one showing wider fluctuations in abundance is more susceptible to extinction. Compounding a normal population fluctuation, a climatic or human-induced stress could bring the species below the threshold necessary for persistence. Third, there is a natural susceptibility of megafauna for extinctions due to their lower population densities and the slower rate of reproduction and population replacement. It is estimated that even among herbivores, there is an enormous difference between the small gazelle that has an annual biomass "turnover rate" of 70% and the large elephant's annual rate of only 9% (see fig. 4.4 and Goudie 1993). For smaller mammals like rodents, the turnover rates are even higher, and consequently, the possibility of extinctions through overhunting is even more remote.

Diamond recognizes that there have always been species going extinct due to changing climatic factors, but these have only occurred over long periods of time in the face of extreme changes. He argues that climate-linked population changes documented in recent centuries are almost all local species impoverishments and not complete extinctions. Given the enormous time depth of the past, there is ample evidence that climate change and other "natural" factors have led to repeated extinctions, yet Diamond asserts that almost no modern cases exist of total extinction due clearly to climate (1984). However, climatic factors do lead to local population expansions and contractions that are important for humans relying on these species, and they also may make the species more susceptible to human-induced pressures that might lead to extinctions.

Diamond reports that of the 4200 modern species of mammals, an estimated 63 have become extinct since A.D. 1600. The majority of the large mammal extinctions have been of continental populations, while the small mammals have largely been those on islands. Of approximately 8500 modern species of birds, about 88 have become extinct since A.D. 1600. The overwhelming majority of these extinctions has been of island populations, and many more island species are near to extinction. Islands provide special conditions and pressures with respect to natural cycles of species. Two of the most dangerous conditions for island-based species are the lack of a refuge population to restore the impacted group, and the lack of suitable alternate settings to which to flee.

Humans have proven to be versatile exterminators in recent cen-

Figure 4.4
Decreasing rate of population biomass turnover with increasing body size.

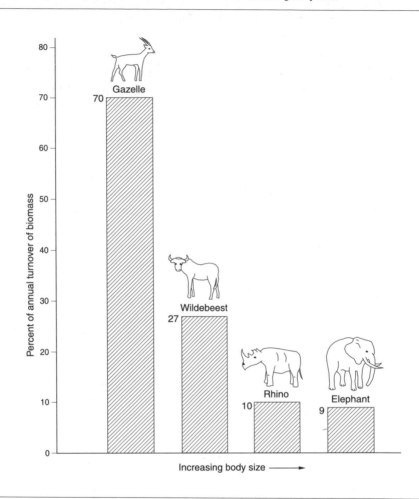

turies, and with the exception of chemical pollution, all of our weapons and tendencies were at work in prehistoric times as well. Six of the major human mechanisms for inducing animal extinctions are reviewed below.

The most obvious of the prehistoric and historic mechanisms was *overkill.* Overkill is often attributed to exploitation of animals for their meat, but there are other factors that may have been equally important in prompting a kill level sufficient to lead to extinction. First, people have found *eco-*

nomically important uses for many animal body parts, such as fur, skin, and feathers. Second, body parts acquired *cultural value* in many societies, such as powdered rhino horns in the Orient and ivory decorative arts in the West. Animals would also come under pressure in human efforts to *protect their agricultural fields and gardens.* Two other mechanisms, certainly present in ancient times, but perhaps not at the level leading to extinctions were *capture of animals for pets* and *hunting for recreation.* Among contemporary examples, overfishing stands out as a clear example of global overkill (Brown 1995; James 1994). It is also a case in which exploitation of this potentially renewable resource was begun in past times, but the rate of removal has far outstripped replacement during this century.

With modern laws against many of the practices that lead to overkill, the greatest contemporary mechanism inducing extinctions is *habitat destruction.* Archaeological case studies, including those in this book, suggest that this was the number one threat to animals species in ancient times as it is today. Clearing vegetation from landscapes to plant agricultural fields or to encourage the growth of grasses for grazing herd animals has had acute impacts on vast tracts of land for at least the past 8000 years. Deforesting terrain to use the timber in construction or as fuel for domestic hearths or industries is also a huge menace and as old as the first village settlements in all parts of the world. Habitats can also be severely impoverished by the presence of domestic grazing animals, especially if the landscape is already vulnerable due to climatic factors or the density of grazing animals is too high to allow natural regeneration of the plants. This is a serious modern problem and probably at least a localized problem around settlements in ancient times. We also know that at least as early as the first historical civilizations, people were undertaking massive land transformation projects to drain wetlands, extend irrigation, and make land more suitable for agricultural production in other ways. Whether or not the last two mechanisms were ever widespread enough to cause the complete extinction of animal species is not certain, but they clearly contributed to the overall habitat destruction caused by humans who were increasingly committed to enhancing agricultural production.

A final habitat destroyer available to humans from the earliest times is *fire.* Fires have destroyed habitats as long as there has been lightning and volcanoes, but humans have been supplementing these naturally caused fires with ones they have set purposefully or inadvertently (Pyne 1998). To some, it is the use of fire that helped set humans apart from other animals and propelled them along their developmental pathway. Scholars are becoming convinced that the use of fire by humans was important not only for early agriculturists, but also for big game hunters, both to enhance the growth of grasses in forested landscapes and to drive herds in order to slaughter them. Hence, the purposeful use of fire is at least 10,000 years old and some would argue 100,000 years old or more (Bell and Walker 1992:154).

Fires clearly have a very immediate localized impact on habitats, but what is more important is that they exert selective pressures on many species. Fires favor plants like grasses that are quick to move back into disturbed areas and fire-retardant species of brush and trees (fig. 4.5; Vitousek et al. 1996). As fires become frequent in a region, the overall composition of the plant, and hence animal, community may change. Some scholars argue that the existence of the vast grasslands and savannas of the world have been favored and extended due to millennia of purposeful burning of those regions by humans.

Humans also have caused species extinctions through the *introduction of predators*. Among predators introduced by humans, the ones responsible for the largest number of extinctions are rats. Europeans carried various types of rats across the oceans during the last five centuries and the Polynesians did the same across the Pacific during the two millennia before that. The introduction of predators is most serious in situations where no analogous predators have existed and the native fauna have not adapted to this type of threat. It is also more severe on islands where refuge is limited and individuals to restore the impacted population are few. Birds that had nests reachable by the rodents or flightless birds whose young could not escape the ravages of the predators were especially vulnerable. Cats and pigs brought by early settlers to new environments also acted as serious predators, as do some species of fish that are currently being introduced into waterways for recreational purposes.

A similar mechanism of destruction is the *introduction of competitors* by humans. These usually economic species are raised in high densities and can drastically reduce the abundance and distribution of native species that rely on similar food sources or terrain. However, it is more likely that their presence would lead to diminished numbers and a retreat to isolated refuge locations by native populations rather than to complete extinctions.

A human mechanism of species destruction that is best known for ravaging human populations, but may also have threatened animal species, is *introduced diseases*. Disease vectors were often carried by the colonizers themselves or by animals or produce transported with them to locations where native human population had not been previously exposed to these diseases and hence, had not built up an immunity to them. Introduced diseases were responsible for tremendous mortality among the indigenous human populations of the Americas, Australia, and Pacific Islands. We can expect that parallel impacts occurred among animals and plants due to intro-

Figure 4.5
Grassland-fire feedback system.

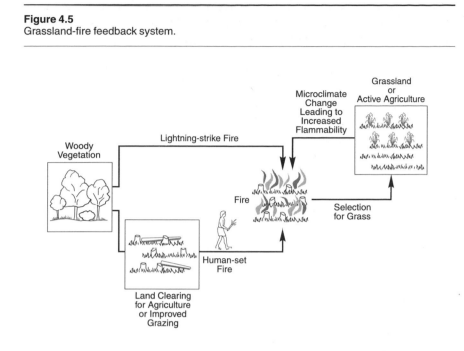

duced diseases, but so far we have collected little evidence bearing on this subject. In the human case these diseases led to extremely high mortality rates, but not to complete extinctions even of a regional nature.

Secondary extinctions, the final mechanism discussed here, could also be considered a form of habitat destruction. The disappearance of one species is likely to produce a cascading effect on other species that used it as prey, pollinator, or fruit dispenser. This process of destruction is often referred to as a "trophic cascade." This insidious type of impact often is not intended in the original action and demonstrates the fragility and interdependence of ecosystems.

Diamond provides us with a series of general lessons about animal extinctions to keep in mind while considering the following case studies (1984):

1. Hunting is merely one of many ways by which humans exterminate animals.

2. Meat is merely one of several motives for hunting.

3. Some historically witnessed cases of overkill happened very rapidly.

4. Population collapses tend to be especially rapid for gregarious species that breed in colonies.

5. Some species survived one or even two human colonization waves only to succumb quickly to later colonists.

6. Coexisting and closely related species differ greatly in susceptibility.

7. Animals that have had little or no human contact do not defend themselves well by fleeing.

8. While fish and mammals have been decimated at sea, there have been no complete extinctions at sea due to the difficulty of finding all members.

Avifauna on Pacific Islands

In recent years archaeological investigation of the Pacific Islands has become extremely active. These islands are relatively small, they are isolated by broad stretches of ocean, and their climates are tempered by ocean forces. Most of the Pacific Islands broke off from continental land masses a very long time ago. Their biota is related to what they had at that time and the distinctive evolutionary pathways followed since then. Some of these islands were created from the ocean bottom by volcanoes, and all of their biota has arrived by air or sea. The climate of most of these islands is damp and temperate due to surrounding waters, leading to specialized forms of plant and animal growth. Because of the isolation of the islands from continental land masses, large mammals are rare and even small mammals, such as rats, may be absent. Similarly, the lack of predators often has allowed species to evolve that were particularly vulnerable to continental predators, e.g., flightless birds or animals that leave eggs or young poorly protected. Each island had evolved ecosystems that were themselves in equilibrium, but were quite different from the major continental land masses of the world.

The islands near Southeast Asia were populated during the last Ice Age by hunters and gatherers whose case studies share similarities with the initial entry into other regions such as the Americas. However, the more distant islands, the ones we are considering here, were only populated during the last two millennia by seagoing Polynesian agriculturists (fig. 4.6). For most of

Figure 4.6
Colonization of the Pacific by the Polynesians.

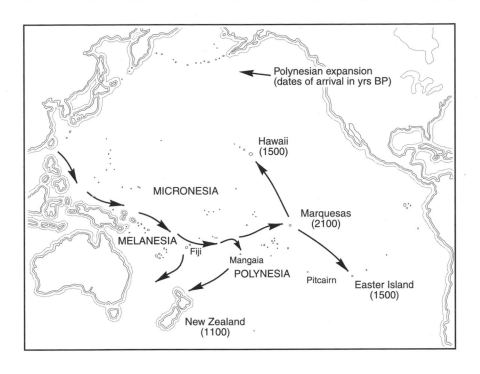

the Pacific Islands, there were two major waves of colonization. The first was primarily people from Southeast Asia whom we call Polynesians, and took place over a several thousand year period leading up to A.D. 1500 when the last islands were settled. The second wave was European explorers, traders, and eventually colonists who reached the area in the early sixteenth century and moved significant populations there during the nineteenth century.

The Polynesians were people from the tropics who cultivated a variety of plants and kept domestic pigs, chickens, and dogs. Since the more distant islands could only be reached by long journeys in boats, the colonists had to carefully select what they brought, although some things still came by accident on the boats. It was clear that even 2000 years ago, these colonists were attempting to reproduce the agricultural systems of their former homelands on the new islands. As discussed earlier in this chapter, Pat Kirch coined the term *transported landscapes* to refer to human attempts at reproducing their familiar surroundings in new locations (1982). As we will discuss in more detail below, this led to widespread habitat destruction on the new islands, including the extinction of large numbers of bird species.

The second wave of colonists, the Europeans, came to islands already inhabited by humans, and hence their impacts were quite different. The first explorers and traders brought with them Old World diseases that were devastating to the islanders who had never been exposed to these vectors (or at least had been isolated from them for a millennia or more). The European settlers brought domestic plants and animals in an attempt, once again, to transport their own landscape (this time Western Europe) to the new territory and to gain an economic livelihood they were familiar with. Once again, these settlers must have accidentally imported other plants and animals that then established themselves on the islands. Moreover, the new settlers often sought to produce not just the things they needed to survive, but products that were economically valuable to be traded back to the homeland. This often encouraged the extensive planting of single economic crops in quantities well beyond the needs of the settlers themselves.

Probably the best known of the Polynesian Islands, the Hawaiian Islands were also among the last to be settled by humans. Hawaii is a chain of islands that has been subjected to considerable recent archaeological research and has rich historical records from the early European contact periods (Sahlins and Kirch 1992). The Hawaiian Islands represent a relatively large landmass for the central Pacific and exhibit tremendous environmental diversity. Due to a mild climate and abundant rainfall on the windward portions of the islands, a rich biota is supported and has entered the popular imagination as a model for a tropical paradise. This generalized view of Hawaii's great potential for growing plants has reenforced the idea of what Captain Cook and other early explorers saw when they first encountered the Hawaiian Islands in the late eighteenth century. They described a rich flora and fauna and assumed it was a *natural landscape* and that the impact of centuries of native Hawaiian settlement on the islands' ecology was minimal due to their conservationist ethic. These views dominate the popular literature and even remain in many scientific circles. However, both positions must be reevaluated in view of the massive new data, largely produced by natural scientists working in concert with archaeologists. Pat Kirch, who has studied the islands, concludes that the "Hawaiian adaptation to environment was anything but passive, for like all human populations, the prehistoric Polynesian inhabitants of Hawaii actively manipulated and modified their habitat."(1982:2).

Polynesians arrived at the Hawaiian archipelago around A.D. 400 or somewhat earlier from islands in the southwest Pacific. They had already lived on those islands for centuries and had developed a *cultural landscape* they were familiar with and which had in turn been adapted from what they had originally brought from Southeast Asia. They brought with them the domestic pig, dog, and chicken. Incidentally, they brought the Polynesian rat, geckos, and skinks, as well as harder to detect insects and microbes. They also brought plants with them, such as the taro, yams, and bananas, as well as a series of weeds that they probably had not intended to bring. By A.D. 1000 there were agriculturally based settlements throughout the islands, and during the following centuries, the success of their productive system led to dramatic increases in population. Kirch estimates that by the century before European contact, the indigenous population had reached as many as 300,000, and they were organized into a highly stratified political structure resembling an early state (1990).

Two kinds of agriculture were practiced on the islands: 1. Water-control farming in valleys for intensive cultivation of taro; and 2. Extensive systems of shifting cultivation using fire for land clearance for yams and bananas. Over the first centuries of Polynesian occupation, these farming systems were adapted and expanded to fill virtually all of the lowland areas of the islands. Population continued to grow quickly on the islands, exerting a constant pressure on productive resources and encouraging the intensification of their farming strategies. The success of their efforts led the Polynesians to expand their shifting cultivation out of the favorable valleys to the more arid leeward areas, resulting in great erosional impacts. The evidence points to the prehistoric occupants of the island extending their agricultural fields to the geographic limits of their plants. In favorable areas they intensified their production by shortening the cropping interval, inputting substantial labor, and using the same lands for domestic animal grazing. These efforts were well rewarded in productive yields, allowing the island population to skyrocket and making available sufficient agricultural surplus to support an increasingly complex social system.

The population curve that Kirch reconstructs from the frequency of archaeological sites found in each period shows a long period of increasing growth reaching a peak about A.D. 1650 and then decreasing during the years leading up to European contact (fig. 4.7). He posits that population peaked before contact and was already heading down before the Europeans landed. Moreover, he suggests that this reveals that a serious diminution in the carrying capacity of the land occurred because of human degradation of the productive lowlands through deforestation and soil erosion. Kirch argues that the greater part of the lowland landscape of the islands had already been converted to a thoroughly artificial ecosystem prior to European contact. The forests had been removed and had been replaced by grasslands. Only at

71

Figure 4.7
Histogram of dated habitation sites from the western part of Hawaii Island (after Kirch 1982).

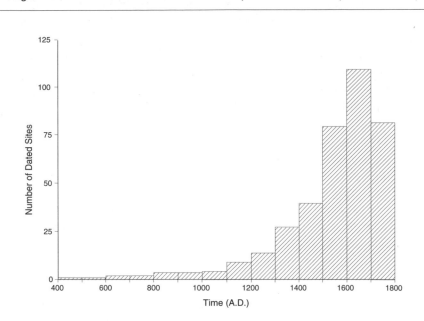

the higher elevations and on steep slopes did the forest remain. Grasslands mixed with pioneering species of plants that regenerated quickly after fires soon covered vast stretches of the island. This situation was in some ways favorable to continued agriculture in that it was relatively easy to re-clear the land, and the open grasslands were good foraging areas for their pigs.

The cutting and burning of the forests to open the land for farming, particularly in the uplands and on the valley slopes, resulted in serious soil erosion. There is clear archaeological evidence of sediments produced by massive soil erosion by A.D. 1200. There have even been instances in which irrigated fields were buried under slope wash, indicating that the erosion not only was hurting the extensive cultivation of the uplands but was burying some of the intensively irrigated fields of the bottomlands. Where palynological research has been conducted, it documents the radical changes in vegetative ground cover that accompanied Polynesian settlement. Cores from lowland areas of the island of Oahu reveal that a forest vegetation that contained abundant palm trees began to change as early as A.D. 800 and was seriously degraded by A.D. 1200 (Athens and Ward 1993). The researchers suggest that in many areas of Oahu, palm forests were replaced by landscapes filled with grasses, shrubs, and ferns, and they attribute these changes to land clearance by the Polynesians for their gardens.

This overuse of the landscape had clear negative impacts on the continued success of the Hawaiians' agrarian system, but our focus in this chapter is on the negative impact it had on native animal species through the well-documented destruction of their habitats. Forests were cleared, grasslands were created, and native food plants were diminished: each of these events put extraordinary pressure on the native fauna of the islands. The primary animals of the islands were a vast array of birds. The Polynesian farmers, in addition to destroying the birds' habitat, hunted the birds for meat, hunted them for plumage, and subjected them to new predators such as the dogs and rats that entered with the colonists. Kirch estimates that no less than half of the bird species native to the islands were driven to extinction in prehistoric times. Among these were flightless birds that had evolved because they had no terrestrial competitors and large flying birds that were vulnerable due to their relatively unprotected nesting habits. David Steadman asserts that fully 60 endemic species of land birds became extinct during that period compared to only 20 or 25 during the historic period (1995:1123). This wholesale loss of avifauna can be partially attributed to overhunting and predation by the newly introduced dogs and rodents, but probably of equal impact was the massive habitat transformation the islands underwent as a part of the Polynesians' food-producing strategies.

An independent means of assessing the scope of habitat transformation during prehistoric times comes from the detailed study of the small land snails that existed in great abundance and are extremely sensitive to changes in the local environmental conditions. Pat Kirch and others have studied these from a number of localities across the islands. The general pattern they have recovered is of a diverse set of species being replaced by a reduced number of species that were tolerant of disturbed conditions (Kirch 1989). These findings reenforce the notion that many lowland forest settings were opened up by removing trees in order to cultivate the area.

Kirch and others do not deny the *conservationist approach to nature* of the Hawaiian Islanders or other oceanic people, but assert that the existence of a conservation ethic and its effectiveness are two different things. Given the demands of a growing population and a limited technology, it was a luxury they could not afford.

To provide an additional case study, Kirch joined with colleague David Steadman and natural scientists Flenley, Lamont, and Dawson to investigate human-induced environmental changes on Mangaia, a small volcanic island in the Southern Cook Islands (Steadman and Kirch 1990; Kirch et al. 1992). At the time of early European missionary contact (in 1822), the

[margin note: conservation ethic in Hawaii?]

Polynesian population of the island was estimated to be about 3000. It is believed that the prehistoric population was at least that high, indicating a density of at least 58 persons per square kilometer. The island is made up of a central volcanic cone surrounded by a ring of elevated limestone escarpments. The radial drainage pattern off the volcano's slopes has led to the accumulation of alluvial sediments in the valley bottoms. The descriptions by early visitors, such as Captain James Cook in 1777, indicated what we would interpret as a degraded landscape in the inner volcanic cone area and intensive agriculture in the valleys. The Mangaian focused their economy on intensive cultivation of taro in irrigated pond-field systems in the narrow valleys as well as on keeping domestic pigs and chickens. Early observers of these islanders identified various social conditions that we may interpret as reflecting pressures of limited land and food resources. Warfare to secure the best taro fields appears to have been endemic in late prehistoric times, including human sacrifice to the war god when a conquest was made.

Through the excavation of Tangatatau rock shelter, the economy from A.D. 1000 through 1600 could be reconstructed (Kirch et al. 1992). This revealed that there was a dramatic reduction in the frequencies of land birds and seabirds over time, matched by an increasing reliance on domestic pigs and chickens. There is also evidence of stress on the local marine species in the form of significant reductions in the size of certain mollusks, such as *Turbo setosus,* and the small size of fish caught and eaten. Both of these phenomena can be best explained in the context of excessively heavy human harvesting of the immediate environs of the island. The late prehistoric strata contain snails that are particularly indicative of irrigation agriculture. The clay sediments from the upper levels also suggest increasing erosion and fluvial deposition originating from the volcanic slopes, indicating a probable clearance of their forest cover. Pollen cores taken from a nearby lake and adjacent swamp confirm this general picture. The core extends back from the present to about 6000 B.P., well before human settlement of the island. The earliest phase reveals a poorly forested island, probably due to cooler weather. During the middle period of circa 6000 to 1600 B.P. on Mangaia, there was more of a rain forest, with occasional erosional episodes that were probably due to weather cycles or naturally caused fires. The final phase (ca. 1600 B.P. to present) indicates sustained disturbance of the forest leading to continual erosion and permanent deforestation, most likely at the hands of humans. Taken together, the evidence from Mangaia suggests a picture of Polynesian colonization and agricultural success, followed by a slow overexploitation of the local marine and bird resources, and habitat transformation with the removal of much of the island's forest cover and increasing soil erosion on its slopes. The interesting implication from ethnohistoric records after European contact is that this environmental situation of slowly diminishing resources may be associated with the observed increase in intra-island warfare and exploitative social arrangements.

Megafaunal Extinctions

Not surprisingly, the situation most frequently cited as the earliest human impact on the environment is also one of the most controversial. The extinctions themselves are not contested, but their cause remains a matter of active debate. The event that is of interest here is the unusually high proportion of large mammals in North America going extinct in a very short period of time at roughly the end of the last glaciation, about 10,000 to 12,000 years ago (Martin and Klein 1984). The question that is hotly debated is whether these extinctions were due to the dramatic change in climate that occurred at the end of the Ice Age or due to the initial entrance of humans into the New World and their hunting these game animals to extinction.

To put this question into a better context, it is useful to take a longer term perspective by looking at previous glacial cycles and the situations when humans entered other regions of the world at earlier times (Klein 1992). There have been as many as twenty climatic cycles of Ice Age proportions during the five million years humans have existed. Extinctions have certainly accompanied the onset and retreat of these cycles, but not on the scale witnessed in North America at the end of the last Ice Age. However, the final Ice Age is the only one during which the humans present were fully modern biologically, culturally, and technologically. Also of interest is the fact that in northern Europe and Asia, where humans were certainly present during earlier glaciations, the rate of extinctions was not as high as in North America.

In looking at the much earlier human entries into Southern Africa and Western Europe, Klein finds that the proportion of extinct genera decline through time and the greatest drop varies from region to region as to when it occurred, suggesting that a worldwide climate change was not at fault (fig. 4.8). However he also sees a general link between the entrance of humans and a sharp drop in the rate of extinctions, with the extinctions preceding human entrance into the region. If any link could be made on the basis of this data, it is that the previously high extinction rates had opened up substantial niches that allowed an easier entry of humans to the region. However, the data from North America and tentative data from Australia show a continuing high extinction rate at the time of first human colonization (Bell and Walker 1992:153). For Klein the conclusion is a combination of climate and human cause, with the humans not killing the animals to extinction, but

Figure 4.8
Proportion of total megafauna genera going extinct in each era (after Klein 1992). Arrows represent approximate appearance of humans in that region.

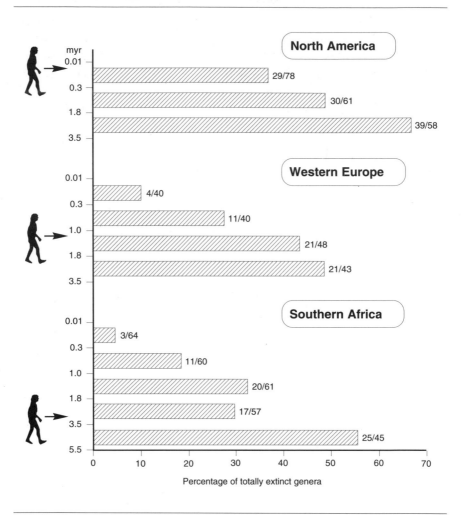

perturbing the ecosystem and putting additional pressure on the megafauna so that more would not survive the climatic change.

The most outspoken advocate for the human-caused extinction theory is Paul S. Martin, a paleoclimatologist (1972, 1984). Although his hypothesis accounting for the megafaunal extinctions in North America sparked a controversy and still has a cadre of critics, it is also a coherent model that has stimulated a generation of study (Steadman and Mead 1995).

Martin proposed that at the end of the last Ice Age, upper Paleolithic hunters of Siberia moved eastward across the Bering region into Alaska and eventually southward, until they traveled beyond the ice sheets into the broad, more temperate vastness of North America, an area of 10 million square miles without humans. Martin's thesis is that the incredible abundance of animals and the well-developed skills of the hunters led to widespread over-kill, rapid human population growth, rapid movement of people south into new territory, continued heavy hunting and further movement (see fig. 4.9). This process continued for a millennium until this *wave of advance* had traversed both North and South America, and its wake left numerous genera of large game animals extinct, most notably American mammoths, mastodons, ground sloths, horses, and camels.

The people involved in this process were the hunters and gatherers of the northeast Asian region who had crossed over the Bering Strait to North America and moved into what is today Alaska. This crossing could have happened over a long period of time during the last Ice Age, probably somewhere between 40,000 and 10,000 B.P. The sea level was sufficiently low through much of that time that what is now the Bering and Chukchi Seas would have been land and largely without ice cover (Jennings 1978). This vast area gave access to the interior of Alaska, which also would not have been ice covered. The environment and available food sources would have been familiar to the hunters and gatherers of northeast Asia, and they probably spread into this region without any particular recognition that they were entering a new continent. Their spread, however, was limited, because during the height of the ice age, when the land bridge would have been available, the glaciation in surrounding regions would have been very thick. Therefore, passage to the rest of North America was blocked. Quite possibly the environment immediately south of the ice sheets would not necessarily have supported the herds of herbivores sought by the hunters. However, somewhere around 15,000 to 12,000 B.P. the climate began to change rapidly with the retreat of the glaciation, and a land route was opened to the south. This period probably also saw the expansion of open grassy woodlands, the habitat of preference for the large herbivores.

This was the environmental setting at the beginning of the Holocene, the most likely period for the first settlement of the remainder of North America. For Martin's theory of what happened at this time to be favored, a few assumptions must be accepted. First, Martin emphasizes the enormity of the megafaunal biomass of North America. He argues there would have been great herds of herbivores similar in quantity to those of the Serengeti Plain of East Africa even in semiarid areas like modern-day Arizona (Martin and Szuter 1994), and densities so great that there are no reasonable models from

Figure 4.9
Human advance through North and South America (after Martin 1972).

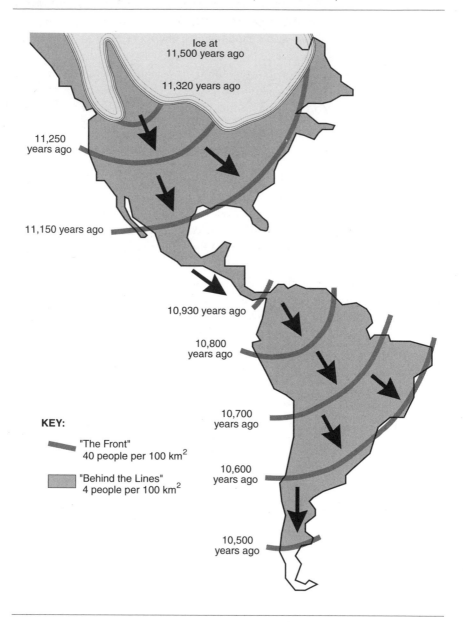

contemporary areas that were more favorable. Second, humans would have to have been capable of expanding their numbers rapidly and of migrating great distances in modest periods of time. The actual rate of growth for a small group entering the New World in 10,000 B.C. to produce a population in the tens of millions by A.D. 1500 is not striking, about 0.1 percent annually.

Martin argues that when entering a new and favorable habitat, any human population, whatever its economic base, could grow explosively, exceeding ordinary restraints. Demographers cite a maximum possible growth rate of 3.4 percent annually for known human groups (based on the Pitcairn Island experience, but being approached by some groups in modern times as well). Even at a rate of 1.4 percent (that is, doubling every 50 years), a band of 100 entering the New World would saturate the hemisphere with 10 million people in 800 years. This is more people than needed and a shorter period of time than the archaeological evidence indicates. Martin suggests that the high population density was restricted to the advancing front. The abundance of fresh game within the front determined the rate of advance, as did the cultural limits to the rate of human migration. He argues that within a decade the population of vulnerable large animals on the front would have been severely reduced or obliterated. As the fauna vanished, the front swept on, while any remaining humans would be at a lower density and would have had to seek other resources. The actual figures Martin uses in his model reflect a frontal arc 160 kilometers deep, with 0.4 people per square kilometer and 16 kilometers of movement per year. This would bring people to the tip of South America 1200 years after their arrival in Alaska.

The third assumption required by this model is that humans were capable of killing a species to the point of extinction. This is based on two ideas from animal ecology: first, that the kill rate for large mammals does not have to be extraordinarily high to cause extinction, and second, that animals unacquainted with humans would not necessarily flee from them. Martin uses a figure of a 20% annual removal rate as being sufficient to push a species of large mammals to extinction. The larger the mammal, the slower its reproduction, so for smaller mammals the percent might need to be substantially higher. However, if the hunting was indiscriminate, such as including reproducing females, then a lower percentage might lead to extinction. Depending on human population estimates and the rate of meat consumption, one could predict that along the front the hunters could take this percentage each year. This would lead to extinction in the region along the front in 10 years. Add to the basic hunting skills the use of range fires and the probable use of domesticated dogs, and one has a superior predator.

The key element that makes this type of hunting possible, though, is the belief that a prey that is not acquainted with humans—their intentions and skills—would have little reason to flee from them. This aspect of the assumption is difficult, if not impossible, to test in the real world, but those who have been in situations where humans have not existed for long periods found many species of animals to be less fearful than under normal conditions. Diamond cites situations in isolated areas of Indonesia in which bird species that normally would flee quickly from humans were quite docile and not scared off by the close proximity of people (1984). Based on this type of assumption, Martin claims that the hunters could wipe out the local prey before they learned to be afraid or to use defensive behaviors.

Some scholars contest Martin's theory, saying that climate change was the primary cause and human presence was not the key. They cite three major kinds of evidence to support this view: first, in North America archaeological sites from this time range with large quantities of slaughtered animal bones are very rare; second, people may have been in the New World 10,000 years earlier than Martin suggests; and third, several non-prey species also went extinct at that time. The first issue is problematic in that there are large kill sites at a similar time in Europe (without the extinctions). The relative speed of movement of settlements posited by Martin, however, might account for this absence. The second issue is difficult to disprove, with frequent claims of an earlier human entry into the New World, but the bulk of evidence is in general agreement with a late entry (ca. 14,000 to 11,000 B.P.). However, Martin's date of about 12,000 B.P. is a bit late given recent discoveries, such as the Monte Verde Site in Chile (Dillehay et al. 1992).

The extinction of non-prey species, especially birds (Grayson 1977), supports an explanation based on climate change, but human overkill advocates suggest that these bird species were ecologically dependent on the megafauna and hence an example of a secondary impact (Steadman and Martin 1984). As one would expect with a hypothesis that posits a comprehensive explanation, it remains in controversy.

The fundamental alternative to human overkill is that climate change was so severe that habitats were reduced or so transformed that they no longer could support the animals and that natural barriers prevented successful migrations. The role of changing global and regional climate patterns in altering habitats by impacting local flora and fauna is not debated here nor denied by advocates of overkill. The position taken by Martin in this case, and by other researchers in case studies presented elsewhere in this volume, is that climate change, if relevant, is still only one part of the picture. Humans have played, and continue to play, a pivotal role in the future of our environment.

5

The Impact of
Agrarian Systems

In looking back over the vast sweep of the human career, there probably is no greater transformation than the introduction of agriculture. The domestication of a vast array of plants and animals allowed the control of food sources so that they could be increased or moved to new locations, altering many constraints that had limited human settlement up to that time. Sedentary villages, overall population increase, and social and political reconfigurations all were a part of the agricultural revolution. With a reliance on agriculture also came a revised set of human-environmental interactions. The plants and animals that were domesticated were altered both morphologically and genetically. Moreover, the human activities involved in food procurement were changed, leading to a much closer interdependence between these particular plants and animals and their human cultivators. To forward that relationship, other aspects of the natural environment were sacrificed. Forests were cut and fields cleared of natural vegetation to allow for newly domesticated plants to be more successfully cultivated. Natural waterways were altered to provide supplemental water for farmed fields, denying their use to other landscapes. Predatory animals were dispersed, or hunted to near extinction, in order to enhance the survival of the domesticated herds. With agriculture the primary characteristic defining human-environmental relations became an all-consuming effort to transform landscapes in such a way that they would produce more crops.

With sedentary village life and the elastic food supplies available through agriculture, human populations began to increase in numbers and to aggregate into denser settlements. This population revolution also redefined human-environmental relations and is the focus of the case studies in chapter 6. Here in chapter 5 the focus will be on the establishment of agriculture and the initial changes that it wrought in the surrounding landscapes.

Sometimes these agricultural pursuits involved primarily plant cultivation, as was the case in North American and Mesoamerican cultures, or it meant both plant cultivation and animal herding, as was the situation in many Old World societies. Before presenting case studies of the regional impact of the establishment of agriculture, it will be useful to review some of the basic principles behind plant communities, as we did for animals in chapter 4.

Plant Life

In any study of human impacts on the environment, vegetation must hold a central position, since people's influence on plant life has led to indirect impacts on virtually all other components of the environment. Moreover, the importance of vegetation is multiplied by the fact that green plants are the primary organisms able to create living matter from inorganic raw materials. They ultimately are the source of organic-based energy that all other forms of life must consume for their own survival. Terrestrial plants succeed in this wondrous task by combining atmospheric carbon dioxide with soil-derived water while converting solar radiation into chemical energy through photosynthesis. This process produces food for all of the world's animals, including humans who require complex organic compounds of nitrogen and carbon for their metabolic synthesis. An additional benefit of photosynthesis is that it produces organic products, such as wood, coal, and petroleum, that can be used to produce heat energy separate from the metabolism that occurs within the body. At the same time that plants are creating these organic compounds by absorbing atmospheric carbon dioxide and water and minerals from the soil, they release into the atmosphere the elemental oxygen that animals, including humans, need to breathe. Fundamental to the growth of plants are the water cycle and the formation of soil, both processes that have been seriously affected by the introduction of agriculture.

Soil and Water

Humans live close to and depend on the soil for their very existence. Soil is one of the thinnest and most vulnerable of natural resources, and it is the one upon which, both deliberately and inadvertently, humans have had many major and often irreversible impacts. Moreover, impacts, such as those described in the prehistoric case studies presented below, can occur with great rapidity in response to land-use change, new technologies, or waves of human colonization.

Soil as an entity is hard to define and is highly variable from place to place, but put quite simply, it is the outer layer of the earth from which living roots of plants obtain sustenance. Soil is the product of a range of factors: parent material, topography, climate, organisms, time. These factors operate to create a rich mix of mineral particles, organic matter, gases, and nutrients that are essential for the maintenance of life. Daniel Hillel (1991) calls soil a self-regulating biological factory that acts to absorb and store water, governs water runoff, acts as a cleansing medium to purify water, and serves as the host for organisms that decompose organic material. Soil is actually formed through the physical disintegration and chemical decomposition of rocks through weathering. Climate, wind and water erosion, and root penetration govern the process of fragmentation of the mother rocks. The components of soil include clay, silt, sand, and organic matter. Clay is composed of tiny particles with enormous surface area that, through combination with other particles such as water and minerals, are the active components of the soil. Silt comprises intermediate-sized particles, and sand is made up of larger particles. Silt and sand are relatively inert; that is, they do not combine easily, but make the soil more permeable and workable.

However, these components themselves do not make a true soil. It is their arrangement through biological and chemical processes that transforms them into a functioning soil. Soil formation is done in place and takes long periods of time — from years to centuries depending on the situation. The soil *body* acquires a characteristic profile consisting of a sequence of horizons. Being formed in place, they have affected each other and are distinctly different from recent sediments that may be layered, but are not functionally related.

The sequence of layers in a well-developed soil is termed *horizons* (fig. 5.1; Montgomery 1992). The O-horizon, or the topsoil, is the uppermost zone and made up of lighter material that has relatively recently fallen to the surface. The A-horizon is home to more biological activity than the zones below. This horizon contains many microorganisms, which help to enrich it with decomposing organic matter (humus from the O-horizon) and nutrients. Normally this layer is darker due to its organic content and is 20 to 40 cm thick. The A-horizon is vulnerable to compaction and to wind or water erosion, which reduces its fertility or may even lead to it being eliminated completely. Ground cover, in the form of vegetation, as well as a thick O-horizon, hold the A-horizon in place. The A-horizon is underlain by the B-horizon, which is a zone of accumulation due to leaching from above and mechanical movement from above and below. It is generally thicker than the topsoil and is home to much less organic activity. The C-horizon is situated below the B-horizon and results from the weathering of underlying bedrock. A *mature soil* is one that has developed in place and has all three well-defined

Figure 5.1
Simplified soil profile.

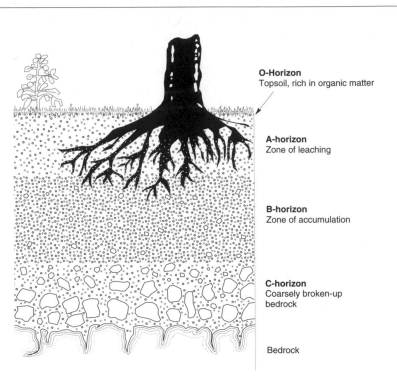

O-Horizon
Topsoil, rich in organic matter

A-horizon
Zone of leaching

B-horizon
Zone of accumulation

C-horizon
Coarsely broken-up
bedrock

Bedrock

horizons. Soils vary widely in characteristics both for the growing of plants and in terms of their vulnerability to human impact.

In contrast to soils, sediments are transported by water or wind from their place of origin to a new location where they are laid down in layers. Depending on the source of the sediments, they may have little organic material and not be fertile or they may contain organic material and nutrients useful to plants. Sedimentation is the opposite of erosion and is the primary way that nature and humans transform the landscape. Rivers, slopewash, and irrigation canals all move sediments around. In some fertile locations, topsoil can be eroded off a terrain and redeposited as sediments in a new location. The source area may thus become less fertile and the receiving area more fertile. In other cases the sediments themselves may not be fertile and may cover up previously fertile soils in the receiving area. Sediments that remain in place for a long period of time may develop into soils.

Even more than soils, water is a fundamental requirement of all life forms. It comprises the majority of the bodies of most living organisms, and it acts as a medium of transport for other essential elements in living organisms. Hence, the availability of water is essential to our life and to the life of all organic things we subsist on. Water movements are also a major force in reshaping the landscapes we inhabit. In addition, water is important in determining the climate, and humans have found ways of harnessing water to provide mechanical energy through waterwheels and dams.

Crucial to the success of plant life and all animals that depend on plants is the continued success of what we call the *water cycle*. In a simple version (fig. 5.2), water evaporates from wet ground, from foliage of plants, and from lakes and oceans (evapotranspiration). It is carried in the air as vapor and then recondenses into a liquid and falls as rain or snow (precipitation). This feeds rivers that return to the ocean, or it percolates into the ground where it is absorbed by plant roots or becomes part of the aquifer and eventually empties itself into bodies of water. The water available for this runoff is the difference between the amounts of precipitation and evapotranspiration.

The soil and vegetative ground cover play crucial roles in the water cycle: rain is broken up by taller plants, which soften the blow to the soil, and organic litter cushions water's impact and acts as a sponge. Much of this

Figure 5.2
Schematic design of water cycle (after Hillel 1994).

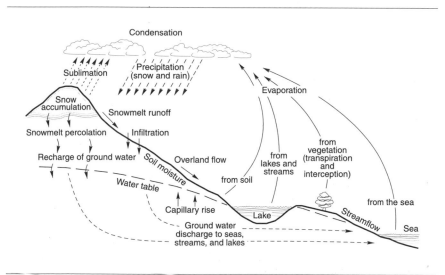

water percolates so slowly that it remains available to the roots of plants and other organisms long after the rain has fallen. Other water slowly finds its way lower until it reaches a geological barrier, where it accumulates as an aquifer and moves along horizontally until it reaches the surface through springs or wells or empties into rivers or lakes. Some falling water remains on the surface and runs off to lower elevations, being drawn by gravity and often carrying local surface material with it. This may start evenly across the terrain as sheetwash, but quickly forms rivulets, gullies, and eventually rivers. The volume of water, intensity of rainfall, condition of the soil, nature of the ground cover, and slope of the landscape are all factors in determining the impact of overland runoff. The extent to which human actions have exacerbated the erosion of soils and sediments caused by overland runoff reflects one of the main sources of human impacts on the environment throughout the world.

Although water is essential to all life, little of it is easily useable by humans, being either too salty or frozen. Humans now use more than half of all runoff water that is both fresh and reasonably accessible (Vitousek et al. 1997:497). Of that water, about 70% is devoted to enhancing agriculture. To meet the enormous demand for fresh water, people have been altering river systems through diversions and impoundments for over 5000 years. This human-induced redirection of the local hydrological regime has been essential to the support of growing human populations, but it has also transformed local environments in very significant ways.

Vegetation

The qualities of soils and the availability of water in a landscape are very crucial determinants to the nature and success of plant life upon which all animals and humans depend. Not surprisingly, plants are very active participants in local ecosystems. Aboveground, a plant's leaves and branches turn and spread to collect light. Their objective is to expose themselves to collect as much sunlight and carbon dioxide as possible. These goals are best achieved through maximizing their surface area and by forming a canopy above other plants to absorb the sunlight. There is competition among plants for available sunlight, leading to a variety of specialized adaptations by plants for them to succeed in this quest. Trees, by being able to reach higher than shrubs and grasses, are able to get at the light before it reaches ground level. When trees grow densely, their leaves may shade the ground below so that lower plants do not do well. Humans who have valued low-growing grasses as food for grazing animals or as their own food crops have often removed trees and other competing plants to enhance the amount of sunlight reaching the grasses.

The roots of plants extend over a wide area to reach for more water, and the plant itself moves water and nutrients from its roots to its aboveground parts (fig. 5.3). Because plants transpire much of their moisture through their leaves back into the atmosphere, they must collect more water than they consume themselves. Just as they play an essential role in consuming carbon dioxide and producing elemental oxygen for the atmosphere, plants are a crucial link in the water cycle. Plants are sensitive to any lack of soil moisture, since they need a relatively constant supply to provide for their own needs as well as for transpiration into the atmosphere. Maintaining this constant flow is particularly difficult in arid and semiarid regions where transpiration is high due to solar radiation and available water is low. Some desert plants have developed special adaptations to reduce transpirational water loss, such as stomata that open only at night. Plants also need carbon dioxide. Since not enough comes through the leaves, they must take some in through the soil. Hence, the soil must be loose enough to allow air to permeate, yet trampling by animals or humans often leads to excessive compaction for adequate airflow. Plants also need minerals from the soil, but too many minerals will cause plants to suffer.

Through millennia of evolution, plants have adapted to these multiple needs with a wide variety of solutions that fit the countless natural conditions of landscape and climate. Some grow more leaves to increase photosynthesis and plant growth, but may be disadvantaged in a drought. Other plants focus on root growth to insure survival during a drought, but may lose in the competition for sunlight and fail to survive. In moist climates where availability of water is not a problem, a plant may maximize the surface area of its leaves to favor sunlight absorption, while plants in arid climates may minimize surface area to conserve water. Trees grow slowly but tall, so they can spread their leaves to form sunlight-absorbing canopies, while low-growing grasses mature quickly to maximize their exposure to sunlight before the leaves on deciduous trees spread above them. Interestingly, many agricultural food crops focus more on root growth than leaf spread, forcing humans to artificially clear the area of competitors to insure their access to sunlight.

Different plants have very different *life cycles*. Of great interest to humans are the *annual plants* that go through an entire cycle (seed to plant to seed) in one year or season of a year. These are very fast-growing plants and are able to withstand dramatic changes in seasonal climate by protecting their germ plasm in a tough seed case. *Perennial plants* go through a longer life cycle, often lasting several years or longer. Some of these plants also have mechanisms for protecting themselves against seasonal climate changes, such as losing all of their aboveground foliage, while others just shed a portion of

Figure 5.3
Cycling of nutrients in a soil-plant system.

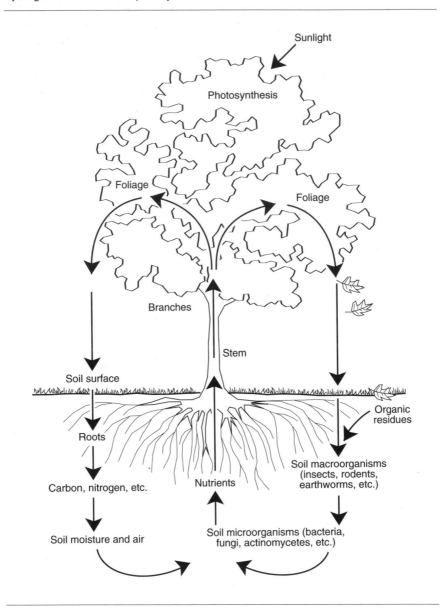

their foliage. These plants often take more than one season to mature, but then produce for several additional years. *Trees* and certain other plants are very long lived. They reach maturity much more slowly, but then live and produce much longer. In human decision-making, planting an orchard is a major investment of time and capital without return for five or even ten years. Yet, once established, orchards may require little labor input and return high food yields. In nature, trees may be slow to colonize an area, but they have an advantage in the competition for sunlight and often replace other plants in the long run.

It is extremely important to recognize that nature is constantly changing. Even without human or animal impacts, plants compete with each other, and the composition of plant communities in any particular habitat changes with the passage of time. We refer to this process as *succession*. Many scientists view succession as an orderly, directional process that works in accordance to rational principles and can be understood and even predicted at least at a general level. For example, in an open area (cleared by a naturally occurring fire or by human agency) of temperate North America, the early colonizing plants will most likely be fast-growing grasses followed by shrubs, and in turn followed by softwood conifer trees. As the trees grow, they will create shade, thus changing the environment itself and putting competitive pressure on many of the lower plants. Over a period of years the species of trees will change, with broadleaf hardwood trees slowly replacing their conifer predecessors.

The actual plants and the sequence of change are determined by the soil, climate, and available species, but several general characteristics of successional change appear to be the same. Generally speaking, over time there is an increase in the plant biomass of the area, greater stratification between plant groups, and greater overall complexity of plants present. It is less predictable, but often there is a general increase in the total production of the plant community. Using cybernetic terminology, succession is a process of *self-organization* that all ecosystems progress through, each according to its own conditions and members. As succession advances, plant communities reach a final stage or a relative equilibrium of the assemblage of plants that some scientists refer to as a *climax community.*

Field studies revealed that several successional sequences that occurred under differing environmental conditions could lead to the same relative assemblage of plants. In fact, early scholars suggested that there were a very limited number of climax communities that existed in the real world. Further research indicated that variations existed within these categories, but nevertheless, some researchers still use the term climax as representing the ultimate expression of plant community development for any particular set of conditions. In this perspective, climax is when the ecosystem supposedly is in equilibrium with the existing supply of plant species and the properties of the local environment. In actuality a total equilibrium is never reached; ecosystems are always in a state of change. Even without human impact, plant communities would still exist in all stages of the successional sequence due to the impact of factors such as animals, pests, fire, erosion, and other biological, physical, and climatic forces. Nevertheless, in recent millennia humans have become the primary cause of increasing numbers of ecosystems being kept at early stages of the successional sequence. Humans, who are anxious to maximize plant material they can consume, act in this way because in a mature plant community more of the energy goes into maintaining supportive tissue (e.g., wood), which is not readily digestible, than into photosynthetic tissue (e.g., leaves) or seeds. In the early stages of succession, the community is characterized by fast-growing plants, including annual grasses that are largely composed of photosynthetic tissue and that devote enormous energy to seed production. This category of plants is the fundamental component of most agricultural systems. When humans introduce agriculture into a region, they artificially push back the extant succession stage to one that is early in the sequence and that has a very high output ratio.

Successional and other studies of ecosystem change reveal how plant communities respond to stresses placed on them through human or natural disturbances. At the same time the changing composition of the plant communities offers differing opportunities for the animals that rely upon them, and changing plant communities also can affect the ambient conditions of the local climate. Succession can be seen as a coevolutionary process with the physical environment, local climate, and plant, animal, and human communities as mutually interacting components. To the extent that successional processes appear to tend toward a limited number of identifiable states, it might be expected that human-natural interactions are also heading toward a limited number of potentially predictable equilibrium conditions. Butzer (1996) points to the "Mediterranean agrosystem" as an example of millennia of coevolution. It is hoped that further evidence of long-term changes revealed by archaeology will help us decide if patterns such as these do, in fact, exist and can be helpful in guiding future decisions, based on those insights.

Fundamentals and Implications of Agriculture

The introduction of agriculture is regarded by many as the single most important transformation in human history. The shift from nomadic hunting and gathering to a settled agricultural village existence heralded changes in almost every facet of life and laid the necessary foundations for the growth of urban society and political hierarchies. The majority of case studies in this volume represent societies from various parts of the globe that chose to pursue an agrarian economy (this chapter) or to intensify the way they already practiced agriculture (chapter 6). Each of these cases will reveal some of the positive as well as negative relationships between people and their local environment that accompany a reliance on agriculture. Of particular interest are the decisions that were made to satisfy short-term objectives that in fact had unexpected consequences for long-term survival.

The introduction of agriculture and the ensuing rise of early civilizations are among humankind's greatest achievements. They have provided us with wondrous things and aided us in reaching our potential in many domains. Without food production, most of what we know as everyday life would not exist, and for that matter, most of us would not exist. Yet, it is also true that the evolution of a food-producing economy has taken a serious toll on humans and on our environment. By examining the development of agriculture, we may learn lessons for our own future.

Food production comprises four basic sets of activities: plant cultivation and/or animal husbandry, harvesting, storage, and control of propagation. In *plant cultivation* the natural vegetation is suppressed or removed, the biology of the topsoil is changed by hoeing or plowing, water is drained off or supplied, and weeds and/or predatory animals are controlled. There is some archaeological evidence that even before agriculture, advanced hunters and gatherers were expending energy to promote the growth of plants they ultimately consumed or were managing their hunting practices to ensure the maintenance of herds of game animals. *Harvesting* involves gathering the edible portion of the plant, slaughtering the animal for meat, or deriving some secondary product such as milk from animals. Preagriculturalists clearly harvested wild plants and slaughtered animals for food. *Storage* involves the treatment and preparation of food resources so that they may be kept for a period of time to even out food availability during lean seasons, or for longer periods of time against future bad harvests. Preagriculturalists certainly stored food, but with the advent of organized agriculture, storage was done on a much larger scale and for a second purpose as well—to retain seeds to plant during the following season.

The *control of propagation* is the key to identifying true domestication of plants and animals as distinct from the experimentation and rational management of resources that came before. Often this control may have happened inadvertently. An example is the consciously selected-for morphological changes that made plants and their seeds easier to gather and increased their food value. These changes, however, also meant that the plants could not reproduce well on their own and had to be planted by humans. With animals, this control of propagation was usually more purposeful and involved separating the sexes and selecting mates so as to enhance desirable characteristics or to suppress others.

The most obvious long-term result of agriculture has been to support the continuing global population expansion. Agriculture facilitated this by providing a potentially larger and more reliable food supply, often more dietary variety, expansion of the range of habitats that people could occupy, increase in the density of population that a landscape could support, and a more sedentary lifestyle that in itself allowed further population growth. This growth in overall population and in the number and size of villages led to a decline in some natural fauna of affected regions. Agriculturists would transform the landscape to suit their needs and would capture or kill animals that competed for grazing land or were predators of the domestic herds. We only have to look at the villagers who today live on the boundaries of Africa's game reserves to see the continual struggle they have with the ravages of the wild animals to their agricultural lands. The natural flora in the vicinity of villages would also suffer, sometimes being eliminated or suppressed to make way for cultivated plants, to be grazed away by domestic herds, or to be used as resources for fuel or building.

Agriculture is perhaps the greatest invention of all time, but it is often argued that the inventors did not recognize the introduction of agriculture as being something new. Instead it is thought that the process was gradual in terms of human life experiences, being the result of many small decisions, each reacting to immediate needs. The cumulative effect of these small decisions, when combined with the nature of the plants and animals and other aspects of human society, was a transformation of epochal significance. The decisions and activities that led to the domestication of plants and animals and the establishment of sedentary village life must have made sense at the time. Looking back from the perspective of today, many of these same decisions had social consequences of debatable merit and long-term environmental impacts that were unquestionably negative and ultimately undermined the very subsistence base they had worked so hard to establish. Many of the changes in human-environmental relationships that characterized early agricultural villages also took place among hunters and gatherers who maintained dense populations and established their own villages based on abundant wild resources. I do not focus on these societies as case studies because they were dispersed in time and space and ultimately succumbed to neighboring agriculturists (see Diamond 1997).

Three basic changes in human organization that resulted from agriculture have transformed society and had especially strong impacts on the environment. First, people settled into sedentary communities, population aggregated into denser settlements, and increasingly, communities relocated themselves to favor certain geographic locations over others. Initially this meant a preference for arable land that could be easily farmed with available rainfall, but even in prehistory the best land was soon filled. Further growth was only possible through the intensification of production, which meant a further aggregation to areas where irrigation was practical. This led to higher productivity per acre, as witnessed by the fact that 40% of modern crop production comes from only the 16% of agricultural land that is irrigated (Matson et al. 1997:506). This increasing productivity has ultimately allowed the movement into densely packed cities. The key point is that over the millennia, as world population has increased dramatically, it has not spread itself evenly over the landscape, but has increasingly favored select locations over vast stretches that remain lightly settled, if at all.

Second, sedentary life and new productive strategies brought about profound changes in family and social values. Permanence of settlement encouraged investment in immovable facilities such as substantial homes, food-processing equipment, and storage facilities. When people no longer needed to carry all of their belongings with them when a settlement moved, they were able to accumulate more and heavier goods, in addition to these stationary facilities. This encouraged the accumulation of material goods beyond the immediate biological needs of the people, and improvements in storage technology made possible keeping both hard and soft goods well beyond what had been known in the past. This trend must have been key in the development of the concepts of private property and prestige goods, both ideas that may not have always existed, but are fundamental to society as we now know it. We can suppose that in very ancient society the value of a good derived primarily from whether it could be eaten, worn, or used as a tool in the immediate future. There was a finite limitation on the amount of valued goods one could eat or wear, meaning there was little need to organize society to produce more than what could be consumed in a reasonable time. However, soon after the agricultural revolution, sedentism, improvement in storage, and the attribution of value beyond immediate consumables encouraged an expansion in production, an expansion in material wealth, and hence, an expansion of the need to protect these goods. This may have been a key step in the growth of social hierarchies as well as militarism and probably led to further movement of people into closely packed settlements that could be more easily defended.

Third, agriculture seems to have led to important changes in the organization of productive tasks and, consequently, to changes in the social and political organization of communities. Early villagers, like their hunting and gathering predecessors, appear to have maintained a relatively high level of flexibility in their productive strategies. Employing a mixed strategy of relying on a diversity of resources gave these communities resilience in the face of failures in one or another of their food sources. Even today, this is seen as a strength of small-scale societies. Although these early farmers retained a mix of food sources, they already were well along on a trajectory toward increasingly specialized tools, facilities, and organizational solutions. The coexistence of strategies that emphasize flexibility and specialization is an apparent contradiction that societies have faced since at least the early years of agriculture. Specialization often results in greater productivity, while flexibility provides for greater security in the face of crises. The resolution that most societies have enacted is to organize themselves hierarchically, with highly specialized lower order productive units and the integration of many of these diverse units at higher levels through bureaucratization and political control. This type of interdependence is at the heart of early complex societies, as it is in our own. This solution has tremendous potential for growth, but it also creates vulnerability by making the system fragile and susceptible to external or internal pressures that might break apart the specialized units. It also presents a situation in which not all members of a society share the same needs, viewpoints, and values. Both of these issues are examples of what Roy Rappaport defined as maladaptations and will be treated further in chapter 7.

Many other communities did not take the route toward productive specialization and amalgamation into larger sociopolitical units. They too sought ways to increase their production in order to feed more mouths, but at the same time attempted to remain independent of the growing urban centers. Anthropologists refer to this agrarian strategy as smallholders (Netting 1993). Smallholders are rural cultivators practicing intensive, permanent, diversified agriculture on relatively small farms in areas with a dense population. The family household is the primary social and productive unit, being largely self-sufficient but also participating in the local market economy and perhaps even housing some small cottage industry. A key aspect of the smallholders is that they own their own land, benefit directly from its productivity, and expect to remain on that plot of land for generations. This has led many scholars to point to this "ideal type" as a model for sustainable agriculture.

Because a smallholder system develops in regions of dense population, expanding the land being farmed is not an alternative to solve food shortfalls. Rather, the smallholders intensify their production through fitting an ever-increasing diversity of crops and animals onto their land. This is accomplished through the increasing investment of the labor of family members in preparing fields, fertilizing, weeding, watering, and carefully tending both plants and animals. Clifford Geertz referred to the process of increasing productivity by smallholders in Java to accommodate a growing population without a hierarchical society as "involution" (1963). The increasing number of people available made both possible and necessary the "fine-comb" techniques of water control and cultivation that still characterize the region. This strategy has proven successful in many widely separated parts of the world, but it does not provide the surplus accumulation or ease of political control that are the basis of complex society. Although not denying the importance of the smallholder in world history, this book focuses more on the agrarian strategies that accompanied the pathway toward complex society.

Our evidence speaks very strongly to the fact that even early agriculturists altered their environment in a serious manner, especially in their immediate locale. However, their overall impact on the larger regional and continental scales remained modest. This was due primarily to the fact that the overall population density was low; their villages were widely scattered on the landscape. In addition, some of the strategies pursued by these early farmers were less harmful to their local environment than practices of their supposedly more advanced successors. One of these strategies, followed to perfection by smallholders, was to plant a diversity of crops, even when dealing with a small field. This may have been done in an effort to reduce the likelihood of total crop failure, but it also had the salutary effect of not diminishing the soil fertility as quickly as single crops and offering the farmers a more balanced diet. The sacrifice they made was that to use a diversity of crops probably required more labor input and also may have produced a somewhat smaller total yield than a single crop. In many ancient, as well as modern, societies the key feature of agricultural intensification has been increasing specialization, that is to focus on the production of a very few crops or animals (Matson et al. 1997:504). The logical extreme of increasing absolute production by specialization is for the farmer to focus on a single crop and rely on a redistributive economy, such as a market, to exchange their produce to meet their own broader needs. Although productivity has been enhanced in many parts of the world by monocropping in this way, so have the risks of increased pests, the loss of beneficial soil microbes, and the growing dependence of farmers on a central political authority.

Environment and Culture in the Early Levant

The earliest food-producing villages seem to have appeared independently in various regions of the world between 6000 and 10,000 years ago. I have chosen to begin with case studies from the Near East because these examples were the earliest, and they influenced developments in many other regions. These early agriculturists lived in nucleated settlements of 50 to 100 or more people. They built substantial, multiroomed, rectilinear homes. They also developed a diverse inventory of tools and containers, most notably grinding stones for food processing, sickle blades for harvesting grain, and ceramic vessels for food preparation and storage. In almost every way that we have come to understand these people, we find them to be extremely creative. They were ambitious and they were problem solvers. The archaeological record is full of evidence of their willingness to experiment: with new tools, new materials, new food-producing strategies, new crops, and new locations to live. I doubt that they clearly understood many of the scientific principles that guided their successful agricultural practices, nor did they have the inventory of experience we apply to solving problems today. Nevertheless, they developed a lifeway that was extraordinarily successful and that many wish to emulate today.

The form of the early agricultural villages that developed in the Near East endured largely intact for millennia and was adopted as a model in many regions throughout the Old World. Three advances were behind the success of this way of life. First, the physiological changes in the domesticates made them more productive and allowed them to be grown in a wider range of environments. Second, the technology of food production, processing, and storage was improved. Third, changes in social values and organization enhanced the effectiveness of village life and the new economy. Whatever were the actual details, this new way of living caught on, and nucleated farming villages became the dominant life unit across the globe from then until the current century.

Environment

The region of the Near East on which we will focus is the Levant (Lebanon, Israel, Jordan, and western Syria). It is the scene of a long and very important history of human occupation that has been well studied. The climate of the Levant is dominated by cool rainy winters and hot, dry summers, what geographers have called a *Mediterranean climatic regime*. Precipitation is not abundant except at the highest elevations and then especially in the north. The modest amount of surface runoff allows for the creation of few real rivers, such as the Orontes of Lebanon and Syria and the Jordan of Israel and Jordan. There are, however, numerous localized springs and sufficient rainfall for dry farming in various locations. The landscape is largely hill country, broken with lowland plains and chains of higher mountains running north–

south. The hill country is the best watered in the region. The land tends toward greater aridity as one moves south past Jerusalem and east past the Jordan and Orontes River valleys. Our major concern with early village life and its impact focuses on the hill country where villages were numerous.

Mediterranean vegetation is naturally very rich. The available genetic diversity is due to its location at the geographical contact point of three continents. It was a botanical conservatory during glacial periods, and the number of plant groupings in the Mediterranean Basin as a whole is several tens of thousands. Over 100 species of trees are native to the region as compared with only 30 in temperate Europe (Le Houérou 1981:486). The Mediterranean has been a center of origin and dispersal for many species, especially those that ultimately were to be domesticated, such as wheat, barley, sorghum, lentil, pea, olive, grape, almond, peach, plum, date, and pistachio. Some of this diversity is due to ecological conditions — being at the contact zone between temperate and tropical regions — and some is due to the long history of human disturbance. The vegetation sorts itself out by elevation and moisture zones. In the higher, wetter elevations there are major forests of cedars, pines, and firs. At the intermediate hilly elevations where the soil is thinner, there is the *maquis vegetation* dominated by deciduous oak and pistachio woodlands. In the drier area *garrique vegetation* is characteristic with smaller evergreen oaks, juniper, and shrubs, while some areas are open grasslands and the driest zones have very little vegetation at all.

Soils of the Mediterranean include *terra rossa,* a clay-loam formed on hard limestone and noted for its red color and favorable structure for plant growth; and *rendzina,* a darkish loam formed on soft limestone and marly bedrock. Both will absorb rainfall, but the key issue for both is soil depth. Although soil accumulates at some depth in lowland basins, on hillsides it is usually less than a meter thick and can be much less. Due to slow formation of soil and the uncertain retention of it in most topographic settings, the vegetation of the region is quite vulnerable. The climate exacerbates this with the long, hot, dry summers that make most plants susceptible to destruction from fire, grazing, or erosion. The general vegetation regression in the region from natural or human-induced activities is toward species that are light tolerant, drought resistant, relatively unpalatable, and able to reproduce from root suckers, cuttings, or produce abundant seed (fig. 5.4; Simmons 1989).

Fire

Due to aridity and the frequency of lightening strikes, fire always has been an important natural force in shaping the Mediterranean landscape. Besides the

Figure 5.4
Vegetation sequence in Levant, following human impact.

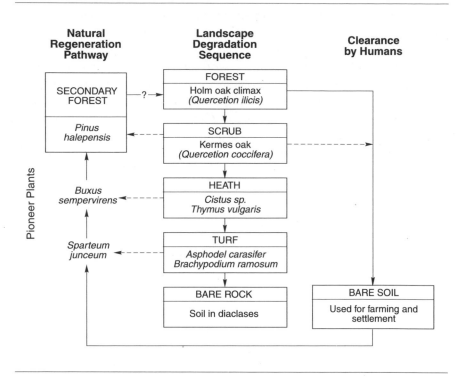

various domestic reasons for using fire, there are several uses of fire that were key to the broader environment. Of special significance for this chapter is that many cultivators used fire to help clear land for planting crops or for enhancing growth of grasses for grazing animals (see fig. 4.5). The most important reasons to use fire are to open up the canopy so light can reach lower plants, to destroy competitive plants, and to break down nutrients stored in woody plant material. In several tropical regions of the world, farmers utilized an integrated approach known as *slash-and-burn,* or *swidden,* to prepare their fields for planting. Known as *milpa agriculture* when practiced by the Maya of Central America, it involves felling the trees of a section of forest, letting the debris dry, and burning it. Not only does that open up the canopy, but it also converts the living plant matter back into minerals that enhance soil fertility, promoting subsequent plant growth. Following the onset of the rains, seeds are planted and crops are grown on that section of land for several seasons. This type of practice exists where there is sufficient land for farmers to move around every few years, and the soil fertility is limited to relatively few growing seasons before requiring a long fallow period for rejuvenation.

This type of swidden system of agriculture is not limited to the tropics. In fact the term "swidden" derives from Old Norse, meaning, "to burn" and came to England with the Norse invaders of the Middle Ages (Pyne 1998:79). In historic England the use of fire in agriculture was quite complex, with slash-and-burn cultivation in outfields, stubble burning in infields, pastoral burning in abandoned plots, and a variety of other uses of fire to promote specific products. Ethnographic and historic records do not document slash-and-burn agriculture being practiced in the Levant in recent times. Nevertheless, we do have evidence for fire being used by early farmers for various tasks, and it may be possible that through continued archaeological research, we will document the use of swidden there.

The risks of natural fire become greater the longer the dry season, so the Mediterranean has a high vulnerability to fire. It is estimated that 3% to 5% of the Levantine forests burn from natural causes each year; therefore it is likely that each plot of forest would burn once every 25 years in a natural setting (Le Houérou 1981:487). The longer the period between fires, the more established the forest cover becomes. The more frequent the fires, the more likely that the same species of trees will not be able to reestablish themselves and that the ground cover will be *degraded* toward more fire-resistant scrub plants and trees (fig. 5.4; see also fig. 4.5). In fact, it is estimated that if the frequency of burning is every 10 years or less, the forest cover will not recover at all and the natural vegetation will become shrubs, herbs, and grasses. Because it does not burn a landscape evenly and each fire is restricted in extent, fire contributes to patchiness. The differentially burned patches will have plant communities of different "successional age" and species composition. The fact that fires often increase the biological diversity of a landscape in this manner has made human-induced controlled burns a favorite tool of forest ecologists today, just as it must have served the hunter-gatherers and early farmers of prehistory.

Grazing

Grazing of vegetation by animals is a natural phenomenon as old as the existence of herbivores, which began well before the appearance of humans. Once again, this is a natural process that was not invented by humans, but has been expanded under their influence. Light grazing may actually increase the productivity of wild pastures. Nibbling and removal of dead stems can encourage the vigor of plants, animals may disperse seeds, and their feces can enhance the fertility of the pasture. Heavy grazing, however, is clearly detrimental in more ways than the direct removal of the plant parts through eating. Among them is compaction from trampling that makes soil more vulnerable to wind erosion and reduces the soil's capacity for moisture infiltration. Grazing may also reduce the plant's photosynthesis ability by removing leaves, or it may kill it directly. As desirable plants are eaten or killed, the reduced competition allows for the spread of unpalatable plants. This usually favors the spread of xeric species, low-to-the-ground plants and "tough" plants in general.

In the Levant it is estimated that about 17% of the land is natural pasture, often in the steppe and predesert zones. This contemporary distribution does not put grazing activity in competition with farmers for land, but we can expect that in the early era of farming, the same lands would be utilized and grazing would be a major factor in the deterioration of potential farmland. The nature of the Levantine climate would exacerbate the effects of grazing. Mild winters with no snow cover would mean that grazing could continue year-round and that there would be no season when the plants and soil were protected from animals. This year-round grazing also meant that the concept of storing forage for the bad season (as is the practice in more temperate climates) was not prevalent; instead, the general attitude was that animals would look out for their nutrition on their own. This lack of concern for the impact of grazing on the plant resources of a region was not a serious problem as long as the population density (and density of animals) was relatively low versus the regenerative ability of the natural vegetation.

This ability to expand the number of animals kept to fill the environment may have been a key factor in animals becoming the major form of wealth in many societies. Moreover, investing available capital in animals often paid a very handsome return. The people of the Levant saw the keeping of goats, in particular, as a great investment. Requiring a very small expenditure, goats multiply quickly, providing a possible return of 15% to 30%. One pair of goats can produce 100 animals in as little as five years. In this same period, sheep would produce 32 and cattle, 10. In addition, the goat is the best domesticate for poor vegetation zones where they are satisfied with a woody forage, agile enough to reach difficult places, resistant to thirst, and intelligent in seeking their own food. The well-known omnivorous habits of goats meant that widespread removal of vegetation would result, and the taste preferences of goats would lead to young shoots and seedlings disappearing first, reducing the chance of new plants regenerating. The productivity of domestic goats was a tremendous resource for the early villagers of the Levant, but their potential impact on the environment was even more awesome.

Erosion

One of the most powerful tools nature employs for reshaping landscapes is water transport (alluvial) and wind-borne (aeolian) erosion. Mountains have been worn down and valleys filled with sediments by the force of gravity and the media of moving water and wind. The susceptibility of a landscape to erosion depends on a variety of factors. Human intervention does not create erosion on its own, but contributes to a landscape's susceptibility. Topography is a key element in the likelihood of erosion, with steep slopes being far more vulnerable than level plains. Also the nature of the potential sediments is important, with small particles, such as clay, being easiest to move. The third major factor, and the one most directly affected by humans, is the vegetative cover of the landscape. Holding other factors constant, the amount of erosion is inversely proportional to the degree of vegetative cover (fig. 5.5; Goldsmith et al. 1990). Studies indicate that the amount of erosion is 50 times higher on bare soil than under a well-developed forest cover. In

Figure 5.5
Effect of ground cover on soil retention.

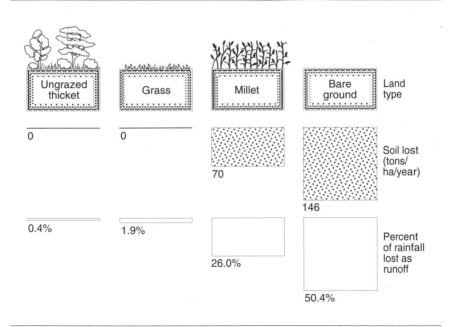

addition, the rate of rainfall runoff is five times higher as well, both contributing a transport medium for carrying the sediments and contributing far less moisture to the remaining soil.

Tremendous amounts of arable topsoil are carried off in erosion each year, even today. It is estimated that in modern Algeria, 40,000 hectares of arable land are lost by erosion every year (Le Houérou 1981:516). Loss of agriculturally productive soil by erosion is among the foremost environmental threats facing the modern world, and archaeological evidence points to this being a serious problem as early as 8000 years ago. Figure 5.6 delineates the interaction of the many factors that influence the severity of wind and water erosion (van der Leeuw 1998a). The physical factors, such as climate and ground cover, interact with human factors, such as food supplies needed and strategies employed to secure them. Crop choice, grazing pressure, and human population will all affect the character of the erosional regime. For the purposes of our inquiry, soil erosion is an ideal yardstick to evaluate the degree of human impact on local environments: first, because it is relatively easy to measure with archaeological evidence; and second, because it is a key to the continuing productive potential of a landscape. Buried sediment profiles can be studied to reveal a datable record of the history of local soil formation and sediment deposition for that locale.

Over the past 10,000 years, virtually all Mediterranean landscapes, especially those of the Levant, have been transformed and in some ways degraded under human influence (see van der Leeuw 1998b for recent overview). This extraordinarily long period of dense agrarian settlement has amplified the natural climate's high potential for soil erosion and other forms of degradation. The harsher and more fragile the environment, the more far-reaching and potentially irreversible will be the damage. In general, soil recovery processes are slowest on shallow soils covering hard rocks and faster on soft rock. The long duration of the recovery cycle in the Levant and other parts of the Mediterranean have led to significant changes in biota. This has encouraged the invasion of more xeric elements from adjacent arid zones and favored the selection for plants with the best adaptive resistance to constant pressure of defoliation by fire, cutting, and grazing (see fig. 5.4). In many areas this has resulted in the natural oak woodlands giving way to a "scrub ecosystem" that is surprisingly resilient under constant pressure. Under continual pressure, this scrub may degrade to something with only low plants like a heath or open turf. Under direct human intervention, bare soil is often exposed in preparation to be used for crops. In either situation, if the soil is left alone it slowly regenerates with secondary plants that would eventually develop into a secondary forest characterized by hardy pines.

Combining the slow recovery of soils and the accompanying changes

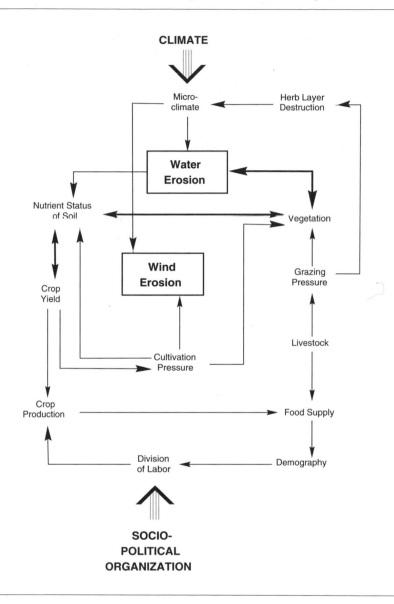

in biota with the sloping topography of the upland Levant, where farming has been practiced for ten millennia, yields a situation in which anthropogenic impacts can be recognized from very early times. The resilience of the human populations and their determination to remain in the region have provided perhaps the longest record of human-agriculture-environmental coevolution of anywhere in the world (Butzer 1996). What resulted in terms of environmental transformation and human accommodation are lessons of enormous significance. Whether we call the changes degradation or not, people have continued to live and thrive in the region and there is a certain level of stability that emerged, at least until very recent times. Do the facts that the vegetation has changed and there has been substantial soil erosion mean that humans have degraded their surroundings, or that a new balance has been achieved that takes into account the objectives and activities of human members of the ecosystem?

People have lived for a very long time in the Levant, at least since *Homo erectus* entered the region about one million years ago. Moreover, due to its geographic location as a land bridge between continents, there have been periodic movements of people through the region, so one could expect that there would be admixture of genes and diffusion of ideas. For almost all of this time, people were hunters and gatherers who existed in small groups that moved about the landscape once or more each year. Among the earliest evidence for fully modern humans comes from the Levant at about 50,000 years ago, as does very early evidence for advanced hunting practices, such as attempts at conserving herd size and organized stalking techniques.

Of great relevance for understanding the nature of human impacts on the environment are the earliest examples of settled villages found in the Levant. Some of the early Levantine villages were surprisingly large, containing 500 to 1000 people or more — certainly the largest found anywhere in the world at that time. All this began to take hold about 10,000 to 15,000 years ago, when there was evidence for people settling into favorable locations for the entire year, building permanent structures in which to live, and aggregating into large groups. Archaeologists have subdivided the time range of interest to us — 10,000 to 6000 B.C. — into periods: the Natufian, the prepottery Neolithic A, and the prepottery Neolithic B (fig. 5.7).

The Natufians were talented folks who lived by gathering plants and hunting animals. Among the important plants for them were wild progenitors of wheat and barley, and among the animals they hunted were wild sheep, goat, and gazelle. They built circular houses with massive stone foundations and aggregated into settlements of 10 or 20 of these homes. These homes often had hearths for cooking and large immovable grinding stones for processing the seeds and nuts they collected. All of these constructions

Figure 5.7
Map of early villages in the Levant and chronology of the prehistoric period.

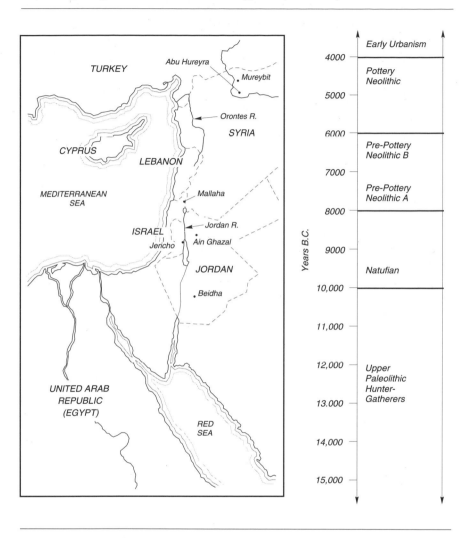

give the impression of sedentism and can be safely called villages. These Natufian villages have been found along virtually the entire length of the Levant in a zone within about 100 miles of the Mediterranean coastline.

In the subsequent prepottery Neolithic periods, especially the B period (ca. 7000–6000 B.C.), there was an increase in the number of settlements, and some of these settlements grew quite large (Rollefson and Köhler-Rollefson 1992). There is evidence that some of the plants were domesticated

Figure 5.8
Contemporary Near Eastern village built with traditional materials in an eroded topographical setting.

by this time period, and there are some scholars who believe that some of the animals were being herded as well. Although both wild and domestic resources were playing a role in the lives of most villagers, the proportion of domestic plants and possibly animals was getting much higher, and village size and the variety of tools used increased. The people who lived in the Levant during the eighth and seventh millennia were at the cutting edge of innovation and could be considered the "most advanced" in the world according to several key criteria. Villages like Jericho, Beidha, Ain Ghazal, Mureybit, and Tell abu Herera grew to hundreds of residents, with well-built rectilinear homes, abundant storage and food-processing facilities, and possibly even some defensive walls (Moore 1985). The effective combination of widely available building materials with utilitarian homes has led to similarly constructed villages for millennia (see fig. 5.8). We have found evidence for trade from Anatolia to the Sinai in at least obsidian and turquoise, and there appears to have been a shared tradition for burial rites over this same region.

The subsequent history of the Levant is a series of ebbs and flows of population size, foreign intrusions, and local resurgence. Of special importance here is the fact that at about 6000 B.C., the number of sedentary villages seriously contracts, suggesting a substantial population decline. Some of that decline may be a result of the fact that many of the former villagers took up more nomadic ways of life and left less archaeological evidence of their presence, but even with that possibility factored in, there was a major decline in settled village life at that time. Village life did expand again starting in about 4000 B.C., and by 3000 B.C. there were large towns and walled settlements we might call cities across this region. History records several more expansions and contractions of settled village life in the Levant, with probably the premodern zenith of population reached during Roman times, early in the first century A.D.

Environmental Impact of the Earliest Farmers

A particularly exciting case study comes to us from the site of Ain Ghazal in southern Jordan. Gary and Ilse Rollefson report on the rise and apparent fall of this very impressive village at about 8000 to 6000 B.C. (1992). Some scholars have suggested that the abandonment of villages like Ain Ghazal around 6000 B.C. was a result of a climatic drying period that made settled farming impractical. The Rollefsons argue that the climate may have changed for the worse at that time, but that more factors were involved in this widespread village abandonment. They attribute some of the blame to human activities and choices the occupants made about their villages. Three factors — the use of plaster in their homes, the reliance on goat herds, and the topography and soils of the region — are singled out as having had extraordinary impacts on the landscape, ultimately undermining its ability to support settled village life.

The early villagers of Ain Ghazal and elsewhere in the Levant built surprisingly substantial homes with stone walls and mud floors, both covered with plaster. Several types of plaster — mud, gypsum, and lime — were used in several of these villages. However, the preparation of lime plaster consumed the most energy, requiring far more burning than gypsum or than mud, which required no fuel in its preparation. The Rollefsons estimate that a ton of lime plaster required four tons of wood as fuel. Despite this heavy drain of what we now know was a valuable and limited resource, the early villagers of the Levant choose to use lime plaster for their homes and to replaster their walls and floors quite frequently. Excavations at Ain Ghazal and elsewhere have revealed homes in which the walls and floors were replastered dozens of times, perhaps even annually. According to their estimates, use of this type of lime plaster would have required enormous quantities of timber to use as fuel. Given the natural density of the local forests, this activity alone would have led to the deforestation of an area 3 km in diameter around the village.

Sheep and goats were the primary domestic animals kept by the early villagers of the Levant. In the north, sheep were the predominant animals, but due to the rougher topography and more arid climate of the south, goats were the animals of choice among the villagers there. Sheep are grazers that focus on eating grasses, while goats are browsers that are happy with coarser vegetation. The goats kept by the villagers would have a serious effect on seedlings and young saplings that were trying to grow in areas that had been logged for house construction or fuel for plaster burning. This would retard the regeneration of forest cover and lead to a degradation of the plants that did return to include more scrub and thistles. These plants were less desirable to many foragers, but this did not prevent the goats from continuing their consumption. It is likely that the farmers kept the goats and other animals off their agricultural fields during the winter growing season, but logically they would let them feed on the stubble in the fields during the arid summers and early fall. This would make the field most vulnerable to erosion just as the rains would begin in late autumn. The overall impact of herding goats as part of the agricultural strategy was to expose more of the landscape to erosional forces at a bad time of year, putting the already fragile soil at greater risk.

The topography of the southern Levant is deeply dissected, with water available only near springs or in *wadi* bottoms (wadi is the Arabic word for a seasonally dry streambed). Hence, human settlements would need to be near water, and farming would most likely be on adjacent terrain. Some farming could be done in the wadi bottoms themselves, but the area was very limited. So from the beginning, the slopes of the wadis were essential to farming success. Areas with sloping surfaces like these would be particularly vulnerable to erosion, and if there was little or no vegetation to hold the soils in place, the fall and winter rains would surely wash away some of the valuable soil.

These factors combined to make a reliance on agriculture the logical short-term choice, but they were troubling in the long term. On an immediate time frame, cutting trees for home construction, plaster burning, and the domestic hearth all helped clear nearby fields that then could be planted with the newly domesticated cereal grains. At first the goats must have also seemed like the perfect complement to agricultural fields, manuring them in the off-season and consuming the seemingly useless stubble of the fields. However, the cumulative effects were quite harmful. During the growing season, the goats would be kept off the agricultural fields. They would have to graze further from the village, hence, putting pressure on vegetative ground cover over a wider and wider area. The same pattern of expanding extent of damage would be true of the ever-present need for fuel wood. Together this would degrade the natural vegetation in an ever-increasing area around the settlement. Among this natural vegetation were plants used as food sources by the villagers as well as for forage by wild animals, which continued to be hunted for food by the villagers. As the fuel and grazing needs pushed the boundary of native vegetation further and further from the settlement, these wild resources became less attractive, and consequently the villagers narrowed their dietary focus by relying more and more on their domestic fields and herds.

The Rollefsons report on a gradual period of decline at Ain Ghazal, leading to abandonment at a later date. Evidence was recovered in excavations that documented the stress on the local environment towards the end of the site's occupation: rooms became smaller due to fewer big timber being available, there was decreasing diameter wood used as fuel in the hearths, there was decreasing variability of wild animals eaten by the villagers, and the lime plaster that required burning was given up in favor of a crushed lime plaster that did not require fuel. These changes were obviously a reflection of a deteriorating natural vegetation in the vicinity of Ain Ghazal, a major factor in causing its decrease in size and the abandonment of many of its sister large villages at about 6000 B.C.

Humans are an industrious species, and although there were negative aspects to this developing agricultural system, the villagers probably sought ways to make it work to their benefit. The land clearance and exposure of the terrain to soil erosion was probably not sufficient cause to destroy this lifeway and lead to widespread village abandonment. Possibly these activities led to an increasing vulnerability of the productive base of the communities and a certain fragility of the economy. In any particular year, this may not have been a problem, but climatic forces vary from season to season. Their increased vulnerability to a series of bad years may have been enough to undermine an entire way of life.

It is likely that at about 6000 B.C. a slight deterioration in the climate led to a series of dry years that were too much for the agricultural villages to absorb, and they were forced to abandon their settlements and lifestyle. Ain Ghazal was fortuitously located at an ecotone where various resources continued to be available, but probably even there the population fell. The abandonment of villages and decrease in size of remaining settlements did not mean that people died off or disappeared completely. Rather, they probably fragmented into smaller groups and took up less sedentary lifestyles.

Steve Falconer and Patricia Fall, who also study in the Levant, see the human-environmental interactions established in this early period as forming the foundation of the characteristic Near Eastern lifeway (1995; see also Butzer 1996). What resulted was a fluid balance of sedentary village agriculturists and smaller groups of pastoralists who followed a less sedentary settlement system. As deforestation and crops pushed the foraging area farther from the village, herds would be kept away full time and those who were responsible for the herds became independent groups. The separation of herders from farming village bases extended the potential area of human impact well beyond the select landscape suitable for farming. This could be seen as positive for the success of people at this time, but it also meant that the negative impacts that came with goat grazing, fuel consumption, and other forms of exploitation occurred on an ever wider landscape. Falconer and Fall use pollen evidence from the millennia following the first establishment of early villages to document the increasing spread of forest clearance activities through the Levant. All of this forest clearance did not result in denuded landscape; often the native oaks were cut down to be replaced by orchards of the newly domesticated olive and vineyards of grapes. These types of crops required a larger investment of labor through the construction of terrace systems and a longer period of waiting for the first returns, but they also led to a stable environmental regime.

Ancient Greece, Italy, and Spain

The countries bordering the northern shores of the Mediterranean Sea were the focus of seminal cultural developments and numerous archaeological investigations. Anyone who has visited Greece or Adriatic Italy knows that they are rugged, semiarid regions with relatively small alluvial valleys and accompanying slopes that are just barely suitable for agriculture. Yet, this is the homeland to some of the world's great civilizations and the origin of many ideas fundamental to subsequent Western Civilization. In particular, agrarian village life is almost as old in Greece as it was in the Levant. Small villages based on domesticated plants and animals were established in Greece by 6000 B.C. and soon thereafter in southern Italy. From then on there have been cycles of growth and decline until the present.

The focus of the first set of archaeological investigations described here is on soil erosion in various localities in Greece (fig. 5.9). As was pointed out earlier, rate of soil erosion is a key aspect in agrarian success and a particularly ominous threat in the hilly areas of the Mediterranean Basin. Greece's climate is similar to that in the Levant, with its topography being more hilly, but without the truly arid zones of the eastern and southern

Figure 5.9
Map of Greece, Italy, and Spain with location of studies.

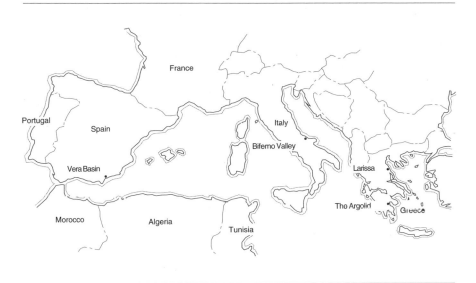

Levant. The major distinguishing characteristics are the numerous useable harbors and the proximity of coastline to almost all land areas of Greece. This led to a focus on maritime trade and resource exploitation, but throughout its history, small-scale village farming has been the core of Greek subsistence. Just as Greek myths speak of golden and dark ages, the archaeological evidence speaks of periods of agrarian success and shortfalls. Although historic events play a major role, some scientists are now linking agrarian failures with the relative rate of soil erosion in the region.

In 1969, a prominent British geologist, Claudio Vita-Finzi, published a summary of sedimentological information from across the Mediterranean. He concluded that the recent history of stream deposition throughout the Mediterranean could be understood as the result of two major phases of alluviations, the Older and the Younger Fills. He dated the Older Fill as late Pleistocene (ca. 50,000–10,000 B.P.) and the Younger Fill as occurring between late Roman and early Modern times (ca. A.D. 400). Each of these episodes silted up stream channels, valley floors, and coastal plains and was distinct from the incision or stream-cutting episodes that came before and after. Both episodes are attributed to climatically wet periods, or pluvials, that would cause accelerated slopewash and stream runoff. The simplicity and explanatory power of these universal climatic events led scholars in various disciplines, particularly archaeology, to employ this model in explaining the ebb and flow of cultures in their own regions.

As might be expected in a region as diverse as the Mediterranean basin, simple explanations are quickly challenged. Additional evidence collected in a diversity of locations began to show that these episodes were not really contemporaneous, especially the Younger Fill where both historical and archaeological evidence was abundant. Clearly, major depositional episodes occurred in most alluvial localities across the Mediterranean, but it was unrealistic to see them as the result of a single synchronic climatic event or even a series of a few events. The pattern was far more complex, and many scholars now argue that the Younger Fill in particular was human induced. Geologist Tjeerd H. van Andel has been particularly influential in overturning this model. His work with archaeological evidence, first in the Argolid plain of Greece (van Andel, Runnels, and Pope 1986) and then comparing that to two other regions of Greece (van Andel, Zangger, and Demitrack 1990), has provided an alternate working model.

Van Andel focuses his attention on sediment columns taken from three separate alluvial valleys in Greece, each with somewhat different cultural histories and depositional records. The sediment sequence in each area is composed of depositional units separated by soil horizons. In the southern Argolid area, for example, the sediment sequence is composed of seven depositional units (fig. 5.10). Each unit represents an episode of erosion in the headwater region's slopes and a resulting alluviation of the valley floor where the sediment core was taken. Each unit ends with a loam and soil profile that indicates a longer period of slope stability during which the slow process of soil formation took place. At that same time, the stream channels became incised and sedimentation ceased, except for intermittent deposits of silt that was carried beyond the streambanks by floods. In summary, there are three phases to each episode: ill-sorted gravels (evidence of catastrophic sheet erosion caused by decreased plant cover), well-sorted gravels (indicating slower erosion), and sandy silt deposits from overbank flooding (usually meaning a period of stability and soil formation). When carbon can be found in the sediment, radiocarbon (c14) dating is possible, and in some cases actual archaeological artifacts are found in the deposits. Where this type of dating is possible the relative sequences can be cross-dated from valley to valley. This has not been possible for all ranges of time represented in the sediment profiles, but sufficient correlations have been made to reconstruct a useful set of histories.

In the southern Argolid, the first three depositional units date to the Pleistocene (272,000, 52,000, and 33,000 B.P.) and the other four are from the last 5000 years (Holocene). The three early units have all phases and may

Figure 5.10
Stratigraphic profile and chronological periods from Argolid core.

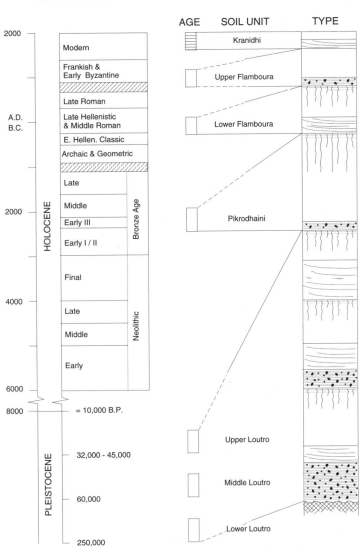

reflect major climatic episodes, since land-transforming human settlement at that early date is unlikely. The more recent Holocene alluvial units are thinner and not as complete, being more closely spaced in time, yet all but the youngest are capped with soil profiles, indicating prolonged slope stability between erosional events that themselves were brief.

Matching this geologically derived sequence with what we know of the settlement history based on archaeology provides some interesting correlations. We know that the deep woodland soils of the hills and some valley bottoms of this region were utilized by Neolithic farmers, but the first of the Holocene erosional units does not occur until about 2000 B.C. This indicates that the settlement density was low or their conservation practices sound enough that for several millennia a balance was maintained. The first erosional episode was followed by a period of population decrease that ended with population increase during the Late Bronze Age of ca. 1400–1200 B.C. Archaeological investigations reveal that there were many people in the valley during this period, yet their presence did not lead directly to soil erosion. This suggests that these people may have introduced some form of soil conservation techniques, probably the use of terracing on the slopes surrounding the valley bottom and checkdams in the gullies. It is also interesting that there is not major erosion during what the ancient Greeks called their *Dark Age* (ca. 1100–900 B.C.). Here the explanation probably has more to do with a decrease in settled agricultural activity and a return of some of the natural forest cover. Growth of settlements resumed with population reaching a historic peak during the fifth through third centuries B.C. During that time farming also expanded to the areas on the edge of the valleys for the first time. These areas were not suitable for the cereal agriculture practiced in the deeper soils, but may have worked well for olive orchards.

The following two erosional episodes occurred during the final centuries before the beginning of the Christian era and then again in late Roman times (ca. seventh century A.D.). Both of these episodes could be viewed historically as periods of settlement contraction following eras of high population and political control. The erosional episodes probably reflect periods of agrarian breakdown when farmers withdraw to their best soils, turning over more distant or poorer fields to pasturage. Without an incentive to repair damage caused by livestock, it takes only a few decades for terrace walls to tumble and gully erosion to strip the stored soil and lay it down as sediments in the valley bottoms (van Andel, Runnels, and Pope 1986). The combined degradation of the hill slope country and burial by sediments of some of the valley bottoms led to contraction of arable lands and partial abandonment of the countryside and some of the major cities. After a period of centuries, soils rebuilt largely due to the establishment of Mediterranean shrub community (maquis) and abandoned areas were recolonized. The fourth Holocene erosional episode is occurring now, and it is interesting to speculate on the similarity of historical circumstances to those of the past. If the pattern holds true, a phase of serious erosion and abandonment may be in store.

The other two regions of Greece discussed by these authors had distinct sequences of erosion and stability complementing the data from the southern Argolid. The much larger Argive Plain shows a major erosion episode in Early Bronze times, late in the third millennium. Since then, there has been overall stability in the plain, but localized episodes of flooding due to specific erosional problems. Both here and in the third area, the Larissa basin, initial land clearance for agriculture does not seem to be the cause of the erosional episodes, but they occur only after substantial periods of farming. In fact, in all three areas, stability characterizes most of the sequence, and erosional episodes are brief in duration and scattered widely through the centuries.

Van Andel, Zangger, and Demitrack reach four basic conclusions from their research (1990). First, the nonsynchrony of the depositional episodes weighs heavily against a primarily climatic explanation of erosion. Second, people were able to farm these lands for long periods of time, probably benefiting from the use of labor intensive soil conservation approaches, especially on the sloping terrain. These would include terracing and other runoff-impeding constructions. Third, after long periods of dense occupation, upland regions appear to suffer serious erosional episodes, that lead to their depopulation and the aggregation of farmers in the still favorable settings. This in turn puts excessive pressure on these locations. Also, the abandonment or relegation to animal grazing of the upland farms and terraces led to more rapid erosion of those zones and deposition of coarse sediments in the lowlands. Fourth, with abandonment of upland zones, shrub vegetation takes over and stabilizes the area, and following several centuries of soil buildup, it is once again suitable for agriculture.

A program of environmental and archaeological investigations to the west in the Biferno valley of Adriatic Italy (fig. 5.9) provides confirmatory evidence for the repeated correlation between intensity of human activity and the rate of valley sedimentation (Barker 1995). Like van Andel who studied Greece, Grahame Barker and his colleagues took the synthetic model of Vita-Finzi as a starting point for evaluating the respective roles of climate and people in shaping the Mediterranean landscape. The valley has been the subject of a long-term investigation through regional survey, site excavation, textual examination, and paleoenvironmental reconstruction. Interestingly, the rate of sedimentation recorded on valley terraces indicates only modest levels of erosion for the early periods of human occupation, with the first major erosional episodes being tied to the spread of rural settlement and agriculture during Samnite and Roman times (the second half of the first millennium B.C. and the early centuries A.D.). The countryside filled in with settlements to an extent unparalleled in the valley's history until modern times. Cereals, legumes, and vines were grown in the upper valley and olives were cultivated in the lower valley. With the beginning of the medieval period, there is good archaeological evidence for a significant drop in the intensity of rural settlement and accompanying land clearance. The valley sediments also document this as being a period of diminished erosion and probably some restoration of the natural forest cover of the hills. It is not until the fifteenth through seventeenth centuries that the Biferno valley experiences its second major phase of intense rural settlement. Once again, the evidence for alluviation also increases at this time, indicating the renewed efforts at land clearance and accompanying soil erosion. Barker concludes that the Samnite/early Roman phase of active alluviation in the Biferno valley does not fit well with the Vita-Finzi model of the Younger Fill that should have occurred some centuries later. Rather, he sees land-use practices as the major agent of landscape change during the later Holocene.

The historical patterns of degradation and desertification of Mediterranean Europe are the focus of a large multinational interdisciplinary project sponsored by the Commission of the European Communities and referred to as the *Archaeomedes Project*. Archaeologists are working together with natural scientists, ethnographers, and economists to understand long-term changes in the landscape of selected regions in Greece, Italy, France, and Spain (van der Leeuw 1998a). Each year thousands of hectares in southern Europe are transformed into near-deserts as a result of contemporary activities as well as patterns that have occurred over much longer spans of time. In one of the study areas, the Vera Basin of southeastern Spain (fig. 5.9), the Archaeomedes team has traced the interacting patterns of settlement, food production, vegetative cover, and soil erosion over the past five millennia. Beginning about 3000 B.C., population increased substantially, with mixed farming communities in the valley floor and grazing in the hilly hinterlands. This pattern continued with evident success until about 1800 B.C., when there was a shift towards a barley-based monocrop agriculture. This seemed to be accompanied by a deforestation of the uplands, a desiccation of the valleys, and the abandonment of many of the settlements, especially in the uplands. By 1400 B.C. the evidence from fuel wood charcoal shows that shrubs and weeds were being used, implying a shortage of available trees. By 1200 B.C. only small, dispersed settlements remained in the lowlands.

Population increased once again during the first millennium, with settlements growing along the coast and mining becoming an economic base. Intense use of the land during this period, including irrigation agriculture, led to its collapse by A.D. 400. Irrigated terrace agriculture became widespread with the eighth century Arab conquest. Small-scale farm holdings characterized the landscape with a multicrop strategy of cereals and extensive plantations of mulberry trees. The region supported a dense population, but with the expulsion of Muslims in the fifteenth and sixteenth centuries, there was a rapid decline in population and the land-holding system changed to fewer, larger holdings. With the depopulation came the deterioration of the irrigation and terracing system, leading to widespread erosion in the uplands and a focus of the remaining population along the rivers. Resurgence in the importance of mining in the eighteenth and nineteenth centuries led to a reoccupation of the area, but as that boom ended, emigration once again began. At present the landscape is seriously impoverished.

The recording of this long series of oscillations in settlement and productivity revealed that after each period of intense human activity, there was a commensurate "environmental crisis." The subsequent reoccupation of the area required a change in exploitation techniques. Intensification of agricultural techniques, mining, and trade all required investment of capital and labor and made the system ever more dependent and vulnerable to socioeconomic systems outside the region. The Archaeomedes Project continues, and they are adding many insights to the simplified summary of events offered above. Beyond all else, they have found that patterns of human-environmental interactions occur at varying geographic scale and temporal duration. Moreover, they also have found that the perceptions of the people at the time, and the social-political institutions that guided them, are crucial in establishing their environmental relations.

American Southwest

The American Southwest has been the scene of intense archaeological investigation for well over a century, and one of the fundamental issues that has confronted scholars from the outset is why so many impressive settlements and even entire regions were abandoned in prehistoric times. The explanations have been varied, but several basic themes have been common. First, changing climatic conditions have been cited, the most dramatic being the "great drought" of the end of the thirteenth century. Second, abandonment has often been blamed on the unsettling influence of new people moving into the region. The mobility of native peoples in historical time periods gave a special credence to this process being key to prehistoric settlement patterns.

Third, without any particular evidence in hand, archaeologists have fallen back on the idea of declining soil fertility, a notion that squares well with the current conditions in most of the region. Recent investigations have begun to look at these and other explanations more closely, and the interaction of human productive strategies and their impacts on the environment are becoming far clearer.

The American Southwest is commonly thought of as the region emanating out from where the states of Arizona, New Mexico, Colorado, and Utah meet at Four Corners. The immediate area of the Four Corners is the high Colorado Plateau, an uplifted zone of modest rainfall. Beyond the plateau are the basin and range complexes of Arizona and New Mexico to the south, the Rio Grande River valley to the southeast, and the lowland desert of Arizona to the far south. In this chapter we will focus our attention on the Colorado Plateau and its prehistoric inhabitants, the Anasazi (fig. 5.11).

The Southwest and the Levant share some important environmental characteristics. They both are governed by a Mediterranean type climate with cool wet winters. In the Southwest, though, rainfall also reaches the area during the summer, being carried by monsoon winds originating over the Gulf of Mexico. Even with this combined rainfall pattern, the total precipitation of the region is modest and is closely correlated with elevation. The soils in most of the Southwest are very thin and fragile, with only a few major river valleys containing substantial alluviation favorable for agriculture. Consequently, vegetation, though varied, is not dense and rejuvenates itself slowly. The upper elevations of the region, including major parts of the Colorado Plateau, are forested with ponderosa, fir, and other pines. The intermediate elevations, being less well watered, are characterized by more open woodlands of pinyon and juniper trees. As one moves down the elevational track, shrubs replace trees as the dominant vegetation comprising a chaparral zone, interspersed with grasslands.

Although people have been in the Colorado Plateau for at least 10,000 years, it was not until the first millennium B.C. that there is evidence for agriculture in the region, and then it is not until A.D. 600 or 700 that farming becomes a dominant supplier of food for some villages. There was a long period during which many people had been exposed to and knew about agricultural practices, yet it remained a peripheral activity with hunting and gathering remaining dominant. Tim Kohler examines recent settlement data from southwest Colorado to suggest that the nature of human-environmental interaction in the Four Corners region both led to the early success of farming and in some areas to the eventual degradation of the region as well (1992). He found that in this region there were basically three types of locations where farming was practiced: floodwater plots in canyon bottoms; broad washes

Figure 5.11
Map of American Southwest with location of Anasazi and Hohokam.

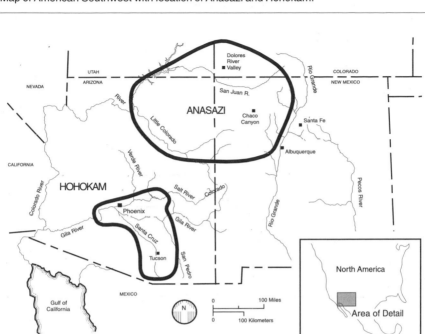

adjacent to flood plains on mesa tops; and mesa tops. For the Anasazi of southwest Colorado, mesa top farming was extremely important, but the soils were thin, supporting a pinyon-juniper woodland vegetation. These trees could be easily removed with the aid of fire, and the soil, especially under pinyons, was found to be reasonably fertile. Unfortunately, long-term cultivation seriously depletes these types of soils.

Kohler's theory is that a form of swidden agriculture was practiced in the upland Southwest. First, the trees in mesa top areas would be burned, and unburned wood would be used as fuel. Second, crops, primarily corn, would be planted there for a few years until mulch was dispersed and nutrient levels of the soil were reduced. Third, when soil was depleted beyond use, settlements would relocate to new plots. Although this strategy was successful over the short-term, it was not sustainable given the very slow regeneration rates for pinyon-juniper woodland terrains and their soils. However, this swidden agricultural strategy did serve to temporarily provide more available calories to support the local human population. To the extent that

unwatch-
able

119

mobility is possible, swidden is an economical strategy in relation to the use of human labor. The point is to harvest slowly renewing resources at an unsustainable rate, then move on to an adjacent area that has not been occupied for a long period of time and repeat the cycle. The first region is left unused, thereby giving it a chance to rejuvenate. If periodic movement were possible due to unoccupied, yet suitable, localities on a large scale, and population density was very low, this system was potentially sustainable. This, of course, assumes that people will move on soon enough and leave the soils fallow for a long enough period of time. Otherwise, the soils may be degraded to the point where rejuvenation is impractical within human life spans.

The actual case study that Kohler relies on is from the Dolores River basin where the Anasazi seem to have moved in about A.D. 600. Over the following couple of centuries the population increased and they aggregated into villages, but by about A.D. 900 the area began to be abandoned. Other archaeologists have cited the immediate cause of this abandonment to be a series of short growing seasons that would have put pressure on corn production at that high an altitude. Kohler, however, asserts that a growing population led to human-environmental interactions that led people to live in villages, intensify agrarian food production, deforest the region, deplete the local soils, and ultimately to abandon the area.

Kohler uses several kinds of evidence to show that human impacts, and not solely climatic factors, were important in unsettling the situation. One key indicator of change in the environment surrounding these prehistoric settlements is the wood that was used there. Archaeological study of wood charcoal found in hearths dating to the various episodes of occupation indicated that the species used changed in a patterned way. Over time there was a decline in the use of juniper and pinyon (native, slow-growing species) and an increase in woody shrubs and fast-growing cottonwood. The species of wood used in construction of buildings also changed. Over time, fewer pinyon were being used, and those that were seem to be from increasingly old trees, while juniper continued to be from young trees. The implication is that the forest that did remain was changing to relatively more junipers, a tree that is more fire resistant, better able to reproduce in open settings, and less desirable for construction than pinyon. Kohler argues that pinyon was disappearing from the locale of settlements and that this put an additional nutritional strain on the population, which used nuts from the tree as well as its wood. The relative proportion of different species of animals hunted by people in the region also changed progressively from animals native to woodlands to those more at home in open or disturbed environments (deer to antelope, cottontail rabbit to jackrabbit). A final source of evidence was the seeds that were found in the archaeological deposits that had blown or been brought to the settlement. Over time there was a substantial increase in seeds from pioneer plants, attesting to both agricultural intensification and to an increasingly disturbed local environment.

This evidence has convinced Kohler of the importance of human impacts in degrading the local environment. His interpretation of the situation is that by about A.D. 840, people had aggregated into villages in favorable settings because of their competitive organizational advantages over smaller units in the face of growing population and depletion of local wild resources. Hence, the very nature of the initial swidden system of agriculture encouraged a further dependence on agriculture and the aggregation of people into nucleated settlements. However, there are costs to aggregation, such as the increasing distance to useable fields, the heavier pressure on local soils, and the accompanying increase in agricultural risk. The Anasazi responded to this by further intensification such as water control mechanisms to feed the increasing population. This trajectory is fraught with risks, but it also is pushed forward by advantages it bestows upon its participants who organize and cooperate. Some of the changes that might have occurred in this situation include the institution of a regular land tenure system and the regular spacing of villages that allowed for recognizable territories that might be defended. People would also be more likely to share food across groups in a village and to invest in facilities to improve the processing and storage of food. Cooperative labor pools and larger social groupings than villages would allow would enable organized long-distance hunts and participation in trading networks. Overall, village life facilitates the management of cooperative activities and the sharing of production risks over a wider set of individual productive units. These advantages made larger and larger villages possible, but they also made the system vulnerable to collapse. A reliance on the management of resources through cooperative action reduced their flexibility of action, so that when poor seasons occurred these people were seriously hurt. In this case an expectable aberration in the climatic regime may have been enough to cause the collapse of the village system in the Dolores area.

Kohler sees a pattern in this situation. That is, cooperation within groups emerges as a response to competition between groups and with nature, in a desire to minimize risks. Because the costs of cooperation may be high, the competition must be intense in order to maximize the total energy extracted from the environment. This resulted in some amazing social accomplishments in the Southwest, but "also contained the seeds of their own destruction. Again and again locally increasing populations degraded their local environments, reached out to larger cooperative spheres in partial compensation for local degradation, eventually creating systems at the extreme limits supportable by contemporary subsistence, transport, and other technologies. Such distended systems were inordinately exposed to, and probably often succumbed to, relatively minor environmental fluctuations affecting food production" (Kohler 1992).

Sustainability, Decision-Making, and Agriculture

This brings up a fundamental aspect of agrarian, or any other exploitation, strategy; that is, sustainability is not a fixed condition, but rather a balance between rates of depletion and recovery (Haggett 1979; Goudie 1993; fig. 5.12). This relationship is always being tested in nature between predators and prey, where depletion is the killing of prey and recovery is related to their birth and survival rates. With soils, the relationships are a bit more complex, with multiple characteristics of soils being important for agrarian success. Also, agrarian success occurs in degrees or relative rates of output, and depends on the productive strategies being employed. As a plot of land is used for farming, the plants extract certain nutrients and others are eroded away due to exposure or other factors.

Virtually all farmed fields are left fallow for periods of time between plantings, and during this time natural or human-induced processes may lead to the replacement of these vital nutrients. The longer the fallow the greater the degree of recovery. Humans can also enhance this recovery rate by artificially adding nutrients through the use of fertilizers or irrigation and by protecting the soils from erosion through terracing or other conservation practices. The actual process of recovery will vary widely between different situations due to differences in the soil itself, the local climate, and the nature of extraction caused by the plants and other factors. For any particular combination of soils, climate, and farmed plants, there probably is a balance between type of plants and their density of planting on the one hand, and the length of fallow and other conservation measures on the other. Given a balance, this plot of land may retain its fertility over long periods of use, and we refer to the situation as sustainable (fig. 5.12A). However, if the fallow is shortened, the density of plantings increased, or the number of seasons planted between fallow periods increased, then as each cycle restarts, the fertility of the plot is diminished and slowly it degrades, its yield diminishes, and over time it no longer is practical to use for farming (fig. 5.12B).

Soil scientist J. A. Sandor and others have sought to measure and compare the extent to which soils used over long periods of time prehistorically have recovered their potential for agriculture (Sandor and Eash 1991; Sandor and Gersper 1988). They believe that the only way to really assess the sustainability of agricultural strategies is to examine their impact over rela-

Figure 5.12
Models of length of agricultural cycle versus soil fertility.

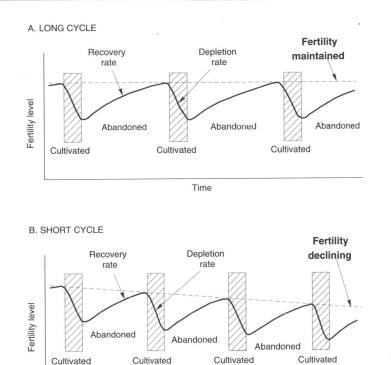

A. LONG CYCLE

B. SHORT CYCLE

tively long time periods such as centuries, an approach seldom practiced by modern scientists. They selected two very diverse settings where ancient agriculture was practiced and examined the characteristics of soils that were prehistorically farmed and compared them to nearby soils that were not. The first locality selected was in the semiarid mountainous region of southwest New Mexico. Agricultural sites dating from A.D. 1000 to 1150 were common in the area, and soil from behind a prehistoric terrace was sampled. Terraces were constructed by placing a series of small rock dams across gentle slopes, with subsequent sedimentation upslope of each dam creating terraced fields. Nearby archaeological excavations confirmed the assumption that corn was the principal crop grown in these fields.

The second locality selected was in the Colca Valley of southern

Per Unlike the New Mexico situation where settings were selected for their runoff potential, nearly the entire Colca Valley was transformed into a terraced landscape for irrigated agriculture. It was estimated that the New Mexico fields had been used for 100 or 150 years at the most and have been fallow for 800 years, while many of the Peruvian terraces have supported more or less continuous cultivation for the past 1500 years up to the present day. The results showed the New Mexico locality to be still significantly degraded, including accelerated erosion, compaction, and losses of organic matter and nutrients such as nitrogen and phosphorus. Moreover, greenhouse experiments comparing the prehistorically farmed soil with nearby unfarmed soil showed the cultivated soil to have not yet recovered to its prefarmed condition. Dry weights for corn grown with it were almost 40% less than from the uncultivated soil. In contrast, the soils from Peru maintained favorable qualities after 15 centuries of agriculture. Even the terraces in the Colca Valley that have been abandoned since the Spanish conquest contained soils with favorable agricultural qualities.

Two very different ecological situations and related agricultural histories are revealed in these studies. First, in the New Mexico situation the soil system was very fragile, and neither ancient practices nor the regenerative forces of the climate act to maintain soil fertility over long periods of exploitation or completely restore its potential after centuries of fallow. Second, in Peru the characteristics of the topography, soil, and climate combined with major labor investment in agricultural practices have allowed a sustainable situation to endure for well over a millennium. Archaeological evidence points to many prehistoric situations where this balance between extraction and recovery must have been maintained as it was in Peru. Settlement there remained vibrant and in one location for centuries, and in other very favorable settings for millennia. However, a far larger number of cases have been found, such as much of the upland Southwest, where settlement was successful for a much shorter period of time—two or three generations or less. Moreover, even under very favorable soil and topographic conditions, virtually all the long-lived settlements were eventually abandoned. There must have been many different specific reasons that settlements were abandoned and people moved to new areas. However, I would strongly argue that despite their excellent knowledge of agrarian practices, these people decided to employ productive strategies that undermined the long-term balance between depletion and recovery.

The question remains, why would people who were able to take into account so many forces make decisions that led to environmental degradation, especially when they recognized that the degradation was occurring? A model of the general elements that go into decisions made by farmers that

Figure 5.13
Model of influences of decisions made by farming unit (after van der Leeuw 1998b).

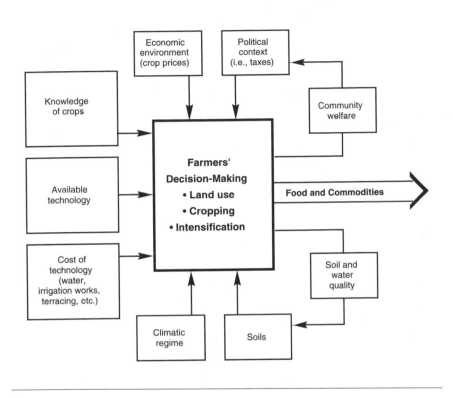

would impact their economic success and the sustainability of their agricultural system may help answer this seminal question (fig. 5.13). Farmers have basically three domains of decisions they can make: how to allocate land-use, what crops to plant, and how intensively to pursue each strategy. The basic output of this system will be the food and commodities required to support the farmer. Additional outputs of the system will impact community welfare (e.g., taxes and food sharing) and future soil fertility and water quality. Guiding the farmer's decisions are a variety of conditions and forces. The local environment with its climatic regime and available soils will provide opportunities and constraints for the farmer. Information on crops and farming technology are key elements in determining courses of action. Much of this knowledge comes from personal experiences or is verbally transmitted. With the advent of written records and the increasing scope of trade connections in early urban society, the breadth of available knowledge increased

125

accordingly. As soon as food produced was exchanged, the external economic and political context played an increasing role in determining a farmer's decisions, as will be seen in case studies presented in subsequent chapters. The price of crops, whether or not in monetary terms, is a crucial element, as is the cost of strategies involved in intensification, such as labor, water, or tools. As society becomes more hierarchically organized, demands made by political entities will become increasingly important either through taxes, rents, or direct demands for certain commodities.

The apparent complexity of this model might lead the reader to conclude that agrarian decisions might be unpredictable. However, the conservative nature of ancient societies and agrarian practices, in particular, make it possible to gain insight from examining only a few elements at a time. A limited number of factors basic to human organization have guided the way agrarian societies developed. The following chapters will examine some of these factors from various perspectives.

6
The Growth of World Urbanism

One of the dominant trends in world history during the past 5000 years has been the emergence, spread, and continued growth of aggregations of people to the point that in modern times, each decade sees a larger majority of people living in cities worldwide. With an increasing reliance on an expanding food base provided by agrarian innovations and improvements in the transport of foodstuffs, it became possible for larger and larger numbers of people to exist and to live in nucleated locations. This process occurred at different times in each part of the world, but there is good archaeological evidence for what we are willing to call cities in at least Mesopotamia by 3000 B.C. and soon thereafter in many other parts of the Old World. The village farming communities continued to be the primary focus of agrarian production in most of these regions, but the new cities provided a nexus for accumulating surplus agrarian production, for industries that relied on specialized labor, and for larger government apparatus. Although not housing the majority of people until this century, cities quickly became centers of production, administration, and innovation. A similar pathway was followed by the prehistoric societies of the New World with cities beginning to coalesce in both South America and Mexico by early in the Christian era.

The emergence of urban society introduced a whole new set of human-environmental interactions. One set of impacts derives from the fact that there were just more people in the world, requiring greater food production. A second impact is the increased need for building materials — wood, stone, and fired bricks — to construct these cities. A third impact is the territory itself that is given over to settlement, creating urban ecosystems. A fourth impact is really a series of newly established interactions caused by the nature of urban society with its industry, trade, and hierarchical administration. Just as settled village life allowed people to invest their labor in permanent facilities and to accumulate more goods, urban life advanced those processes to new levels. The creation and concentration of goods and the productive capacity to create more became the hallmark of urban society. All of this took a heavy toll on the environment and solidified a new set of relationships between humans and their environment.

The increased demands put on local environments by growing urban populations were partly mitigated by the greater labor invested by these people to transform their landscapes to sustain a higher level of production. Among the many efforts employed to increase productivity, irrigation of bottomlands and enhancing hill slopes through terracing are two of the most fundamental innovations of humankind. Redistributing available surface water through the construction of irrigation canals made agriculture practical in many otherwise unsuitable regions and often increased the productivity of those and other regions several-fold (fig. 6.1). The construction of irrigation works was limited to favorable geographic settings where potential farmlands were relatively flat and the river or other sources of water were elevated sufficiently above the fields to allow for gravity to carry the water through the newly dug canals. Other, more complex water-management techniques were also used, such as underground canals (quanats, see English 1966; Schreiber and Rojas 1988), or raised fields (chinampas, Coe 1964).

Irrigation must have started on a small scale with rather simple constructions, but as its value became apparent, more effort was invested in new construction to divert more water into the canals and to extend the canal system to reach greater areas of potential farmland. Because of changing water levels and clogging by waterborne silt, canals and their intakes required substantial additional labor to maintain, in addition to the normal labor required to guide water from field to field. Beyond this, some personnel had to be devoted to making decisions about the allocation of available water among the users and insuring that these directives were carried out. With irrigation water also came potential problems, the most obvious being the susceptibility of low-lying farmlands to disastrous flooding and the longer-term problem of salinization. To combat flooding from rivers that had agraded above the level of the surrounding fields, people from early historic times until today have constructed protective levees between the river and the settlement or fields to be protected. This, of course, is effective up to a certain level of flooding, but changes the basic hydrology of the area and can multiply the damage when the flood level exceeds the height of the levee.

Salinization is caused by an accumulation of salt in the soil near its surface. This salt was carried by river water from the sedimentary rocks in the mountains and deposited on the Mesopotamian fields during natural flooding or purposeful irrigation. Evaporation of water sitting on the surface

Figure 6.1
Irrigated date palm orchard in modern-day southern Iraq, the heartland of ancient Mesopotamia.

in hot climates is rapid, concentrating the salts in the remaining water that infiltrates through the soil to the underlying water table. In southern Mesopotamia, for example, the natural water table comes to within roughly six feet of the surface (Gelburd 1985). Conditions of excessive irrigation bring the water table up to within 18 inches, where capillary action brings it to the root zone and even to the surface, where the high concentration of salts would kill most plants (see figs. 6.2 and 6.3).

Solutions for salinization were not as straightforward as for flooding, but even in ancient times it was understood that the deleterious effects of salinization could be minimized by leaching the fields with additional water, digging deep wells to lower the water table, or instituting a system of leaving the fields fallow (Adams 1978). The first two cures required considerable labor and the third solution led to a diminished productivity, not often viewed as a likely decision in periods of growing population. An effective irrigation system laid the foundation for many of the world's early civilizations, but it also required a great deal of labor input and often favored societies that were centrally controlled.

Another major option available to growing agrarian societies to

129

Figure 6.2
Waterlogging and salinization (from Hillel 1991).

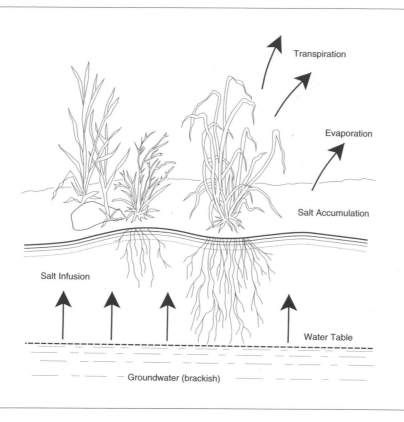

meet their food-producing needs is to expand the land under cultivation, which often means to farm less-desirable hill slopes surrounding the favored low-lying valley bottoms. Since bringing irrigation water to a hill slope is usually impractical, the key is effective utilization of rainfall. Rainfall either soaks into the soil or runs off of it led by gravity. A soil that is deep, well-structured, and covered by protective vegetation and a mulch of plant residues will normally absorb almost all of the rain that falls on it, given that the slope is not too steep (Hillel 1991:97). However, soils that have lost their vegetative cover and surface mulch will absorb much less, with almost half the water being carried away by runoff in more extreme situations. This runoff carries with it topsoil particles, nutrients, and humus that are concentrated in the topsoil. The loss of this material reduces the thickness of the rooting zone and its capacity to absorb moisture for crop needs. Sufficiently violent runoff erodes away the soil until bedrock is exposed, leaving only protected patches of soil and diminishing the overall productive potential of the landscape. This erosion may in turn have a deleterious effect on the lowlands that receive this runoff, often clogging waterways and burying productive soils below sediment of coarser material. Hence, for growing urban populations to expand their farming endeavors to the surrounding hill slopes, they had to devise ways to impede runoff and maintain the depth and fertility of the soil.

The most direct solution to this problem of slope runoff was to lay lines of stones along the contours of the slope and hence, perpendicular to the probable flow of water and sediment. These stones would then act as small dams (the name checkdams is used in the American Southwest), slowing the downhill flow of water and allowing more water to infiltrate and soil particles to collect behind the dam. This provided a buildup of sediments for plants and improved the landscape's water-retention qualities. The success of this type of approach led to its use in many different circumstances and societies. Among many early civilizations, including those of the eastern

Figure 6.3
In the mound in the background are the remains of an active agricultural center in southern Mesopotamia from 4000 years ago, whereas in the foreground one can see that today the land is so thoroughly salinated that salt has reached the surface.

Mediterranean, elaborate constructions we refer to as terraces were an essential element of their agricultural systems (fig. 6.4). They were widespread in the Levant as early as the second millennium B.C. and at least in a simplified form they were probably employed millennia earlier (Simmons 1989).

The objective of building terraces was to transform sloping ground into a series of nearly horizontal arable plots with adequate control of water runoff and minimal erosion of the soil (fig. 6.5). When these terraces were constructed, the natural patterns of drainage were altered, as was the development of soil behind the terrace walls. Overall, the impact of well-planned terracing was to allow farming in otherwise unusable areas and to increase the sustainability of plots that already were in use. The costs, however, were great both in terms of labor for initial construction and for the continual maintenance needed to keep the walls intact. Beyond labor costs, terracing also created a situation in which the productivity was enhanced, but the risks were as well. If the terraces were not adequately maintained, and the terrace wall was breached by runoff, the artificially increased height of the soil would lead to rapid erosion and further gulleying of the slope.

The use of both irrigation and terracing to increase agrarian production is a good example of an idea suggested by Boserup (1965): by increasing labor input one can increase overall production, but the costs in terms of labor input are high. Early civilizations, as well as our own, have continually

Figure 6.4
The origin and distribution of terracing.

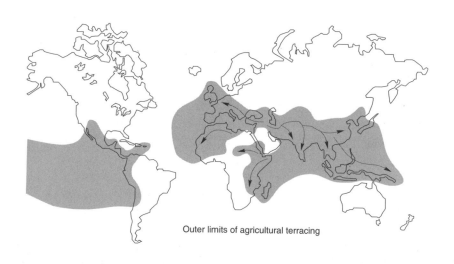

Outer limits of agricultural terracing

Figure 6.5
Hillside terrace construction (after Butzer 1982).

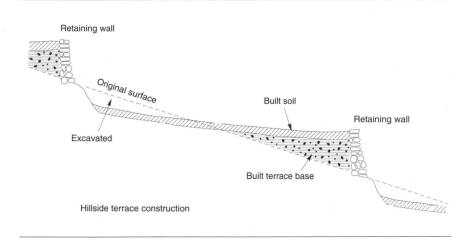

Hillside terrace construction

made the decision to devote more labor if it meant increasing production. With these increases came increasingly dramatic transformations of the landscape, greater regimentation of labor requirements, and greater risks if the system was challenged.

Mesopotamia

It was a study conducted in the Near East that first demonstrated the value of archaeology in understanding human impacts on the environment and possible methods to ameliorate these problems. In 1958 Thorkild Jacobsen and Robert McC. Adams published an article in *Science* that spoke directly to the problems caused by salinization of farmlands in lower Mesopotamia 4000 years ago and what modern inhabitants of that region might learn from the past (Jacobsen and Adams 1958). Over the years since 1958, sporadic papers have continued to appear on this subject (Gibson 1974; Gelburd 1985; Dickson 1987; Redman 1992), and salinization is often expressed in textbooks (Redman 1978; Nissen 1988) as a major problem leading to the reduced political importance of southern Mesopotamia, even though there remains considerable debate (Powell 1985) over the cultural context that led to this environmental "catastrophe."

The case study focused on here is that of the Ur III Dynasty of southern Mesopotamia (fig. 6.6). Information on this is gleaned from the

133

Figure 6.6
Ancient river courses and site locations in Mesopotamia reconstructed from air photos and field investigations.

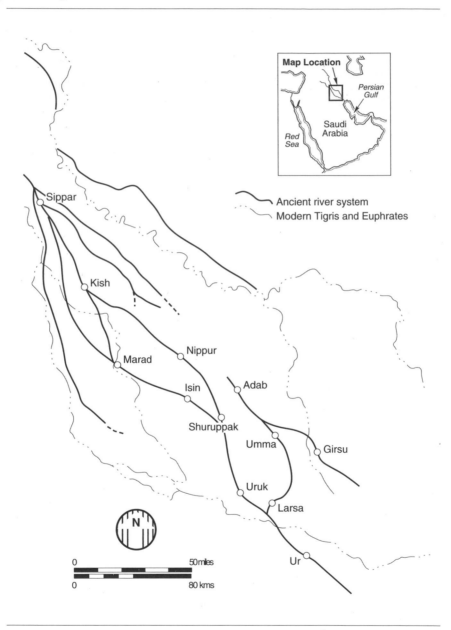

original Jacobsen and Adams article (1958) as well as subsequent pieces by each of them (Jacobsen 1982; Adams 1978). There remains some controversy over whether the changes cited were as grave as suggested or whether these causes were in fact at fault. The use of early textual accounts and incomplete archaeological investigations often leave the most interesting interpretive models as hypotheses rather than confirmed facts. If we were to avoid these still tentative reconstructions because of their uncertainty we, as archaeologists, would be ignoring what might become our greatest contribution to modern society. Whether or not subsequent studies show that this view of the Ur III situation holds true, it is likely that other Near Eastern civilizations experienced similar cycles of political and economic growth followed by environmental and subsequent social decline, both before Ur III (as suggested by H. Nissen, personal communication) and after it (Adams 1978).

Four thousand years ago, the Ur III Dynasty was situated in the southern half of Mesopotamia, and consisted of numerous cities, each inhabited by several tens of thousands of people and supported by an associated hinterland of farms and villages. This was one of the great early societies of Mesopotamia with well-developed writing, a system of laws, extensive trade networks, and ambitious builders, and it was a period of strong centralized political control (Edzard 1967; Nissen 1988). The economic system relied heavily on irrigation agriculture with vast field systems along the Euphrates River and canals leading from it. Winter-cultivated cereals were the main crops, although there were many secondary crops. Herding was also important, with contemporary records indicating as many as two million sheep were being kept.

The aspect of Ur III society emphasized here is the rapid rise in the centralized control of the political hierarchy and paradoxically how that contributed to an era of declining agricultural productivity and environmental damage. Centralized control of the once independent city-states was a logical objective of the growing power of the Ur III rulers. Centralization gave them greater access to labor pools, military conscripts, trade goods, and agricultural produce. More telling from our perspective, centralized control increased the potential for the production of food and other goods. Some of this increased productivity was achieved through increased specialization of production, but the majority resulted from centralized management of the construction and maintenance of water works and the allocation of water in the growing irrigation network that fed the Mesopotamian fields. Moreover, it was a logical decision for Ur III rulers to extend the land served by irrigation and to increase the capacity of the existing canal system so more water could be brought to the fields. This would allow more water to be used, particularly in flood years. Another decision that would have seemed logical under pressure to produce more, would be to shorten the period of time fields were left fallow. But the same decisions that brought short-term increases in production, as evidenced in the high population density and great construction projects of the Ur III period, rapidly undermined the agrarian base and led to a long period of diminished productivity. The major villain was salinization of the soils. Although there is general agreement that salinization was, as Hans Nissen says, "one of the greatest countrywide catastrophes," there remains considerable debate over the causes. (I largely have accepted the ideas of Jacobsen [1982] and Adams [1978], but the reader should be aware that other scholars are less convinced of this view [see Powell 1985 for a critical examination of Jacobsen's original thesis].)

Written records of temple storehouses of the period allow scholars to reconstruct with some certainty the relative productivity of fields and the crops being planted. A long-term decrease in productivity occurred between 2400 and 1700 B.C. At the outset of this period, wheat was an important crop, accounting for at least one-sixth of the cereals produced. But as salinization increased, people slowly shifted to the more salt-tolerant barley, so that by the end of the Ur III Dynasty in 2000 B.C., wheat made up only one-fiftieth and by 1700 B.C., it appears that wheat was totally abandoned in the region (Jacobsen 1982). The end of this decline in wheat production coincides with a long period during which centralized political control had broken down. Many cities were abandoned or reduced to villages, and the emphasis in agriculture shifted. Whereas during the height of Ur III control maximizing surplus production for central rulers dominated, during the subsequent political breakdown, the object became satisfying the needs of local populations in a more self-sufficient localized production mode.

The evidence from the uplands surrounding Mesopotamia that is only beginning to be collected by a couple of projects has provided a consistent set of results. Naomi Miller has examined macrobotanical remains from two widely separated sites in upland Iran and Turkey (1992a). She found that over time during the second and third millennia fuel wood was brought into the settlements from farther and farther away. There was also a shift to a greater reliance on dung over wood as a source of fuel. Both patterns indicate that forests were being clear-cut in the vicinity of the settlements. As was suggested for the vicinity of Ain Ghazal (chapter 5), domestic needs, goat browsing, and field clearance would essentially deforest the immediate vicinity of the villages, while lime production and charcoal making would consume additional quantities of wood, probably cut at a location farther from the settlement. This would extend the effective area of deforestation even more.

Another study, this time of pollen taken from a core from the bottom

Figure 6.7
Primary components of a pollen diagram from eastern Turkey.

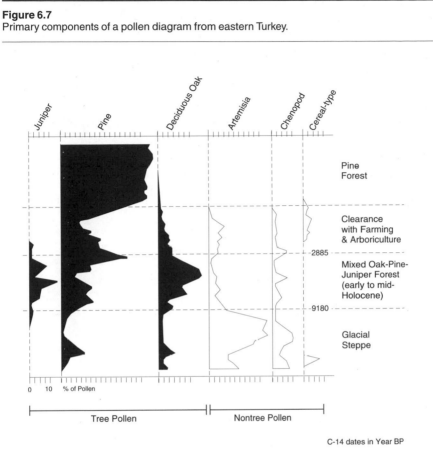

of a lake in south central Anatolia, reveals a more broadly regional pattern of vegetative change over the past 10,000 years (van Zeist et al. 1975). During the last Ice Age, the region was a glacial, steppe environment with few trees and mainly grasses (characterized as *cheno-artemisia*; fig. 6.7). During the early Holocene (ca. 9000 B.P.), when the first farming villages would have been established, the region hosted a mixed forest of oak, pine, and juniper. By the mid-Holocene (ca. 3000 B.P.) the oak in the forests was drastically reduced; pine, whose pollen can travel great distances, continued; and cereal grasses increased. Recent pollen evidence is dominated by pine pollen that is traveling from mountainous refuge areas and a modest occurrence of cereals, reflecting the reduction in agriculture in the region.

The traditional lore today in the Near East to explain deforestation

137

Figure 6.8
Young villager gathering vegetation for her domestic hearth in the western Mediterranean region.

and localized failures of farming blames it on the Ottoman Rule of the region during the last few centuries. It is said that the denuded lands are largely the result of overgrazing of goats during the period of Ottoman Rule and that in ancient times these were the lands of "milk and honey." This assertion is probably true to some extent in that the Ottoman political system discouraged local infrastructure development and encouraged small-scale social groups that would rely on herded animals. However, this interpretation is an oversimplification that takes our attention away from the needs of the domestic hearth and industrial kiln from as far back as the earliest civilizations 5000 years ago. The goat is the most destructive of the grazers, but its effects are largely secondary; that is, it usually is not the one to destroy the trees themselves, but only the shoots, leaves, and young sprouts. This does diminish the primary production of the trees as well as keep young trees from reestablishing themselves. Thus, goats are strong contributors to keeping an area from regenerating trees and ground cover and consequently exposing it to the elements and leading to degradation of the fertility of the topsoil and, ultimately, to complete loss from erosion. Complementing these pressures is the hearth and kiln that need not just twigs and thin branches, but timber as well. The heavy weight of wood also dictates that when possible, people will completely denude local sources, rather than draw on larger, more distant sources in an effort to conserve forest growth. The importance of securing fuel for the domestic hearth continues to this day to force the gathering of forage from great distances (fig. 6.8).

Mexico and Central America

Mexico and Central America were home to a wide variety of impressive prehistoric societies. The Maya to the south and a variety of central Mexican societies to the north each built strong agrarian systems that supported very high populations and elaborate urban centers (Coe 1982). The main New World crop in North, Central, and South America was corn. First domesticated about 5000 B.C., or somewhat earlier, corn started out as a very small cob, not economically viable as the dominant food source. This differs from Old World species like wheat that were nearly as productive in the wild as under early cultivation. Early forms of corn were pioneering weeds basically used by Central Americans as a back up or famine food. However, over a long period of low-level use, the nature of corn changed, with larger cobs and kernels being selected for by the early users. It took three or four millennia of slowly increasing the size of the cob, the number of kernel rows, and the size of individual kernels before corn as a crop become so productive that people could depend on it as their primary food. With this change, somewhere around 2000 to 1000 B.C., it became practical to invest the labor to clear fields and to establish year-round villages that could rely on corn harvests and stored corn for their primary subsistence. During this same period other crops were also experimented with and ultimately domesticated by New World groups. Gourds, squash, and beans are among the most important, but altogether more than forty species of economic plants were domesticated in the New World.

Once well-developed, corn and other New World domesticates offered people an abundant source of food leading to increasing population and social advance. The Maya of Central America were among the most innovative people of the Americas, having many accomplishments in the arts, science, and human organization. Well before the beginning of the Christian era, the Maya and their associates had built enormous ceremonial and administrative centers throughout their lands and developed into a tightly controlled society that thoroughly settled the landscape between centers with scattered farming households and hamlets. The geography of the Mayan homelands did not lend itself to centralized irrigation works, but rather was most suitable for extensive fields of slash-and-burn (milpa) agriculture. This ensured that the agrarian population would have to remain scattered to be close to their fields and that a maximum amount of land would have to be under tillage to support the growing population. In fact, as many as 8 to 10 million people lived in the Mayan domains 1000 years ago, a figure not surpassed until the recent decades of this century.

The Mayan homelands of the Yucatán, Belize, Guatemala, and parts of Honduras were well watered and primarily lowlands (fig. 6.9). The upland zone, focused in Guatemala, had relatively well-drained soils that were favorable to maize agriculture, especially in the valley bottoms. The Mayan lowlands were characterized by less well-drained soils in an environment of flatlands with scattered lakes. Classic Mayan civilization, best known for its ceremonial centers with earth-filled pyramids topped with carefully ornamented temples, was well established by A.D. 300. The construction and decoration with stucco relief of pyramids and temples absorbed tremendous amounts of Mayan labor and resources. These centers were the focus of religious activities, trade relations, and whatever political integration existed at the time. The Maya were remarkable astronomers and regulated religious events with a sacred calendar that was calibrated by an extremely accurate secular calendar. Public ceremonies utilizing the temples, pyramids, and ritual ball courts demonstrated the power of the elite, as did the rising tide of militarism. Despite their many talents, the zenith of Mayan ceremonial centers and the organized society they represented was not especially long lived.

Figure 6.9
Map of sites discussed in Mexico and Central America, a region commonly called Mesoamerica.

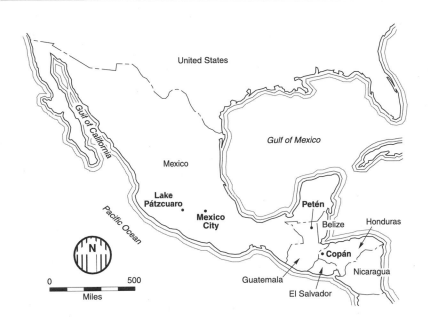

By A.D. 900 to 1000 there is widespread archaeological evidence for the abandonment of most of the major centers and an overall drop in the population of the region. Clearly there is a breakdown in the political and social organization that had led the Maya to such impressive accomplishments. Various theories have been put forward as to the cause of this "collapse." Primary among them is that degradation of the environment through excessive agricultural practices played a major role (see Culbert 1973). Archaeologists are beginning to accumulate evidence to evaluate the importance of human impacts.

The Petén region of lowland Guatemala was the subject of a pioneering study of prehistoric human-environmental relations by the Central Petén Historical Ecology Project (CPHEP; see Deevey et. al. 1979; Rice 1996). This project was designed primarily to learn about the genesis and change of the tropical forest, rather than focusing on the prehistory of the Maya. However, the Maya were clearly one of the central agents of environmental transformations, being a "strain" on the natural ecosystem. One of the goals of this

141

study was to delineate changes in the forest ecosystem that could be attributed to climate change versus those resulting from human impact. May to October is the rainy season in the Petén, with 70 to 90 inches per year. A high canopy of mahogany, breadnut, and sapodilla trees dominates the landscape with a middle canopy of avocado and other small trees and shrubs. In temperate regions, such as those we discussed earlier in this volume, forest soils contain most nutrients that sustain plant growth. When a temperate forest is cut down, it is the soil that stores the nutrients until they are utilized by subsequent growth.

In contrast, it is the vegetative cover rather than the soil that holds most of the nutrients in tropical forests, such as those of the Petén (Rice and Rice 1984:8). More than 75% of the nutrients in a tropical forest ecosystem are in the living vegetation and the dead organic matter on the ground, which is rapidly recycled into new growth rather than enriching the soil. Because of this a tropical forest can regenerate almost all of its biomass within a 10-year period, versus up to 100 years in most temperate settings. If the trees and vegetation that are cut are also burned, this recycling is even faster. Hence, a slash-and-burn strategy can transfer the abundant nutrients in the tropical cover to newly planted crops and yield impressive returns. At the same time, slash-and-burn exposes the soil to potential erosion and therefore is best conducted in selected topographic settings and under close management.

We know from historic periods that this region can efficiently support a swidden or milpa agricultural system, where trees are cut from a plot of land before the dry season and burned at the end of the dry season. Then it is used for two years of crops and left fallow for three to six years. This type of rotation has been known in recent times to comfortably support a density of about 25 people per square kilometer. However, archaeological evidence from this region suggests that at certain times and in some locations, the population density attained 250 people per square kilometer (Rice 1996:196). Obviously, Mayan farming strategies were well developed and closely attuned to the potentials of the environment. Houses were dispersed across the countryside to allow farmers easy access to the maximum amount of arable land. Instead of transforming the entire landscape to increase production, the Maya grew a diversity of crops on the same field and may have focused on the naturally low-lying areas, or *bajos,* with their relatively fertile soils for labor investments such as raised fields. The efficient production and centralization of farm products allowed the growth of enormous ceremonial centers such as Tikal, which thrived from 100 B.C. to A.D. 900. However, even Tikal entered a period of decline in A.D. 800, with the last dated monument being constructed in A.D. 909. The general belief is that the land had been filled up for some period, and with declining fertility, the dense population could not be supported and fell into rapid decline, requiring emigration. Archaeologists estimate that within a few centuries, population had fallen by 80% and most of the formerly majestic ceremonial centers had been abandoned.

As part of the Central Petén Historical Ecology Project, Don and Prudence Rice and Bill Deevey studied several lake basins from a number of perspectives: archaeological settlement patterns, pollen record, erosion of sediment, and chemical loss of soils (Rice and Rice 1984). Their unit of study was the lake and its drainage basin. One can relatively easily define the surface boundaries of each lake basin and then monitor the movement (flux) of nutrients and sediments between the terrestrial and aquatic portions of the system (see Binford and Leyden 1987). Their model views an ecosystem as sustaining itself on the flow of chemical elements drawn by vegetation from rocks, soil, and air, carried either in dissolved or suspended form in water into the lake. The presence of humans increased this flow. Thus a lake basin can be thought of as a *trap* in a closed system, revealing activities that influence the terrestrial components of the catchment basin.

By examining sediment cores taken from lake bottoms, these authors found that the deposition of phosphorous and silica were both amplified over normal levels during the period of Mayan occupation, indicating a significant disturbance of the surrounding landscape. Phosphorus is rare in the lowlands and is crucial for agrarian success; hence tracing its movement through the environment is a meaningful measure of impact on chemical nutrients. Erosion leads to a permanent loss of phosphorus from the soil, since it is generated very slowly from underlying bedrock. Because of this, in modern times phosphorus is one of the major elements added to soil in the form of chemical fertilizer. It is believed that activities such as burning vegetative cover and constructing stone buildings released large amounts of phosphorus into the soil (Rice and Rice 1984:21). Phosphorus deposited in lake bottoms reflects the active transport through erosion of the chemicals from surrounding topsoil, where it exists both because of natural generation from bedrock as well as from human waste, food products, mortuary, and disintegration of stone building materials. The researchers found that the phosphorus deposition in the lakes increased roughly in a linear relationship with the archaeological evidence of population increase, reflecting probably both more phosphorus in the soil and more erosion of this soil into the lake bed (fig. 6.10). This loss of a key element, and other components of the topsoil as well, led to a slow, but progressive undermining of the productivity of the lands around the lakes, particularly the uplands that would be most vulnerable to slope wash.

Silica, being a relatively large-grained component of soils, is a reasonable indicator of the rate of transport of soil in a lake basin (Binford and

Figure 6.10
Impact of long-term Mayan settlement on the terrestrial and lacustrine environments of the central Petén lakes (from Rice 1996).

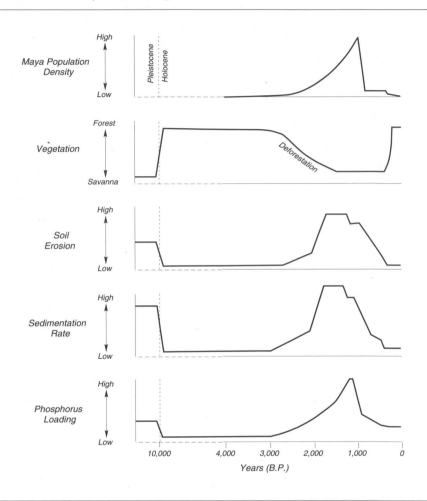

Leyden 1987). It might reflect a variety of landscape-altering activities that would make the soil more susceptible to erosion, such as deforestation, cultivation, and settlement construction. The researchers found that in Lake Sacnab and especially in Lake Yaxha, silica deposition increased several fold during the height of Mayan occupation (Rice, Rice, and Deevey 1985). Despite this evidence of soil erosion and the implied reduced productivity of local lands, the Maya lived here and elsewhere for a long period of time. Clearly the Maya understood the tropical forest ecosystem well enough to maximize the exploitation of the region and to conserve available resources so as to thrive for centuries in most locations. Researchers have suggested that the Maya tried not to completely clear the land and to plant it with diverse crops to maintain fertility and minimize exposure to erosion. They also invested heavily in water control to minimize the destabilizing aspects of water flow while maximizing the flow to fields to increase crop yield per hectare (Rice and Rice 1984:27). And finally they organized themselves to move food around the region, buffering localized risks and allowing for concentrations of population.

The picture that comes together from studies of the Petén and the adjacent Mayan area of the Mexican Yucatán reveals an anthropogenic ecosystem through much of the Holocene. The high forest that prevailed in much of that region was largely removed by the farming and settlement building activities of the Mayas as early as 3000 to 4000 years ago (Islebe et. al. 1996). This resulted in a shift toward more open vegetation during much of the Mayan occupation with the maximum deforestation between 1000 and 2000 years ago. The basic drain on the land of dense population, intensive agricultural manipulation, and construction of massive settlements increased to the point were the system was no longer sustainable. Declining productivity must have had a multiplier effect, leading to food shortfalls, reduced labor investment, and political instability. By the end of the tenth century A.D., most of the large settlements of the Mayan uplands and southern lowlands had been abandoned or at least seriously depopulated. The deterioration seems to coincide with a relatively dry period that would have also put pressure on productivity, making it difficult to determine whether the primary influence was climatic or human (Hodell, Curtis, and Brenner 1995). Without denying this uncertainty, I believe this "collapse" was primarily due to the extended period of intense human exploitation, albeit aided by microclimate variability.

Similar inferences have been drawn from the large research project focusing on and around the Mayan center of Copán in neighboring Honduras (Abrams and Rue 1988). Based primarily on evidence taken from a pollen core in a local bog, Abrams and Rue see a major era of regional deforestation during the Classic Mayan occupation when the forest was replaced by grasses, and then a regeneration of the forest about A.D. 1300, and finally a disturbance once again during this century. They attribute several important uses for wood products that outstripped the supply as the major cause of deforestation. First, the domestic hearth required a continual supply of fuel; second, the production of lime plaster for houses and monuments required fuel; and third, the construction of homes relied on quantities of timber. All of these demands would be tied directly to the size of the local population as would the need to clear or partially clear lands for agricultural fields. Their conclusion is that the deforestation was basically the result of a growing, dense population, and once that declined in the tenth century A.D., the soil and forest regenerated over time. The forest was not threatened again until the twentieth century, when the population once again soared. An interesting footnote to these two studies, that we will return to in the last chapter of this book, is that the tropical rain forest of Central America is only about 600 years old and has grown on the location of what was a largely anthropogenic, agrarian landscape (Islebe et. al. 1996:270).

Another case involving the study of lake sediments from the Pátzcuaro Basin west of Mexico City has received considerable attention both from scholars and the popular press (O'Hara, Street-Perrott, and Burt 1993; 1994). This was within the region of the Tarascan State, a powerful pre-Hispanic group that at one time controlled as much as 75,000 square miles of territory. These were contemporaries and adversaries of the better known Aztecs of the Mexico City area to the southeast. Unlike the Maya, the people of this region and central Mexico in general lived in more aggregated villages, and their agriculture was a mix of intensive irrigation in the valley bottoms and more extensive rain-fed farming on the surrounding hill slopes. The capital of the Tarascan State was Tzintzuntzan, a city that reached a population of 30,000 people before European contact. Tzintzuntzan was at its height from about A.D. 1350 until European contact, although a smaller version of the city had existed at least since A.D. 1000. The interesting aspect of this case study is that we know this location to be in a naturally forested region that would have been covered with pine and oak trees, yet early historic accounts report that the area was largely barren of trees. The question facing investigators is if the reconstruction is correct, was the deforestation due to the prehistoric Tarascans or to the colonists who introduced Spanish agricultural techniques in early historic times?

Researchers recovered two primary kinds of evidence bearing on human impacts on the environment. First, the pollen in the sediments revealed the composition of vegetation in the vicinity of the lake during prehistoric times. Second, the accumulation of sediment was a rough measure of the rate of soil erosion in the basin. Palynological analysis of the sediment core recovered from Lake Pátzcuaro revealed a decrease in alder tree pollen at about 3000 B.C., coinciding with an increase in herb pollen, such as chenoam. The implication is that the alder were being cleared from areas along streams, where they would naturally grow, to make room for early agricultural fields. The next significant event noted in the sediment is a short-lived erosional episode that coincided with the earliest evidence of corn pollen about 1200 B.C. This may represent an intensification of the early agricultural practices to include significant proportions of maize crops. Unfortunately, we do not know much about the archaeological record at this early time range. The next identifiable erosional episode took place about 500 B.C. to A.D. 800, and O'Hara and her colleagues suggest that this may have been the result of farming on steeper slopes leading to erosion of the subsoil and possible gulleying. Soils in the Pátzcuaro area are highly susceptible to erosion. Archaeological evidence indicates that this was a period of major cultural changes. First, there was a rise in the number of people who relied on lake resources as well as some evidence of social ranking. Between about A.D. 400 and 900 there was the appearance of ceremonial centers where there had previously been only autonomous villages. This may signal the emergence of territorially discrete and competing polities. This transformation in the social and political landscape may have been prompted by the rise in population and power of the city of Teotihuacán, the greatest of early Mesoamerican centers.

The heavy impact on the environment was followed by a period of stability between about A.D. 800 and 1150. Sediment accumulation decreased and the lake level dropped by about four meters. A prolonged or intermittent drought may have caused the partial abandonment of the region as well as a lowering of the lake level. Archaeologically there is evidence not of abandonment but of a nucleation into defensible locations, leaving major parts of the landscape vacant. The natural vegetation returned to these areas and helped impede the erosion that had characterized the preceding period. Another erosional episode began about A.D. 1150 and was characterized by higher erosion rates linked to further deforestation of the region. Fir trees disappeared from the pollen record, indicating lumbering or another cause of tree removal from quite a wide area around the lake. It was during this post A.D. 1150 period that true urbanization took place in the basin. Contact with central Mexico appears to have diminished and a regional culture, the Tarascan State, developed. The fortunes of the Tarascan State waxed and waned, largely in response to their eventual conflicts with the newly emergent Aztecs in central Mexico. The demands of a high population, craft production (including metallurgy), and the ravages of warfare all must have taken their toll on the stability of ground cover and associated soil erosion.

As with other areas of the New World, the indigenous population levels decreased sharply soon after European contact. This was largely due to newly introduced diseases, but there probably was some effect from the breakdown of the pre-Hispanic administrative and economic systems. The lake sediments indicate that immediate post-conquest times saw a cessation of erosion. This probably reflects the overall decrease in agricultural activity that accompanied the population decline. As the Spanish colonized this region, they probably introduced plow agriculture and domestic herd animals. Both of these activities are often cited as the cause for widespread erosion in Mexico, but the evidence from the Pátzcuaro Basin does not point strongly to this being a problem, at least in the early decades. However, later in colonial times erosion did resume, reflecting an increase in population and accompanying agricultural activity.

Hohokam of Southern Arizona

The Hohokam represent one of the great cultural traditions of the American Southwest. Archaeologists have characterized them by the red paint on buff-colored pottery, the fact that they built platform mounds and ball courts, and their highly efficient irrigation agriculture (Gumerman 1991; Crown and Judge 1991). Their settlements are found along the lowland river valleys in the desert region of central and southern Arizona. Their occupations of parts of this region are very long lived, beginning before the Christian era and lasting until almost A.D. 1400. Some of their settlements were occupied for only a few generations, but in selected locations, such as the basin occupied by the modern city of Phoenix, Hohokam communities were present for a millennium. These were very successful farmers who built impressive irrigation systems; their homeland received only six or eight inches of rain per year, far less than corn requires. The Hohokam supplemented their irrigation crops by gathering plants and hunting game. They also developed a regional trading network that brought them products from the uplands to the north and east. Although the population density of the Phoenix basin ebbed and flowed, the persistence of the Hohokam in that location is truly impressive, and to the Hohokam themselves, their existence must have appeared sustainable forever.

The centerpiece of the Hohokam's success was their irrigation system, which was built around the two rivers — the Salt and the Gila — that traversed the broad Phoenix lowland basin. These rivers ran year-round, but their volume varied enormously in response to runoff from rainfall and snowmelt in their catchments during the spring. When these rivers were in flood, they carried substantial quantities of suspended sediment from the uplands. When the fields were purposely watered or accidentally flooded, they received a load of nutrients and new silt that served to regenerate the soil's fertility. This was extremely important in the Southwest, where soil development was slow and remained shallow. The Hohokam took advantage of this resource by building hundreds of miles of canals, some as long as

Figure 6.11
Reconstruction of location of Hohokam canals in the Salt River Valley near Phoenix, Arizona.

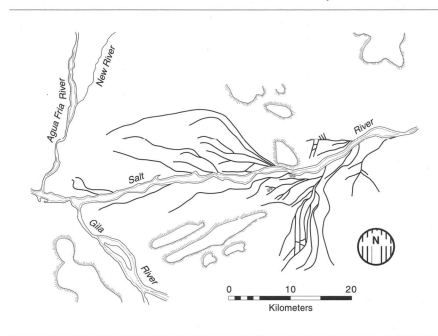

30 km, to bring water and sediments to increasingly distant fields (figs. 6.11 and 6.12). Hohokam settlement focused in the wide valley bottoms of the Salt, the Gila, and their tributaries. However, they also utilized the sloping uplands, the bases of alluvial fans, and the arroyo bottoms, where storm runoff could be channeled and would bring major organic and sediment additions to the desert soils (Fish and Fish 1992).

Other aspects of the Hohokam's food-producing strategy were designed for enhancing productivity and maintaining sustainability. Use of surface water was essential for Hohokam survival, and sources of this water in the desert Southwest were extremely localized. Moreover, locations suitable for water diversion or canal headings in association with downstream flatlands for farming were even more restricted. This made it very disadvantageous for a settlement to move frequently. In addition, the major labor invested in constructing canals and runoff gathering features, and the fact that population was increasing and filling up alternative locations, made it very important for Hohokam settlers to conserve the long-term productive potential of their immediate surroundings. The fact that intensive agriculture

Figure 6.12
Simplified diagram of a Hohokam irrigation system.

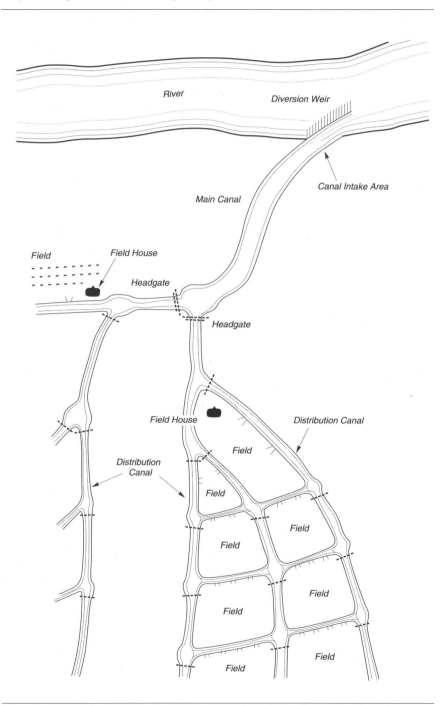

River

Diversion Weir

Canal Intake Area

Main Canal

Field

Field House

Headgate

Headgate

Field House

Distribution Canal

Distribution
Canal

Field

Field

Field

Field

Field

Field

Field

Field

Field

results in reduced mobility options for human groups is key to understanding the human-environmental interactions of the Hohokam and many other groups around the world.

The removal of ground cover plant material was mediated by the fact that the Hohokam were "direct gatherers"; that is, they consumed what they gathered rather than depending on domestic animals that consumed the plant material. This meant that a wide range of plants not eaten by humans that might be consumed by domesticates would be spared. It also meant that when humans did consume wild plant material, they often focused on the seeds or fruits, leaving the plant intact. This, combined with the fact that the Hohokam homeland had a relatively warm climate (minimizing the need for fuel to heat their homes), meant that the vegetative ground cover was favored. Potential sources of fuel, such as mesquite trees, were also spared because they produced seedpods that were important sources of food. Wood for fuel and for construction would have had to come from elsewhere. Also, transplanted desert species supplemented the corn, beans, and squash that spread from Mexico. Local varieties of beans were grown, agave was harvested for food and fiber, and other crops like cotton and little barley also contributed (Fish and Fish 1992). Animals hunted were usually small and found in the vicinity of settlements, such as rabbits. Trapping them may have been a regular part of the daily farming regime. Large artiodactyls, like antelope and deer, were hunted when available, but over time it appears that long-distance hunting parties were needed to bring back these animals, implying that they were no longer available locally. Also over time, the shift in type of rabbits eaten (from cottontail to jackrabbit) reflects increasingly open habitats. Both of these processes show that despite the conservation efforts of the Hohokam, their presence in high numbers took its toll on the natural vegetation.

Archaeological evidence reveals that there was a dramatic increase in riparian species consumed during the Classic period (ca. A.D. 1250–1400), a time by which the other terrestrial fauna would be depressed in the vicinity of settlements. Although the overall climate and environment of central Arizona has not changed significantly since Hohokam times, the riverine ecosystem along the Salt and Gila Rivers has changed dramatically as a result of human-induced alterations, primarily during the past century. In prehistoric times the rivers would have had some water year-round, and they would have flowed actively for substantial periods of time. There would have been lakes and swamps along the river courses, and the riparian areas would probably have been lush and large. Nevertheless, the use of muskrat, beaver, birds, and fish implies a food crisis for the Hohokam. Fish ranked second behind rabbits as a source of animal protein for the Classic period Hohokam (James 1994). In measuring the size of the fish taken during Classic Hohokam times, Steven

James found that they were smaller than the modern examples, suggesting to him that already these fish were under pressure and the larger ones had been fished out, leaving only relatively small fish to be caught. James' overall point is that long-term, dense occupation of the Salt-Gila River Valleys by the Hohokam led to the impoverishment of large game in the region, forcing them to use less desirable small game as a source of protein. It even led to the degradation in the river fish available. But this was probably not enough to lead to the abandonment of the region by A.D. 1400.

The Hohokam developed important social institutions to help overcome the difficulties in their environment. As the number of Hohokam settlements grew in an area, they developed coherent groupings we call the Hohokam "community" (Fish and Fish 1992). In the denser situations, this resulted in large central sites with public architecture, such as a ball court and/or platform mound that would be the focus of ceremonial and civic activities. Small settlements, and even distant, part-time hamlets, were involved in the success of these "communities" by being located nearer the agricultural fields and wild food collecting stations. Community organization provided the framework for allocating water from canals and mobilizing labor for construction and maintenance of the canal system.

In sum, the Hohokam developed a distinctively enduring settlement system that outlasted most of their southwestern and North American neighbors. Renewal of fields through waterborne additives permitted a seemingly sustainable agriculture. The yield of domestic crops was supplemented by tended and weedy indigenous species. Because settlements were localized along watercourses, the large surrounding expanses were left uninhabited, allowing for the continued growth of wild vegetation for fuel, craft materials, and edible wild resources. Added to these procurement strategies was an overarching social organization that acted to spread agricultural risks over a sufficient number of environmental zones and allowed for temporary shortfalls that would be buffered through social connections. An example of this relationship is the fact that agricultural fields in the uplands would benefit from a year of heavy rainfall that might cause destructive floods in the lowland fields. This is clearly a lesson in human organization that adjusted to the requirements of its environment to survive for what, to its inhabitants, must have seemed like an eternity. Nevertheless, Hohokam society came to an end in the fourteenth century, and it is informative to examine the possible causes.

To suggest a possible set of reasons for the demise of Hohokam society, it is useful to look more closely at the relation of environmental factors, irrigation strategies, and social responses. A study of tree ring variability taken from the upper drainage of the Salt and Gila Rivers provides new insight into this complex set of relationships (Nials, Gregory, and Graybill

Figure 6.13

Reconstruction of flow level of Salt-Gila River during Hohokam times based on tree rings (after Nials, Gregory, and Graybill 1989).

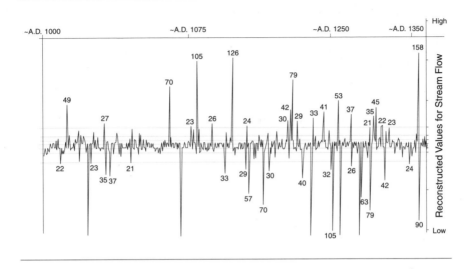

1989). The basic assumption of tree ring studies is that trees will grow more (i.e., thicker rings) in wet years and less in dry years. In the lower valleys where the Hohokam irrigation system was centered, this should correlate directly with stream runoff and consequent levels of flooding. Although there may be intervening variables, this assumption seems reasonable, and moreover, it provides archaeologists with a useable surrogate measure of annual environmental cycles, at a level of accuracy we seldom attain for the past.

In the Salt-Gila River Valley, settlement grew as people were able to develop irrigation systems using the river floodwaters to advantage. The rivers themselves probably braided as well as ran in a deep channel. Settlement appears to have been along the channels and the main feeder canals. These feeders and the ultimate distributor canals were located some distance downstream from the initial intakes, making each major canal that took water directly from the river the feeder to an entire system of canals that often stretched for many miles downhill. Communities were located along these feeder canals, and it is hypothesized that because they all depended on maintaining the same source of water, they also were held together as a social or political unit (Abbott 1994).

According to the tree ring records (fig. 6.13), there were some big variations in flood levels before A.D. 800, but after that date for over two centuries (until ca. A.D. 1075), there were relatively consistent water levels.

This condition favored the construction of an expanded irrigation system in the lower valley. This climate predictability would have encouraged a period of great growth in population and organization. Archaeological evidence confirms this hypothesis, documenting not only a filling in of the Phoenix basin and other lower river valleys, but also the appearance of settlements well up the tributary rivers that displayed Hohokam characteristics. Archaeologists consider these as potential colonies where materials and goods were exchanged with the central valley settlements.

During the next century and a half (ca. A.D. 1075–1250), tree ring evidence indicates that the variability of floods increased with dramatically higher or lower water levels occurring each 20 years or less. Although this situation is less favorable for growth than the preceding centuries, it is within limits that the Hohokam were able to handle without major disruption to their society. Although droughts must have been hard on these people, if they were spaced years apart and reasonable quantities of corn were stored, they could be weathered without enduring trouble. Floods might have had a more serious impact on the system, because they would likely inundate whatever crops were in the fields and destroy irrigation facilities that would take substantial labor to replace. Regional trading partners were probably sufficient to get the Hohokam through drought years, and the destructive flood years must have been far enough apart for irrigation works to be reconstructed without discouraging the inhabitants.

In the century following A.D. 1250, the climatic situation appears to have become even more erratic, with floods or droughts coming at least once every 10 years. This put tremendous pressure on the survival of the entire system. Crop production in the valleys was seriously diminished, and labor required to maintain the irrigation works dramatically increased. The reduced surpluses of the valley people led to the dissolution of the regional system, which put increased pressure on the valley residents in bad years. To make up for these shortfalls, it is likely that the valley farmers overplanted in their good fields, extended planting to marginal fields, and cut back on fallow periods. All of these strategies would lead to decreases in soil fertility and subsequent productivity. It might also have led to salinization of the formerly most productive soils in the lower valleys. To increase the fields watered during favorable water years, the canal intakes may have been built larger, but during serious floods this would only increase the destructive force of the flood and require even greater labor to replace. At this same time, there was most likely a transformation of the sociopolitical system that emphasized more centralized control, possibly as a response to the increasing environmental threat to the agricultural system (Abbott 1994).

Over the centuries, the Hohokam had developed a very effective human ecosystem. It centered on an agricultural system that relied on major crop production from an efficient but costly irrigation system, supplemental goods from the immediate area and regional partners, and an organizational structure that managed the parts to maintain stability in the face of a naturally variable climate.

The human presence and agricultural activities of the Hohokam on and around the floodplain also contributed to basic environmental problems. Stream channel entrenchment seems to have occurred more frequently and more severely during late prehistoric times than one would expect from climatic factors alone (Waters 1991:155–156). By clearing vegetation from the floodplain and surrounding slopes (*bajadas*), the Hohokam would have inadvertently increased the volume and velocity of surface runoff. Compacted foot trails, short ditches, and even the canals themselves would have concentrated the runoff and further increased its velocity. Taken together, this would seriously enhance the likelihood of serious soil erosion from the slopes surrounding the valley and siltation of the canals on the valley floor.

The longer the Hohokam existed in the same location, the more pressure they put on floodplain dynamics and on the fertility of the soil, but they maintained it through various conservation methods and by supplementing local food with goods brought in by exchange systems. However, when the climate entered a long period of greater variability, including disastrous flooding, it put an additional pressure on the Hohokam system that could not be easily sustained. Their response was to invest more labor in extracting the maximum from the land, but that made the system even more vulnerable to climatic extremes. The production shortfalls also diminished their ability to maintain their regional trading partners and threatened their local organizational control as well. Energy and resources devoted to ceremonial activities and other cooperative ventures helped hold the system together for generations, but at a cost. To provide for these activities, the agricultural extraction was continually maximized, which cost enormous labor investments and weakened the underlying resilience of the system. When an infrequent but extreme climatic situation arose, the system now could not recover from it, as it probably would have recovered if it had happened a century or more earlier. Nials, Gregory, and Graybill (1989) believe such an event, or series of events, occurred around A.D. 1350. Two years in succession witnessed the highest flood level they had recorded and were followed immediately by one of the driest years on record. The system, already weakened by a century of disruptions, obviously did not overcome this one-two punch. Archaeological evidence shows very sparse settlement in the valley after that date, and the disappearance of many of the traits we have identified as Hohokam from the record.

Human-Land Relationships in Early Civilizations

The main point of the Mesopotamian and Hohokam examples, and I believe of the Mesoamerican examples as well, is that at least in these preindustrial societies, short-term political stability and economic maximization were only achieved by weakening the capacity of the productive system to react to internal and external challenges, and hence, undermined its long-term survival. Cooperative activities in many contexts may help survival of small-scale systems, but as those cooperative ventures become larger and more formalized, their adaptive potential does not always operate. The archaeologists responsible for the Mesoamerican case studies have not yet suggested the social context of the environmental problems they observed, but I would not be surprised if they paralleled the Mesopotamian and Hohokam situations. State ideologies asserted at that time, as do many today, that everyone's interests were served when the interests of the central rulers were served. Yet, many people may not share the rulers' objectives and all elements of the population may not benefit equally from a particular productive strategy. The issue, therefore, is the effective locus of decision-making within the society, how these decision-makers gain their information, and how they perceive their needs.

What does the bigger picture look like from here? Generalities begin to make sense as we compare the various examples already available in the archaeological literature with the case of southern Mesopotamia. Lowland irrigation settings, like Mesopotamia, are vulnerable to problems of salinization and siltation from upland erosion if major energy is not invested in combating these processes and maintaining the long-term productive potential of the soil. The underlying cause of this mismanagement seems to emanate at least in part from the hierarchical nature of complex societies. Whereas in a small-scale society the primary producers make the major decisions and are guided by a conservative, risk minimization strategy, in complex societies the elite appear to have a very different strategy. It may be to minimize risks as they see them, but it may not act to minimize risks for the majority of the population, and hence, may in fact pose a serious risk to them. The elite often acted to increase surplus production to support themselves, frequent military activity, major construction, and the crafting of specialized prestige goods. To meet these demands, it was logical that the elite would encourage excessive allocation of irrigation water (especially during wet years), shortening fallow periods, extending cultivation to new areas (requiring herding to be done at more distant locations), and deforestation of uplands to provide fuel wood for newly emerging industries and a growing population. The history of the Ur III Dynasty may contain a lesson that is as relevant for us today as it was 4000 years ago.

As successful agrarian societies began to develop managerial and hierarchical social systems, they set in motion forces that reshaped the agricultural decision-making process, which in turn guided human impacts on the environment. There were benefits to these changes, but in many cases they appear to have threatened the long-term stability of human-land relationships. As discussed in chapter 3, anthropologist Roy Rappaport considers this type of inefficiency in the flow of information a "maladaptation" that exists in many complex societies and often undermines their continued survival (1978). Gifts to religious orders, taxes for political leaders, or even unequal exchange values in a market are all ways a surplus can be culled from the producers for the benefit of the elite. For these types of asymmetrical flows of goods to exist in a society, there must also be a strong ideology that convinces the producers that it is in their benefit, or at least necessary, to provide these goods to the elite. The promulgation of these ideologies helps to hold together complex societies.

A useful framework for the discussion of the Ur III Dynasty and the other case studies in this chapter is to think of long stretches of history as a series of cycles of growth, stability, and decline. The idea of regions and their dominant societies oscillating in a cyclical pattern is not new, having been proposed by the fourteenth century geographer Ibn Khaldun (1967). This pattern can be measured in terms of any number of key variables, such as population, energy consumption, other technological indicators, centralization of political power, changes in social organization, or agricultural productivity of the landscape. It is likely that many of these factors are interrelated through feedback mechanisms that act to limit excessive growth in order to regenerate overdepleted situations; hence, the appearance of cyclical behavior.

It is generally agreed that population level is a key variable in understanding the seriousness of human impacts. This is true for any animal species: if the population grows too large, the readily available resources in their environment are no longer able to support it. What alters this relationship for human groups is that through agricultural technology we have been able to enhance the natural productivity of an environment, and through trade or warfare we have been able to move resources from areas of availability to areas of high demand. The actual population numbers in any particular community or for an entire society reflect a variety of biological and social factors that govern fertility, mortality, and migration. The archaeological and ethno-graphic records clearly demonstrate that although human populations are biologically capable of growing quite quickly, they equally are able to limit that growth through social and other mechanisms (Cowgill 1975). This pro-duces a situation in which population growth is not seen as an unremitting pressure, but rather as a flexible variable responding to many factors by increasing, remaining stable, or even declining. The impact of population growth will be dealt with in more detail in chapter 7.

7
Forces That Grew
with Society

In chapter 6 several successful agrarian societies that grew to urban proportions were examined to see what new types of relationships they developed with their environments. Relationships that were only hinted at in the village level of development became the hallmarks of the more complex urban-based societies. Primary among these was the expansion of food production to support a growing population that could live together in dense aggregations. The new levels of population attained and the decision to live closely together in cities brought into focus several other situations that transformed human-environmental relationships. Contagious diseases became a serious threat to general health and even to life itself; life in densely packed cities required new forms of organization and administration; and the need to supply this enlarged population encouraged the rise of mass production industries. Implications of population growth, changing community health, emerging industry, and new forms of government are the subjects that will be discussed in this chapter.

As indicated in chapter 1, many forces that have developed with the growth of complex society appear at first glance to be negative in terms of our long-term relationship with the environment. However, in many other ways these forces were part of the "improvements" in human society that made us the dominant animals in the natural world and continue to enhance our productivity and enrich us in many ways. These relationships are not simple, and the decisions that have led us in these directions were not made without cause. To effectively understand and potentially act to improve our relationship with the environment, it is necessary to look at these forces from a number of perspectives and not immediately assign positive or negative values to them.

Expanding Food Production

The growth of urbanism, and modern civilization as we know it, would not have been possible without major increases in our ability to produce food. The model in figure 7.1 is a summary of the activities and responses concerned with expanding food production to support a growing settlement system. This is constructed to parallel most closely settlements in irrigation-agriculture locations such as those of the Sumerians of Mesopotamia, the Hohokam of Arizona, or several of the Mesoamerican cultures. In these and other similar cases, agricultural strategies relying on water-control mechanisms were able to support large, dense populations for long periods of time, yet in each case success seems to have also been followed by environmental degradation that ultimately undermined these societies.

The introduction of irrigation is the starting point for examining the growth of a society in a potentially favorable setting for agricultural production. The abundant food produced using irrigation could be used to support either a growing population of food producers, or a mix of food producers and non-food-producing specialists involved in the creation and/or consumption of items and activities related to status and hierarchical social arrangements. The evidence again and again reveals that ancient societies decided to divert produce and personnel from the food production system and allocate them to the support of activities, items, and individuals not themselves producing food. The repeated presence of this tendency is a key factor in defining the course of human history since the origin of agriculture and sedentary lifestyles. Although the choices made and the mechanisms to implement them have been nearly as diverse as the number of societies in the world, there has been a general trend toward an increasing proportion of the productive potential of human communities being devoted to non-food-producing pursuits. What allows this, and what must be maintained or even expanded to support these growing complex societies, is the ability for a limited number of people to grow enough food for many others, and for it to be efficiently collected and redistributed.

It is possible to simplify this situation into four general strategies by which communities have expanded their food production, each with its own implications for the environment and for the institutional growth of the society (fig. 7.1). The most direct means of increasing food supplies is through *intensified production*. This typically involves some combination of planting more densely on current fields, using fields for more seasons before leaving them fallow, or shortening the fallow period (Boserup 1965; and see later this chapter). Over time, this would almost certainly lead to diminished soil fertility, which would necessitate a variety of labor-intensive activities to maintain

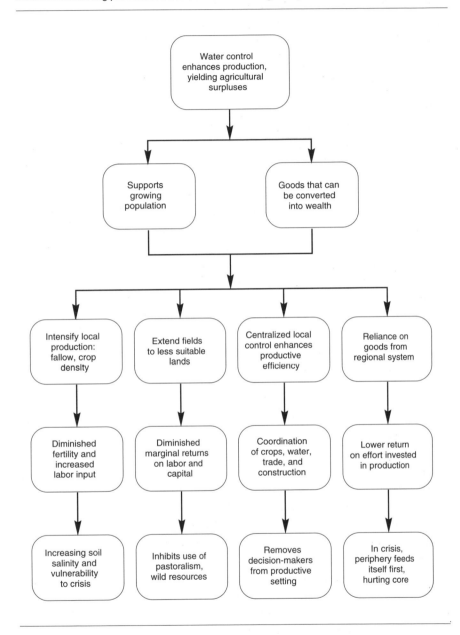

reasonable production. In some locations, the increased use of irrigation water would also cause soil salinization, further weakening the productive potential of the region.

A second strategy to increase food supplies would be to *extend fields* to less suitable and/or more distant lands (see fig. 7.2). Many traditional societies have a system in which individual families work multiple small fields (Netting 1993). This type of organization is a preadaptation to expansion. However, as these fields were located at a greater distance from the laborers' homes, more labor per hectare would be expended in commuting to the fields, preparing them, and keeping them fertile than on the closer fields of equivalent size. Hence, even though the total community production would increase, the marginal productivity per labor unit would decrease as less suitable and more distant lands were put under cultivation. There is a secondary problem with extending the fields: it takes them out of use for pasture, hunting, and wild plant collecting. This diminishes the variety of the community's diet and further requires its dependence on agriculture.

A third strategy that anthropologists often cite as a means to increase food production is *centralized control*. Efficiency might be gained within a region by promoting the specialization of production of particular goods in each community or even by groups within a community, and then the exchange of the goods to meet everyone's needs (Adams 1966; Sanders and Price 1968; Fish and Fish 1992). Centralized management could increase productivity by coordinating the allocation of irrigation water and the choice of plants grown, and by organizing labor to expand and maintain facilities. Many scholars believe that the emergence of this type of redistributive economy is one of the fundamental beneficial characteristics of a complex society. There are, however, potential problems in terms of environmental degradation, because this managerial arrangement distances the decision-makers from the productive setting (McGovern et al. 1988). In situations of diminishing soil fertility, a local producer might promptly undertake additional conservation activity. A decision-maker primarily concerned with the community's volume of collectable surplus per season, however, would be less likely to allow production to be purposely decreased, even if such restraint might pay off in the distant future.

A fourth strategy for increasing food supplies, particularly in urban systems, is to *rely on goods imported within a regional system*. The regional system can be built on colonists moving out from a center, on the center providing goods desired in the periphery, or on the center being sufficiently powerful to coerce the movement of goods from the periphery. All of these situations can be seen in the archaeological record. The net result is that more food and other goods are available to the occupants of the urban centers,

Figure 7.2
Schematic representations of a village and its fields undergoing growth.

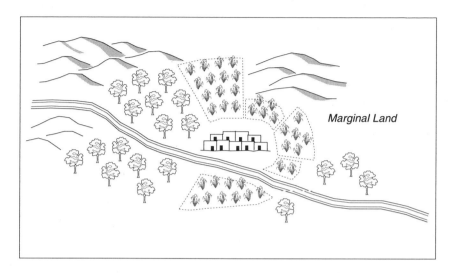

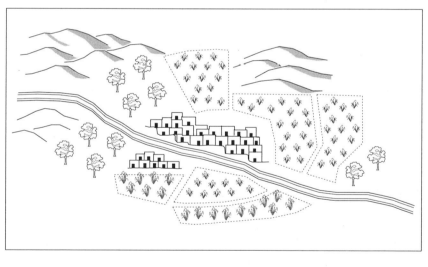

allowing a greater proportion of their population not to be devoted to food production. This is a pattern that started at least 5000 years ago in many parts of the world, including those discussed in the case studies in this chapter, and has continued to gain momentum ever since.

At least at the outset, each of these four basic strategies did act to increase the amount of food and other goods available to a society, facilitating the growth of its population and an expansion in the energy it could devote to "civilizational" institutions. However, these same strategies demanded increases in labor input, which often led to an overutilization of the landscape, diminishing its long-term productivity and, at the same time, potentially stimulating social unrest. The very structure of decision-making in a complex society exacerbates the tendency to overexploit both laborers and the landscape by building a system that benefits from increasing quantities of goods. Around the world, complex societies are based on food-production systems that rely on these strategies, and they have developed institutions and supporting ideologies that act to keep the society integrated and operating in a reasonable manner. However successful these strategies are at most times and in most places, they do introduce several weaknesses into the system — maladaptations that make them more vulnerable to crises. Slowly diminishing soil fertility, lack of alternative food sources, decision-makers who are removed from the scene of production, and reliance on outside groups for essential goods are all conditions that weaken the resilience of a society when it faces trouble and have taken their toll in countless situations.

Population

In every case study in this volume, the growing number of people is a factor in creating an imbalance between society and the environment. This is not a new idea — it pervades much of the environmental literature and goes back at least as early as the writings of Thomas Malthus (1878). Malthus was among the first and most influential of a series of scholars to try to explain the fundamental interactions of population, environment/land, and agricultural methods/technology (Netting 1993:276). He suggested that human populations had a natural tendency to grow, but that they would reach a limit that depended on the productive technology available. In this perspective, a change in technology — the introduction of irrigation agriculture, for example — would allow an increase in the population that could be supported. The technology was the independent variable and population was the dependent variable. Few scholars would completely agree with Malthus' somewhat cynical and overly deterministic theory, but the basic notion of population being limited by available technology has found its way into many modern perspectives.

A more useful formulation of this idea is the notion of *carrying capacity*. For any particular landscape and climate, there exists a reasonable approximation of the biomass it can support. Hence, we can use the concept of carrying capacity to estimate the number of carnivores a region can support based on expected availability of plants and herbivores. This concept becomes more relevant when one adds in human food-producing strategies appropriate to the landscape and known by the people living there. It is possible, therefore, to categorize the kinds of terrain in the vicinity of a human settlement according to what food resources each could yield given the local climate and the state of agrarian knowledge. Factoring in the least-cost principle that people will rely most heavily on lands close to their settlement, it is possible to estimate the total likely productivity of any region and thus, the number of people it could support (Higgs and Vita-Finzi 1970).

In Malthus' theory, when a human population reached the carrying capacity of the land, its numbers would be kept in check by disease, warfare, or starvation. Anthropologists have suggested that it is very unlikely that a society would grow to the point where it cannot feed itself and its members begin to die of starvation (Catton 1993). Rather, societies appear to implement other means of limiting their numbers in advance of starvation, such as out migration or restrictions on birth. Either way, the point remains roughly the same: given the characteristics of the environment and the state of human food-producing strategies, any particular region has a limit to the number of people it can support. At the surface, this theory seems to be a reasonable approximation of reality, but how does one explain the many situations in which regional populations appear to have kept on growing? Malthusians would say that could only happen under circumstances in which the technology of food production has improved significantly, allowing more people to exist. Other scholars have looked at this same situation and insisted that population is not the dependent variable "waiting" for technology to change, but is the independent variable, growing on its own and "encouraging" technology to change in order to accommodate the increasing number of people.

A very influential advocate of population being the independent variable is the Danish economist Ester Boserup, who presented her views in the book, *The Conditions of Agricultural Growth* (1965; see also 1981). For Boserup, population growth is a major factor determining agricultural developments. She points strongly to the rapid rise in population growth rates

Table 7.1
Boserup's five land-use types and the implications for cropping and population.

Land-Use Type	Period Sown	Period Fallowed	Frequency of Cropping (%)	Population Density (People/Km²)
Forest fallow	1–2 yr.	15–25 yr.	0–10	0–14
Bush fallow	2–8 yr.	8–10 yr.	10–40	4–16
Short fallow	< 2 yr.	1–2 yr.	40–80	16–64
Annual cropping	1 crop/yr.	few mo.	80–100	64–256
Multicropping	≥ 2 crops/yr.	no fallow	200–300	> 250

Source: Boserup (1965); Netting (1993).

since World War II, and insists that they are not likely to have been caused by technological innovations alone. Whereas for Malthus and many classical economists, the supply of food was considered to be inelastic, and its lack of elasticity considered the main factor in governing the rate of population growth, for Boserup it is elastic. She insisted that the basis of the misconception was considering the key decision farmers made about land-use as two separate choices: (1) extending cultivation to new lands, and (2) intensifying cultivation on current fields.

Unlike Malthus and most subsequent economists who based their ideas on information from Western Europe and North America, Boserup studied the tropics, where the traditional agricultural strategy was swidden. In a mobile swidden system, the distinction cited above did not exist; the major choice was how often to use any particular piece of land. Land not being farmed was considered as vacant by a classical economist, while for Boserup and the swidden agriculturists she studied, land being left fallow was still a part of the farming system and was, in the meantime, being used for hunting and other forms of procurement.

Boserup's key contribution is the idea that productivity of any particular parcel of land is tightly tied to labor input on that land. The land's fertility is not some constant value, unaffected by human use, but is tied to frequency of cultivation and input of human labor to pursue such strategies as irrigating, terracing, or fertilizing. Viewing the diversity of land use in the tropics, Boserup suggests five types of agricultural land use in order of increasing intensity of exploitation (table 7.1):

1. Forest-fallow cultivation.
Plots of land are cleared in the forest, sown for a year or two, and then left fallow for a number of years (20 or more) for the forest to regenerate before clearing again.

2. Bush-fallow cultivation.
The fallow period is much shorter, between 6 and 10 years, and no true forest returns. Also, the cultivation period may extend to as long as the fallow period.

3. Short-fallow cultivation.
The fallow period lasts only one or two years with only grasses returning before reuse.

4. Annual cropping.
Land is left fallow only a few months between harvest and subsequent planting. This may also include a rotation in which one or more successive crops are sown in an annual cycle.

5. Multicropping.
The most intensive system of land use, with the same plot bearing two or more crops every year.

Boserup challenges the previously held assumption that the soils in the tropics are only fertile enough for long-fallow cultivation, and because of that, the population had reached the land's capacity. Her idea was that particular fallow systems are not tied to particular types of soil or climate — human land-use is a dynamic process. She also expanded her own studies to include temperate zones and more permanent agriculture (1981). Boserup argued that under the pressure of increasing population, there has been a shift in recent decades from more extensive to more intensive systems of land use virtually everywhere in the underdeveloped world and historically in Europe as well. She also argues that there is a close connection between the system of fallow employed, the techniques for fertilization, and the tools for cultivation, and that some techniques of soil preparation and cultivation will require substantial human labor input. Following this line of reasoning, it could be asserted that some forms of human use, with sufficient labor input, have *improved* the soil, increasing its fertility and its ability to support more crops, and hence more people. In fact, many scholars have taken Boserup's five-part sequence of agricultural strategies as something of an evolutionary scheme with more intense systems being practiced by more advanced cultures in the past.

An essential element of her proposition is that food output per labor hour input decreases as one shortens the fallow and increases the intensity of cultivation. At first glance, this seems a bit illogical — that is, more advanced systems would require more labor per unit returned — and some scholars have contested whether it actually stands up to empirical examination (Bronson 1972). However, if one did get more food for less work by intensifying, then one would expect every group who learned about intensification to instantly adopt it. We know from agricultural history and prehistory that this is often not the case. Boserup's essential point is that a group will only go toward intensification if they have to. She sees the long-fallow farmer as having considerable leisure time, but this is increasingly lost as the fallow is shortened and field preparation and attention to cultivation, irrigation, weeding, and fertilizing all increase. Even though overall output increases so that more people can be fed, the hours of labor invested increases even faster.

In this scenario, technological advances are not an inherent part of the human experience, nor are available ones adopted in all circumstances. Rather, population growth is seen as the natural process, and when that results in situations that abut on regional carrying capacities, people are encouraged to invest the extra effort needed to intensify their agricultural systems in order to reap more food. This general position, that technological fixes can be found for the problems of growing population and other environmental threats, certainly has currency among many modern thinkers.

There are other scholars (e.g., Cowgill 1975, 1996) who were uncomfortable with a theory that saw steady population growth and its attendant pressure on resources as a natural condition and as the prime mover in explaining many important cultural developments. A closer look at various ethnographically known societies shows that they have regulated their numbers in a variety of ways. Out migration is an important factor when one is examining a limited geographic region, but if the spatial framework is large, then people moving about is less important. The key to population change when taking a broad perspective is the balance between fertility and mortality rates. In premodern times, and in most developing countries today, fertility and mortality rates are both very high when compared with modern North America or Western Europe. Hence, a small change in one or the other rates can have a substantial effect on resulting rates of population growth or decline. Changes of a year or two in the age of marriage, a year or two in the reproductive life of females, or three or four months in time between pregnancies can lead to drastic changes in overall growth rate. And a change in the growth rate compounded over a long period of time in terms of generations can lead to enormous changes in total population.

From the perspective of thousands or even millions of years, the growth in the number of people inhabiting the earth has been quite spectacular. However, when one looks at the changes from a human perspective — that is, a single lifetime in a particular region — then the process is not so overwhelming. In fact, rates of growth vary widely between regions and over time, and there have even been numerous periods of population decline on a regional level. Several geographers have assembled the historical and archaeological evidence for population patterns in four major regions of the world and compared these with three general models of population change used in their field (Whitmore et al. 1990 and fig. 7.3):

1. Arithmetic-exponential.
This is the most popular model and divides the history of population growth into two stages: first, an infinitesimally slow monotonic growth up to the Industrial Revolution followed by, second, a staggering acceleration up to the present.

2. Logarithmic-logistic.
This model is comprised of three disjunctive sections for the population trajectory. Each section is a population growth outbreak that is associated with a technological revolution. After each era of rapid growth there is a stabilization at a new higher level, that is, each technological revolution increases the carrying capacity of the earth. This approach is consistent with some of the ideas of the Malthusian approach coupled with a multilinear model of social evolution.

3. Arithmetic-logistic.
In this model global population history of the last 12,000 years can be seen as cycles, each with three elements: growth, overshoot, and stabilization.

The underlying assumption of all three models is that there has been a global synchrony to population growth and that declines have not been significant. Whitmore et al. attempted to examine the available evidence for long-term population change in four key regions of the world and found that the regional patterns were not synchronic and that substantial regional declines were normal and may have been associated with human overuse of the environment. They also suggested that the patterns of population growth in each region could be better understood in terms of *waves*. These wavelike undulations in population numbers were of differing length and amplitude in each example, but they were similar enough so that the authors refer to them as *millennial long waves*.

A brief look at the pattern from each of these four regions reveals some of the basic issues governing population. The Tigris-Euphrates River valley, setting of the world's oldest cities, experienced several minor population declines during the first long wave that began about 4000 B.C. with

Figure 7.3
Mathematical models of global population growth.

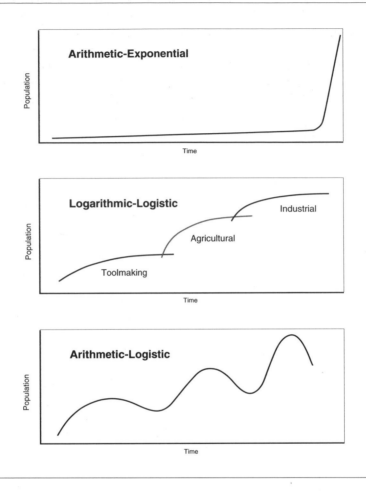

the first major occupation of the valley and lasted until about 500 B.C. (fig. 7.4A). The growth and decline was more accentuated during the second wave that ended in the Medieval period. The third wave is still on the rise today, and up to this point, it appears even more accentuated. Even from this one case study, it is possible to infer that there is a pattern over time. Going from the earliest to the most recent cycle, the wavelength decreases (i.e., time elapsed), the amplitude increases (i.e., number of people involved), and consequently, the rate of change becomes more rapid. The demographers interpret the Mesopotamian trajectory as one reflecting a society that is *resilient*;

that is, capable of absorbing change, fluctuating greatly, yet persisting over a very long period. The Nile Valley reveals a similar pattern, but one in which the first wave is far longer and more gradual (fig. 7.4B). It begins earlier and lasts 1000 years longer. The second wave is quite short, with modest amplitude, and the third wave shows an abrupt increase in population in the last century. The geographers see this pattern being one of stability over most of its duration with more resilience apparent in the third wave. They also see it as providing a good example of the second general model of global growth: logarithmic-logistic. The population grows slowly, and then reaches a limit that it doesn't surpass for many years, until there is a breakthrough that allows a new surge in numbers.

In the Basin of Mexico, the two and a half waves seen in the first two examples seemed to have occurred in much less time — about 3000 years (fig. 7.4C). These waves were of declining wavelength, increasing amplitude, and increasing rates of change, suggesting a pattern of increasing resilience

Figure 7.4
Estimated population change for major regions (from Whitmore et al. 1990).

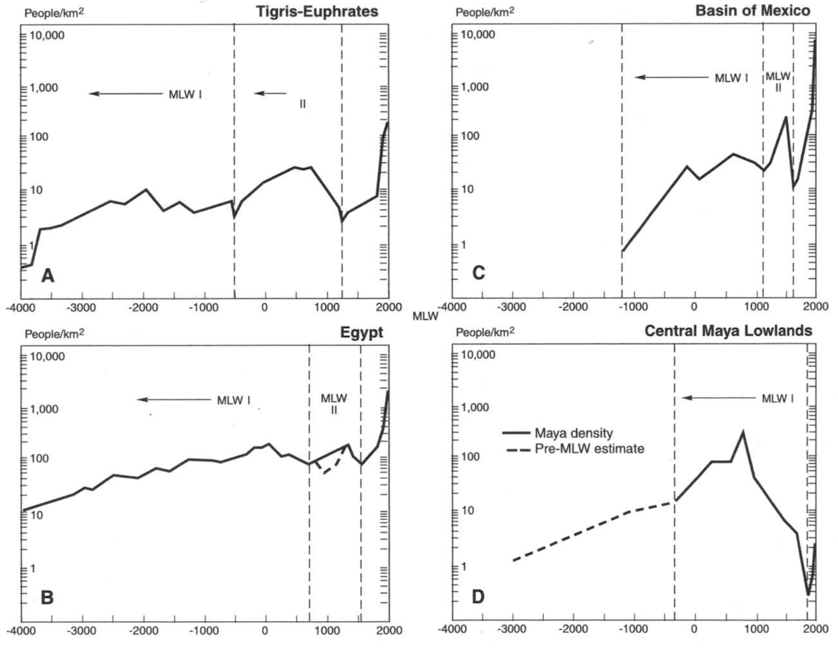

and low stability similar to the Tigris-Euphrates Valley. The fourth case study, the central Maya Lowlands, offers a pattern different from the others (fig. 7.4D). It appears to be only in the middle of the second wave, and modern era population has not reached that of the prehistoric peak. There was a wave of growth with agricultural expansion and the environmental alterations it necessitated, but this led to a massive depopulation and a situation that did not quickly rebound. Hence, the geographers see this region as exhibiting little stability and very little resilience.

The overall pattern that these examples portray is of nonsynchronized periods of repetitive growth and decline. The growth rates appear to double from the first to second wave, but then the current wave appears to represent growth about five times faster. The decline of the second wave seems to be steeper than that of the first, but we do not yet have the decline for the third (current) wave. If the model holds, it will be quite steep. In fact, the authors are willing to hypothesize that the world is heading toward a global population peak of 10 or 11 billion by about A.D. 2155.

In each of the four regions, major environmental alterations accompanied the growth phases, as settlement expansion and intensification of agriculture are the major components of population growth. In some parts of these regions, such as southern Mesopotamia, the environmental alteration was serious enough that the region could not recover. In other regions, such as the Nile Valley, the deterioration was never permanent and intensive land use could recover or even continue unabated. In the Maya Lowlands the environment was radically altered during population expansion, but with population decline, the forests returned. Yet population growth did not quickly resume. These examples demonstrate the complexity of possible interactions between population and environment. They also show that population growth and decline sometimes are associated with major political shifts, but that they also seem to crosscut these upheavals. The conclusion that Whitmore et al. reach is that although population is a key factor in understanding environmental transformations, it is by no means the single cause of these impacts, nor does it play out the same in each situation.

One of the reasons that environmental potential as expressed by carrying capacity does not map directly onto population numbers is that treating demand for food as if it reflected the "needs" of a society as a whole is not a completely realistic approach. There are two aspects to this confusion. First, a society's needs are in fact the cumulative needs of many individuals who are organized into various groups, each with differing characteristics. Second, people too often conflate need with demand, as if a social stress (need) automatically generated an effective demand. Rather, demand is experienced by producers and relates to the consumers' ability to compensate producers for their efforts. Looking at historical examples, the reality is that food shortages often lead to hoarding, a rise in prices, and starvation rather than to innovation in technology as Boserup suggested (Cowgill 1975). The key to both issues is who is experiencing the stress, who is in a position to do something about it, and why might they see it to be in their interest to do what they do. That one's situation within society is so important in determining perception of issues, choices available, and logical responses is a fundamental insight into the nature of human-environmental interactions and will be returned to in the final chapter.

Disease and Community Health

The human impact on the environment is often measured in terms of soil erosion, deforestation, or species extinction. These are each essential measures of the viability of the environment for plant and animal survival, which usually reflects the environment's potential for food production as well. Equally important are measures of the quality of life experienced by humans; one key parameter of which is the condition of community health. We have touched on the impact of various decisions and human activities on the productive potential of the landscape and will evaluate this issue in a more general perspective in the final chapter. However, decisions that may be made in large part to improve food production or settlement structure may have had unforeseen impacts on the community's health. Given today's emphasis on air quality, water quality, and overall quality of life questions when evaluating environmental impacts, it seems necessary to look at the implications for ancient societies as well.

Two key cultural advances — the introduction of agriculture and the growth of urban society — have been the focus of the last two chapters with respect to their impact on the environment and the potential for producing food, but they also had dramatic effects on human health. The epidemiology of the rise of civilization, like its impact on the physical environment, is largely a series of negative consequences of what are widely thought to be two of the most positive advances in human history (Boyden 1970; Cohen and Armelagos 1984; Cohen 1989; Newson 1998). The origin and spread of diseases has had a fundamental impact on human history. For example, until World War II, more victims of war died of war-borne microbes than of battle wounds (Diamond 1997:197). Moreover, disease has reshaped settlement patterns, undermined the growth of particular societies, and, as we have discussed for the European entrance into the New World, was instrumental in determining the fate of a hemisphere. What makes this phenomenon even more crucial for the issues treated in this book, is that it appears that the origins, spread, and evolution of the most dangerous infectious diseases are closely tied to decisions humans made to domesticate animals, intensify agricultural production, and pursue an urban way of life.

Several fundamental aspects of civilization are relevant to considering impacts on community health. First, civilization is characterized by cities that have large and densely packed populations. Cities are heterogeneous, often depend on food from outside, and may engage in trade with quite distant communities. Second, the reliance on agriculture is almost total, leading to more intensive strategies such as irrigation and the transformation of large areas of natural landscape to the service of food production. Although there are many aspects to changing human health, the following discussion focuses on only two: the spread of infectious diseases and the general quality of community nutrition.

To understand the impact of human activities on infectious diseases, it is necessary to recognize that the pathogens themselves have a life cycle in which they compete for survival and reproduction like all other organisms. Moreover, they often spend a part of their life cycle in a host animal like a mosquito or sheep before infecting a human. Hence, a change in human behavior that affects the survival or habits of either the microorganism itself or its vector (host) may facilitate or retard the spread of a disease (Diamond 1997:198–200). Probably the most basic way that a disease-causing microbe can be spread is for its current host to be eaten by a new host, which has then infected itself. Examples of this type of transmission would be salmonella bacteria that we contract by eating infected eggs or trichinosis that we get from eating infected pig meat that is insufficiently cooked. Another common means for the microbe to be transmitted is through the saliva of an insect that bites the old host and flies to a new host to infect. Malaria, the plague, and typhus are examples of diseases that are spread this way. Other microbes are transmitted by the "symptoms" they cause in those inflicted. Skin lesions (smallpox), genital sores (syphilis), coughing (influenza), and diarrhea (cholera) are all effective means for infecting new hosts who come in contact with or proximity to infected individuals.

The proximity of humans to animals was certainly a factor in the increased transmission of animal-borne diseases to members of farming communities. In fact, the presence of high numbers of domestic animals in sustained contact with humans was instrumental in the origin of key infectious diseases and their evolution to new forms. What started as an animal disease may have, through mutation, developed strains that preferred a human host. Experts believe that smallpox and tuberculosis originated with cattle, measles with dogs, influenza with pigs and chickens, and the common cold with horses.

Probably the single most significant human decision to impact the nature of disease was the widespread adoption of sedentary urban life, with the rapidly growing number of people choosing to live together in densely packed cities. The success of most pathogens depends on the number and proximity of host organisms, both vectors and victims (Newson 1998:49). Having more people around provides greater opportunities for the offspring of pathogens to find a new host. Consequently, the pathogen will not die out, even when a particular host dies and ceases to function as a suitable host. Moreover, since already infected individuals are more vulnerable to other infections, the effect of a dense population is compounded.

Evidence gathered by paleopathologists shows that many, if not most, infectious diseases had little impact before people began to live in dense communities (Black 1975). Before that, only chronic diseases and those that had nonhuman hosts were real problems (e.g., herpes virus and yaws bacteria, both of which remain inactive for long periods of time). Chronic diseases were successful even in circumstances of low population density, because the impact on their victims was relatively mild and the host survived for long periods, allowing for transmission. Diseases with animal hosts — zoonoses — could exist in situations with small human populations even though their effects were often serious and sometimes even fatal. Diseases like rabies, malaria, and the plague could thrive even if their human victims died quickly, because the host animals lived on to spread the disease to new humans.

The sedentary aspect of village and urban life also had a major effect on the spread of infectious diseases. Sedentism enabled parasites or vectors to maintain continuous contact with human hosts, so that the organisms could complete their life cycle in proximity to the people they ultimately would infect. This is key for parasites that spend some of their life cycle outside of the human host, such as cholera and diarrhea that are transmitted via fecal-oral infections. Hookworms also thrive in sedentary situations because the worms spend time in the soil. Villages and cities rely on stored food that provides a source of sustenance for carriers, such as the rats that are famous for carrying bubonic plague. The accumulation of garbage from sedentary living may also provide a spawning ground for both microorganisms and hosts.

Other human impacts on the environment directly affected the animal hosts for diseases, leading to varying effects on humans themselves. Village life and widespread land clearance took us out of close proximity with some parasites, such as the ticks that might live on deer, but brought us into continuous contact with others, such as the fleas that might be carried by domestic dogs. In other cases, land clearance, irrigation, and standing water all encouraged the spread of hosts like mosquitoes that led to the success of devastating diseases like malaria and yellow fever (fig. 7.5; Woods 1979). Recent archaeological evidence indicates that the first widespread occurrence of these diseases came with the agricultural revolution and the establishment of village life. Malaria in particular has a long history in places such as Mesopotamia and may have played a key role in undermining the productivity of the southern part of that region. In southern Mesopotamia, the land slope is very gentle and water would stand on fields and in canals for long periods, providing an excellent opportunity for mosquitoes to breed. Moreover, animals are preferred as prey by these mosquitoes, and herds of domestic cattle and sheep in close proximity to human settlements and standing irrigation water would provide a favorable setting for completing the life cycle of both the mosquitoes and the disease's pathogens they carry (Ives 1994).

We might suggest that the low gradient of the landscape and tendency of water to pond in the agricultural fields of the lower reaches of the Tigris and Euphrates Rivers in southern Mesopotamia favored not only salinization of the soil in farmed areas as discussed in chapter 6, but also the spread of malaria. Both of these processes would have diminished the productivity of the people in the south and both may have contributed to the region's abandonment in favor of settlement to the north. There may have been other diseases that became serious threats in early irrigation societies such as southern Mesopotamia. Standing water, especially in irrigation canals, would have been a major cause of the spread of diseases such as schistosomiasis, which is transmitted via snails that spend part of their life cycle in the mud of the canals and need to make direct contact with humans, which happens while people are irrigating their fields or maintaining the canals.

Several other factors that are associated with civilizations have been important in spreading diseases. Cities are characterized by, among other things, their proclivity toward reliance on trading goods with partners in their own region and beyond. This encouraged people and goods to move over great distances, serving as carriers of a disease from one city to another. The density of people in a city might have provided the critical mass of population to enable some acute viral infections to survive and spread. Diseases such as measles, smallpox, and mumps would attach to a human who would then become immune or die; in either case they could only be a carrier for a short period. Hence, for these diseases to thrive they must have lots of potential victims. Hygiene in early civilizations may have helped slow the transmission of some diseases, but the accumulation of garbage, the widespread sharing of water and food sources, and some customary ways of relating may have encouraged the evolution of some diseases to more virulent

Figure 7.5
The cycle of malaria transmission (from Woods 1979). Copyright © 1979 by Mayfield Publishing Company. Reprinted by permission of the publisher.

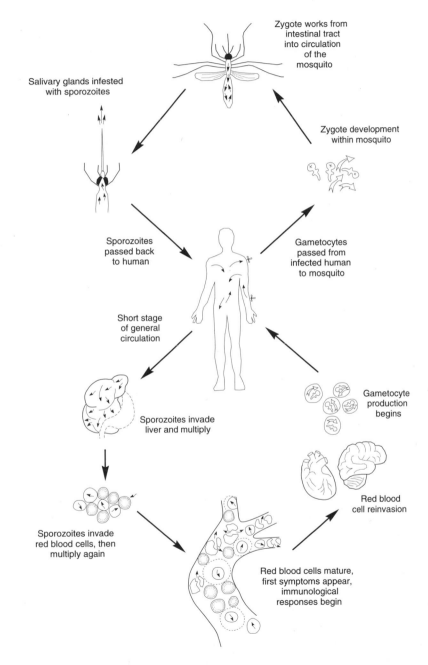

Zygote works from
intestinal tract
into circulation
of the
mosquito

Salivary glands infested
with sporozoites

Zygote development
within mosquito

Sporozoites
passed back
to human

Gametocytes
passed from
infected human
to mosquito

Short stage
of general
circulation

Gametocyte
production
begins

Sporozoites invade
liver and multiply

Red blood
cell reinvasion

Sporozoites invade
red blood cells, then
multiply again

Red blood cells mature,
first symptoms appear,
immunological
responses begin

forms or encouraged them to attack older individuals where their impact would be more serious.

Community Nutrition

A question of major significance is whether adopting agriculture as a way of life and subsequently intensifying its practice actually benefited a community's health. There is a generally held assumption that with agriculture there came a general improvement in the human diet and, consequently, in many aspects of human health, but physical anthropologists have questioned whether nutrition actually improved (Cohen and Armelagos 1984). There is evidence supporting both sides of this question. Skeletal evidence recovered by archaeologists reveals repeated examples of long bone cortical thinning and porosity of the skull among farmers, both indicative that the individuals had suffered from anemia. There also appears to have been many circumstances in which increased frequency of Harris lines on teeth and enamel hypoplasia indicated serious disruptions in nutrition during early growth of individuals in early farming communities. Complicating this picture is evidence of these same maladies among some preagricultural hunter and gatherer bands. The evidence does not produce a clear picture, but there were numerous cases in which the farming community's nutritional balance was as bad as that of their hunter-gatherer predecessors.

It is likely that in the early stages of agriculture, when domestic plants were primarily a supplement to the gathered array, community nutrition may have improved. However, once farming became dominant, especially in parts of the New World where corn was the almost exclusive source of food, the dietary balance would have diminished significantly. In addition, the normal abundance of agricultural yields may have allowed the population of these communities to grow excessively large, so that during periods of low harvests, nutritional stress would be more severe. These shortfalls would be more serious because the collected food sources that hunter-gatherers had relied upon to buffer shortfalls were no longer used or even available. To the extent that adoption of agriculture provided a greater potential return of food, coupled with a greater risk of serious nutritional deficiencies, the implications of the decision to become an agriculturist become extremely ominous. We will return to this seminal question in the final chapter.

Skeletal evidence does seem to point to less physical stress among agriculturists, as measured by robustness and frequency of arthritis and physical injury. There is new evidence that with the introduction of agriculture in some societies, there was an increase in the physical stature of women, but not of men, leading to diminishing sexual dimorphism (Peterson 1994). It is interesting to contemplate the likely causes and the consequences this change prompted in gender relations.

Overall, the various studies suggest a decline in the quality of life and possibly even a shortened life expectancy associated with the adoption of agriculture, despite a decline in the physical demands placed on the body (Cohen and Armelagos 1984). This conclusion requires us to reevaluate several generally held propositions about the advantages of agriculture over hunting and gathering. The simplistic notion of unimpeded human progress is ill founded. There was not a progressive increase in life expectancy; the picture was actually more complicated, with individuals in many hunting and gathering groups outliving those in agricultural groups. We have also found that hunter-gatherer groups were often better buffered against episodic food stress and sometimes had a more balanced diet than their farming counterparts. Nevertheless, since the advent of farming, regional and global population has grown dramatically. Moreover, much of this growth has included the repeated adoption of farming by former gathering people to the point where societies that rely on gathering are virtually extinct. This global population growth was accomplished *in spite of* a general diminution of both child and adult life expectancies, a questionable advance in human diet, and a quantum increase in contagious diseases. This suggests that the forces, social and otherwise, that encouraged the adoption of agriculture and eventually of urbanism were extremely powerful, being able to override the negative impacts of early farming on those who attempted it.

Ancient Industry and Trade

With the growth of early urban societies came the increasing specialization of labor within communities and specialization of production between communities and regions. These processes have continued to increase to the point where they are essential characteristics of modern society, with the context of production and trade today being global. At the outset of agriculture and village life, the family or some other small organizational unit was probably the basic self-sufficient unit of production in society. Food sharing and long-distance hunting or procurement are very old activities, but the institutionalization of specialized production and subsequent exchange dates only from the time of the earliest cities. The growth of these activities has had, and continues to have, profound effects on the environment.

Although the location of much early industry and certainly the consumers of most of its products were in the early cities, such as those in lowland Mesopotamia, the most profound environmental effects can be seen in the peripheral regions, where resources were being extracted and processed. We have reasonably good archaeological evidence of the relation between the early cities of Mesopotamia and the communities that existed in the upland regions to the north and east. Although separated by many miles, the upland, forested areas that fringed Mesopotamia were in regular contact with the lowland cities due to the movements of goods and people and the pressures of economic demand and military threat.

Since agricultural village life began in these uplands several millennia before the rise of cities in the lowland, the human-environmental interactions in the uplands were probably locally driven at first. As we discussed in chapter 5, deforestation would have already been a serious problem in the vicinity of early villages where land had to be cleared for agricultural fields. With long-term occupation and the slow growth of these villages, the forests of the uplands would have come under considerable pressure. In the vicinity of villages, trees most likely would have been eliminated, and even shrubs would have been under pressure for use as fuel and forage. Nevertheless, in the two millennia — 6000–4000 B.C. — of widespread village development before the spread of urbanism, the communities of the uplands appear to have reached some balance with their environment. Villages thrived in settings with access to good arable land, and the forest cover in those localities was seriously reduced, but not completely eliminated. Soil erosion must have been a periodic problem, but the longevity of settlement in these localities indicates that regeneration was possible and some sort of stability existed. Land clearance to create agricultural fields; use of woody vegetation for the domestic hearth and plaster and ceramic production; and consumption by domestic animals certainly degraded the composition of the local vegetation (Miller 1985, 1992a). Nevertheless, population and demand must have remained sufficiently low that regionwide abandonment was rare and conditions appeared relatively sustainable. In fact, Karl Butzer points to the human-environmental situation that coevolved in the Levant as an example of a human-degraded environment that attained a balance that has sustained itself for millennia (1996).

Beginning about 4000 B.C., the situation established by villagers in the uplands began to change in select locations. The imbalance can be detected at different times in various places, but its underlying cause was the same — the growth of urban centers and the demands they created. Among those demands would have been a demand for building timbers where they were available, and metal ores where they could be mined (fig. 7.6). These added to the local demand for wood and fuel and, in many cases, set the natural situation sufficiently off balance that for the local settlements to

Figure 7.6
Source locations of raw materials imported into Mesopotamia.

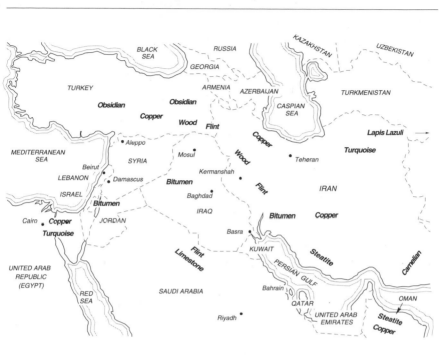

survive, they would have to adopt dependent relationships to secure basic commodities such as food. Metal production is a particularly instructive example since the sources of ore were in the uplands of Turkey and Iran on the margins of Mesopotamia, yet the bulk of the consumers were in the cities located some distance away. From the earliest urban times, metals were a highly valued commodity for use in weaponry, tools, and prestige goods. Thus, the successful procurement of metal justified the establishment of new relations between producers and consumers, even if it meant the movement of people and fuel to make extraction possible. It is not easy to separate the impacts of early industry from those of village life, but modeling these behaviors allows us to make reasonable guesses.

One simulation model attempts to estimate the relative impacts of the demand created by local industry versus the domestic hearth on the forests surrounding an archaeological site in Turkey that we know was a center of tin production for use in bronze metallurgy (Chadderton 1994). The model incorporates modern estimates for the density of oak forest in that type of environment and the growth rate. Ecologists suggest that the maximum rate of growth is not achieved in an oak forest for 50 years after it is cut. From historical and ethnographic sources, the model estimates the amount of wood and fuel required for each of the basic activities in the community. Historical evidence points to charcoal being used for almost all purposes throughout the region, which has the effect of multiplying the amount of wood that would need to be cut. The four basic needs for fuel were: (1) domestic (i.e., cooking, ceramics, plaster); (2) mining; (3) smelting; and (4) metal item production. The model then incorporates estimates for local populations and the number of people required to mine various amounts of tin.

The central question of the simulation was how much tin could be mined and people supported while allowing the forests to rejuvenate. (Put another way, it is a question of how much area could be deforested while still yielding a sustainable pattern.) Chadderton's conclusion was that the interval of cutting would have to be substantially longer than 50 years for there to be any measurable regeneration of the forests. (This would result in an area 8 km in radius around the settlement being cleared.) The smaller the economy, the more likely that reforestation will occur. Hence, if the community could manage with only cutting each forest grove once every 105 years, regeneration would be maximized and an area only 3 km in radius around the settlement would have to be cleared. Two additional insights became clear from this analysis: first, during downturns in the economic cycle the forest would regenerate; and second, the domestic consumption of fuel was close in volume to the industrial needs. This second point means that local population growth can be as much of an environmental problem as the presence of extractive industries such as metallurgy. The author suggested the most likely solution to fit the empirical situation is one where production increases over time, reaches a peak, and then slowly declines as fuel becomes scarce. The entire cycle takes about 500 years, at the end of which there are no useable forests, the soil is eroded, and the region must be abandoned.

The question facing the ancient villager again and again was not whether or not wood was needed — it was always needed. The question was: under what food-producing strategies would the need for wood and other plant forms of fuel exceed the rate of replacement? Decisions about the use of wood for domestic hearths or about how many goats to graze on the nearby countryside were made by the local people, enabling the participants themselves to develop mechanisms for balancing this consumption against potential regeneration. Metallurgy and other extractive activities that were prompted by demands from distant cities were harder to keep in balance with local supplies. This structural problem, which emerged as an integral element of industry and trade within an urban society, has far-reaching implications and will be examined more generally in the final chapter of the book.

Recent research has documented the fact that even in ancient times industrial production of some minerals was substantial enough to produce significant hemisphere-wide air pollution. A team of French and American scientists have found a record of serious lead air pollution in an ice core taken from Greenland (Hong et al. 1994). Lead production became common about 3000 B.C. with the improvement of the technology for smelting lead-silver alloys from lead sulfide ores (galena) and then removing the silver from the alloy. The use of silver, and hence the smelting of lead ores, increased dramatically during Greek and Roman times largely due to the widespread use of silver in coinage. At this maximum, about 2000 years ago, it is estimated that about 80,000 metric tons per year of lead were produced—given that it was as much as a 300 to 1 by-product of silver production—and that about 5% of the smelted lead entered the atmosphere as pollution. The fact that it was found in the arctic zone of Greenland at an elevation of over 3200 meters above sea level indicates that this lead pollution was carried hemisphere-wide by the middle troposphere.

The concentration of lead during Greek and Roman times was four times the level considered to be natural and about 15% of the level that has occurred during the past 60 years due to the widespread use of lead additives in gasoline. Given that the source of lead pollution in ancient times was limited to Europe and the Mediterranean region alone, it could be expected that local and regional pollution levels were much higher, possibly approaching those of today. The ice core data show a significant drop in lead pollution as the Roman mines were exhausted and as Roman power waned. There was a gradual resumption of pollution levels during late medieval and Renaissance times as new mines were worked in Germany and, ultimately, the New World. By the Industrial Revolution, atmospheric lead concentrations had once again reached the level of the Roman period. It is difficult to determine whether these levels of atmospheric lead pollution had a serious impact on worldwide human health or plant growth, but it does seem possible that in the locales where this smelting was taking place, health and environmental impacts were severe. It has even been suggested that lead poisoning was among the significant causes of the fall of the Roman Empire (Nriagu 1983). Having now recognized the reality of large-scale hemispheric pollution long before the Industrial Revolution, scientists must pursue further skeletal and elemental studies to evaluate the impact of industrial pollution on ancient peoples, a possibility that up until now was seldom taken seriously.

Craft and industrial production would not have grown into major activities without mechanisms for distributing these goods to large populations.

These exchanges, both of bulk commodities and small precious items, provided the basis for increasing specialization of production among communities and a means by which wealth could be accumulated. As human groups became less self-sufficient and more dependent on traded goods, this process also conferred an element of power onto those who controlled trade. In some ways the growth of trade may have had a benign effect on the environment, because the production of goods may be more efficient in a situation with specialization, large-scale production, and exchange rather than self-sufficiency. Areas best suited for certain goods and people best trained to transform those goods would specialize in their production, thus conserving resources and maximizing output per person.

Whether or not there are gains in efficiency, there are clear impacts of growing trade on the environment and society. With trade comes an impetus to specialize in the production of foodstuffs and other basic commodities, such as wool or olive oil. The efficiency gained by focusing on a single crop is counterbalanced by more serious environmental impacts caused by intensively grown single crops versus a diversity of crops. Moreover, farmers are now producing for a market (or administered) economy rather than for themselves and hence, are susceptible to control by market forces. In other words, when producers are largely self-sufficient (or deal with a closely related community), producing only what is needed can be easily monitored and makes economic sense. When producing goods for a market where prices can change and wealth can be accumulated well beyond what one can "eat," the producer may be encouraged (or perhaps forced) to produce more goods, thus putting a further strain on the environment.

Just when did significant trade begin? This is not a simple question to answer. We do know that even as early as the first farming villages in the Near East (ca. 7000 B.C.), obsidian was procured for tool-making from distances of several hundred kilometers (Renfrew, Dixon, and Cann 1966). The actual mechanism of moving this material over these distances is debated, but it is clear that already these communities recognized the special value of the obsidian. They went to the extra effort of producing additional goods to exchange for the obsidian with outside traders, or to supply their own people so that a long-distance journey could be made to extract the obsidian. There is archaeological evidence that, as village life developed in this region, other exotic goods were traded, such as turquoise and native copper. Due to the difficulty in documenting the movement of bulk goods, like foodstuffs, or perishables like wool, our best evidence for early trade comes from materials that are exotic to a region and usually were imported in small quantities. This type of trade may not have had a substantial impact on the environment, but it did help develop the context for trade to grow dramatically in the following millennia. Trade routes, knowledge of distant resources, human relations, and a willingness to assign value to items that could be accumulated well beyond what was needed for sustaining life all were essential to the ultimate expansion of trade activities.

It has been suggested that as early as the fourth millennium trade had developed to a new level, where it played a major role in the evolution of society (Adams 1974; Wright and Johnson 1975). It is argued that the newly emerging urban society of southern Mesopotamia had established a system of interaction between their resource-deficient homeland and the resource-rich, but politically less developed, highland regions around their periphery (Algaze 1989). To achieve this growth, urban trading centers were developed midway to the highlands, and smaller trading outposts were established in the highland zones themselves. The flow of goods, such as metal, timber, stone, oils, and rare items, was essential to the maintenance and growth of the increasingly stratified society in lowland Mesopotamia. A class of administrators and bureaucrats relied on the managerial activity and wealth created by this trade to maintain their exalted position within society. At various points in later Mesopotamian history, this trading network was supported by military conquests and formal integration, making it into a political empire. In its earlier incarnation, however, during the fourth millennium, the impetus was probably less formal and more directly driven by interpersonal relations and economics.

Whatever the actual method of establishing and maintaining a far-flung system of trade in both basic commodities and prestige goods, the impact on both the urban core and highland periphery regions was substantial. In the urban core area of lowland Mesopotamia, this process meant that goods could be imported that would both enrich the material aspects of life there and also supplement basic subsistence supplies. These imports were essential to the creation of the material trappings of a hierarchical society in two ways. First, the trade brought in exotic goods and raw materials that could be closely controlled and were converted into goods of high value to enhance the prestige and represent the wealth of the upper classes. And second, the movement of certain basic commodities that were not locally available allowed the population of the lowlands to grow in numbers beyond what it might have in isolation.

The impact of this trading system on the environment was related to the potential it offered to the social classes that benefited if they encouraged its growth. To sustain an increased level of trade, the core region had to increase the production of what it had to offer, which basically was grain and manufactured goods like ceramics and textiles. This meant that agricultural production had to increase well beyond what would have been necessary to support the society, in order to support the combined needs for food to trade to the periphery, for workers in manufacturing, for administrators of the trade, for a military, and for a class of traders. Thus, the maintenance of the trading system became a strong stimulus to the upper classes to encourage, if not force, an increasing amount of agricultural production. This led to over-planting, shortening of fallow, extension of fields to marginal lands, and salinization. As we saw in chapter 6, these pressures eventually undermined the productivity of the land. By the end of the third millennium, the very underpinnings of the hierarchical society in southern Mesopotamia were threatened, and we hypothesize that this may have caused the downfall of the earliest cities involved in the fourth millennium expansion as well.

The environmental impact of trade on the peripheral areas was equally severe, but happened in a different way. Guillermo Algaze, in his discussion of the fourth millennium, suggests that this trading activity led to little positive economic benefit to the peripheral areas beyond an initial surge in their social hierarchy and personal wealth to those who controlled the extraction of local materials (1989). The trade did not create a significant economic infrastructure in the peripheral lands. In many regions the focus was on the extraction of irreplaceable materials, such as metal, or slow-to-regenerate resources like timber, which were removed from the region to be processed into manufactured goods in the cities of the lowland. Although there may have been significant labor required for extracting these local natural resources, this labor was not organized into craft or industrial ac-tivities that would produce value locally. Because the rulers of the peripheral areas benefited from increased trade, they encouraged a focus on these ex-tractive activities at the cost of developing a more diversified economy. This reduced the resilience of these upland areas, diminished their natural re-sources, and primed the entire system for collapse. The environmental im-pact would result primarily from the exploitation of the timber, stone, and metal sources of the uplands, and the imbalances the focus on trade created in the rest of society.

In situations where the peripheral region production focused on agricultural goods, the environmental impacts were quite different. In the fourth millennium Mesopotamia case, the colonization of neighboring Susi-ana to the southeast did not provide unavailable natural resources as much as it multiplied the agricultural land available and provided a pool of human labor. Throughout history, militarily and economically powerful states have subjugated peoples in regions much like their own, who then provided sur-plus agrarian production to the central state rather than to their local hier-archy. Hence, the environmental impact would not be different in kind from indigenous use, but probably exerted unrealistically high demands on the countryside and the population that would have sped up whatever process of degradation might already have been underway.

In other colonial situations, the peripheral region could provide crops or products that were deemed valuable to the people of the core area, but were not basic foodstuffs. This trend toward focusing on a "cash" crop has become very important in many developing countries today, where it has diminished local self-sufficiency and sometimes even threatened survival. An example of this is the production of olives for oil and grapes for wine that has been ubiquitous around the Mediterranean since at least early urban times in the third millennium. It reached a peak during the Roman rule of the basin roughly 2000 years ago. Neither olives nor grapes provided a major portion of a family's diet, and both required a substantial investment in field preparation and a long period before the first harvest, so they were a difficult choice for a self-sufficient farmer to adopt. Once processed, however, these crops had tremendous market value, and in the sophisticated Roman Empire, there seemed to be no end to the demand for both products. In regions like the Levant where major parts of the landscape were hilly and covered with thin soils that did not provide a good basis for grain production, orchards of olive trees in particular became very widespread. This was a successful crop, if the farmer could wait several years for the first harvest and had the labor available for building and maintaining terraces on the hillsides. A large portion of the Levant was turned into orchards, with a serious decline in its natural forest cover and ability to produce other goods. This situation of becoming a part of a market system that relied on the global exchange of goods was not necessarily a problem, but it did make the local economy directly dependent on the price and demand for a product of which the producer could consume only a small proportion.

Falconer and Fall (1995) have examined both pollen and macro-botanical evidence on the changing forest cover and land use of the Levant from the earliest cities through modern times. Several processes are revealed in this data (fig. 7.7). First, there was a natural oak-pistachio forest in the region during early Holocene times and a residual steppe zone from the cooler, drier late Pleistocene era. With the growth of urban centers in the Early Bronze Age, there was the development of a four-part settlement system in the region: coastal or oasis trading centers, cereal agriculture in the limited alluvial flatlands, orchards and vineyards on the abundant hilly slopes, and pastoralists using the intervening terrain. During periods of political stability, this diverse strategy seems to have fit well into the environmental setting, and human population grew. As can be seen from the pollen core from Lake Kinneret in northern Israel, there was a decrease in oak and an increase in olive well beyond natural levels. This most likely resulted from

Figure 7.7
Pollen diagram from Lake Kinneret, Israel.

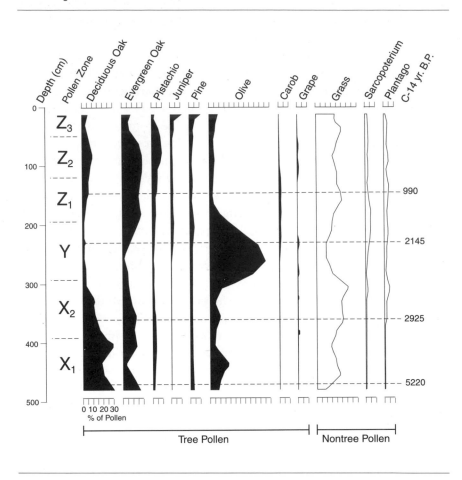

substantial areas being transformed into olive production, which required massive labor inputs, but yielded a high value crop from land that was not nearly as useful otherwise.

The detailed pattern shows an alternation between olive and oak that seems to parallel the rise and fall of urban society in the region during the Bronze and Iron Ages. However, it is in the deposits that are about 2000 years old (pollen zone Y on fig. 7.7) that the most graphic evidence of human impact on the environment is revealed. Olive pollen frequencies rapidly increase to 60%, while oak recede to roughly 5%. At this same time, grape pollen increases, probably indicating that the olive/grape orchard complex dominated the landscape. It is estimated that the Levant had its highest premodern population during Roman colonial rule when, despite the extraction of substantial resources for tribute, the landscape could still support a dense population and eventually a resurgence of the wild forests as well.

In post-Roman times the presence of olive fell dramatically and natural forest cover returned, but largely it was evergreen oak, not the deciduous oak of former times. The multistemmed evergreen oak appears to be better adapted to existing in regions of high human use, because it can cope with browsing and wood cutting better than the single trunk deciduous oak (Falconer and Fall 1995:89). Although areas of the Levant may have been originally deforested due to the growth of early agricultural villages, the more widespread, regional deforestation may be the result of orchard planting for trade commodities by the later urbanized society. Consequently, the return of natural forest cover, albeit at a degraded level (see fig. 5.4), resulted from the breakdown in global economic systems of trade. This inverse relationship between expanded agrarian production and regeneration of natural forests in marginal agricultural areas is a pattern than has revealed itself at several times in the past, as well as during the twentieth century. We will return to discuss the implications of this situation in the final chapter, but the reader should take special note of evidence from this region, because it both may have been the most *humanized* of any in the world due to its long and continuous settlement by agriculturists, and also was disproportionately important in forming Western Civilization's attitudes toward the environment due to its pivotal role in forming three of the major religions of the world.

Hierarchical Government

As has been suggested earlier, societies are made up of individuals and groups of people who have their own views of how to best serve their needs and the needs of the society at large. The two fundamental aspects of a complex society, or state, are, first, it is comprised of many people; and second, it is run by elite who derive disproportionate benefits from the productivity of the more numerous commoners. What puts this elite into such a favorable position? Among the many possible reasons, four stand out as particularly important in securing the elite's favored position (Adams 1966; Diamond 1997:277). First, they could redistribute much of the goods they collect back to the commoners in popular ways. Second, they could arm themselves and disarm the commoners. Third, they could use their monopoly of force to maintain order, thereby improving personal security. And fourth, they could formulate an ideology or religion to justify their position and the advantages it confers.

Each of these activities can act to strengthen the state by bestowing various benefits on respective elements of the society. Minimizing random violence, organizing economic specialization, providing group identity, and facilitating communal decision-making not only conferred advantages on the elite, but also improved the lives of the commoners. In fact the evidence of the past is that in virtually all situations where large numbers of people lived together, they eventually developed a complex social organization and a state run by an elite. History and archaeology have also demonstrated that these forms of organization were favored over simpler ones either by choice or force, so that today, all of the inhabitable areas of the globe are characterized by territorially defined states. As we discussed in chapters 3 and 6, this widespread emergence of complex society may have had both positive and negative impacts on human-environmental relationships.

With the growth of early states and the administrative hierarchy that characterizes them, the definition of the elite became more formal, and often they were most easily identified by their role in the government or economy of the society. Decisions by the elite, or of any other segment of the population, are made in order to serve self-interests. It also should be acknowledged that the "common good" might be seen as being served by different alternatives, based on one's perspective on, and position in, the social unit. Needless to say, decisions reached by different segments of the population may not only be different, but they may be conflicting and seem illogical to one or another group. Most governments have mechanisms for adjudicating these disagreements or ideologies to explain them, but which party holds the wealth, access to information, or the allocated power ultimately determines outcomes.

As in the case of Mesopotamia, the rulers of these societies benefited from a continual increase in local agrarian production, an increasing flow of traded goods from the periphery, and an increasing captive population that could farm the land and work in the factories. The increasing production did not necessarily benefit the farmers themselves, as the increase probably went into the surplus that was taken by mid-level and upper level rulers. The increasing production also diminished the fertility of the farmland and the ease of access to natural resources in the periphery, so that the laborers would have to work harder just to keep up, let alone meet increased production objectives. As was discussed in chapter 6 for southern Mesopotamia, this led to diminishing soil fertility, salinization of fields, the eventual ruin of the agricultural system, and the downfall of the elite classes based upon it. It may have been clear to the farmers that the environmental situation was deteriorating, but the real decision-makers were far removed from the agrarian situation, and it was not in their own immediate interest to change course based on views from people they may never have even met. This type of situation is not limited to the Mesopotamian case, and we will discuss its more general implications in the final chapter of the book. Before that, it is instructive to look at another case study of human-environmental interaction that illustrates this type of situation.

A Failed Experiment

Viking-Age Scandinavian populations expanded into the North Atlantic between about A.D. 800 and 1000. The Eastern Islands of Shetland, Orkney, and Scottish mainland were the first occupied, and then the more distant Western Islands of Iceland, Greenland, and Vinland (fig. 7.8). The colonial experience on Greenland has been the subject of interdisciplinary studies by the North Atlantic Biocultural Organization, which focuses on developments in the North Atlantic region since the Iron Age (McGovern et al. 1988; McGovern 1994; Pringle 1997). The initial Norse settlers brought with them a chiefly political organization, a well-developed seafaring tradition, and an economy based primarily on domestic cattle, sheep, goats, pigs, dogs, and horses as well as cereal cultivation of barley and oats. On Iceland and Greenland the cereals did not do very well, so those settlers imported grains, tried to grow feed, and consequently, were higher on the food chain. However, even these Western Islands supported stands of willow, alder, and birch and a range of nonarboreal species suitable for pasture. Between A.D. 1000 and 1260 was considered the "golden" age of these settlements, while from A.D. 1250 to 1300 was the "little ice age," a slight cooling period that may have *transported landscape* had serious negative effects on these colonies. The entire region is marginal for cereal agriculture and the other components of the transported continental agricultural systems. Nevertheless, at their peaks, Iceland probably *deforestation* had a population of 50,000 and Greenland, 5000. However, overstocking of *erosion,* domestic animals, fuel collection, iron working, and construction activity *but also* seems to have rapidly depleted the dwarf trees, and probably the soil was seriously eroded by the Norse land-use practices (McGovern et al. 1988:225). *little ice age* By the late middle ages, the Greenland communities had been completely abandoned and Iceland experienced a major loss of population.

Pollen records from Greenland show a marked decline in willow and birch with the establishment of the early colonies. Wood would be particularly valuable to these settlers for smelting and smithing iron, use in domestic hearths, and in building. We know from statutes and records from the mainland that the Norse were sensitive to conservation issues and tried to space

Figure 7.8
Map of North Atlantic region with location of Norse colonies in Greenland.

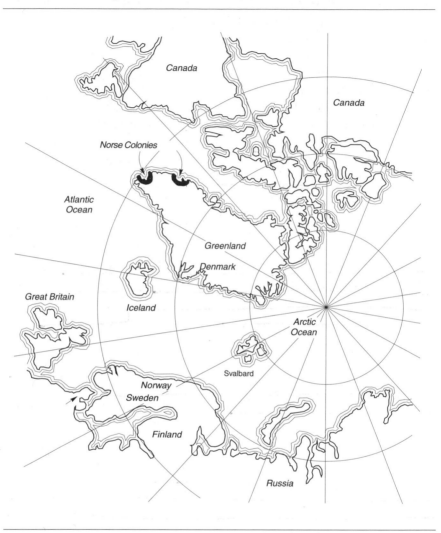

their farms, manure their fields, and pay attention to the number of animals being grazed. Despite whatever conservation efforts were made, the situation deteriorated, which led the researchers to ask several related questions:

1. Were Norse land-use practices causing adverse ecological impacts, outweighing the effects of their conservation efforts?

2. Were impacts on land use sufficiently widespread to cause significant, sometimes irreversible degradation of components of the ecosystem important to the Norse economy?

3. If they were destructive of vital economic resources, why did Norse farmers fail to perceive and correct the problem?

The investigators concluded that "humans react not to the real world in real time, but to a *cognized environment* filtered through traditional expectations and a world view which may or may not value close tracking of local environmental indicators. Humans are also not always willing or able to forego short-term personal advantage for long-term common benefit." But what impediments to management blocked effective responses? A perusal of organizational literature reveals six factors that would lead to apparently poor decisions. First, the model used in making a decision might be based on another ecosystem that had surface similarities, but critical differences. Second, insufficient detail of information might be presented, leading one to overgeneralize the problem. Third, there may only be a short observational series, because it is a truly new situation where there is little realistic experience. Fourth, the managers might feel detached, being socially and geographically distant from the producers. Fifth, the reaction of the managers might be out of phase with the problem; in other words, too little too late. Sixth, the managers may perceive the potential problem, but not feel obligated to take action: "it's someone else's problem."

I would expect the first three factors to have been most serious in the early years of the colonies and to fade as knowledge was gained. The last three factors became more of the problem as the administrative structure shifted from chiefly local involvement to a more formal, geographically separated patron-client relation. At first, most colonists owned their land and used slaves from their conquests. As the presence of slaves diminished, more farmers lost their land and became tenants or wage earners on someone else's farm. The tenant farmer no longer was free to make his own agricultural decisions. In order to hold onto his lease, he would have to attempt always to maximize. This shifted land-use decisions up a rank in the new social hierarchy, giving real authority to absentee landlords who were locked in their own power struggle in the homeland. They were also distant from the ecological feedback that might have warned of impending doom. Even if information flow had been better, it is unlikely that they would have had sympathy for strategies involving reduction of current production levels in favor of long-term conservation. The ecological warnings of the Little Ice Age and the progressive environmental degradation of the islands may have been recognized only by those who were politically powerless. Even for those settlers, it might have been possible to save their colonies if they had taken up serious fishing or the subsistence pursuits of the Inuit who had recently immigrated to Greenland and relied heavily on sea mammals. Despite the logic of this response, the Norse did not change their ways, probably because it was not culturally acceptable to them. What it would have taken to reverse this situation is a difficult question that we will leave for the next chapter. The reality was that Greenland was abandoned, never to be resettled, and Iceland's population and pasturage were dramatically cut.

This chapter has discussed a number of processes that are closely associated with the growth of complex, urban societies. The adoption of agriculture is a process that began about 10,000 years ago and has continued to the present day with virtually the entire population of the world relying on this as their major source of food. The growth of cities and hierarchically administered society followed quickly on the heels of agriculture and has become the dominant social form on the earth. Even for those who do not live in cities, the impact of the urban system is pervasive. Tremendous and diverse environmental impacts accompanied the introduction of agriculture and urban life. Chapters 5 and 6 detailed some case studies of these processes. Some of the environmental impacts furthered the course of culture change, making it more difficult to return to a former lifeway. Other environmental changes had less immediate impacts, but ultimately undermined the very life-style they had helped establish. In this chapter we have looked at several seminal processes initiated by the urban revolution 5000 years ago that are still with us today. Population growth, community health, industrial production, trade, and hierarchical government are the cornerstones of modern civilization, each of them an essential element of social change, each of them with dramatic environmental implications.

8

The Past as Prologue

Since the beginning of organized society, people have been drawing on the past to provide insights and models for contemporary behavior. Whether it was the poet Homer recounting the adventures of the heroes of Greece's "Golden Age," or your own parents regaling you with stories of how hard they worked in their youth, we as a species have refashioned events in the past to suit our needs for guiding behavior in the present (Hodder 1982). The results of archaeological research are a rich and objective source for lessons from the past, appropriate to almost any question and tied closely to almost every region of the world. This resource is one of the great potentials of archaeology and cannot be ignored if archaeology is to take its place among the essential social sciences. However, there are risks inherent in the use of the archaeological record in this manner. The interpretation of past events as models for contemporary behavior is a subjective endeavor that relies both on a firm knowledge of the past events and an explicit recognition of the objectives guiding the application of this knowledge. The point of this book is not to provide goals for using the past, but to provide an empirical basis for interpreting the past and to highlight the key relationships and processes involved in human-environmental interactions. I cannot prevent the misuse of the past, but I can make the past more accessible to those who want to use it rationally.

The condition of the Americas before and after European contact is of great interest, because it is where many of us live and it relates to the ideas our nation was built upon and, ultimately, who we are. It has a broader significance for this book because it could help answer the question of whether there existed a "Golden Age" of conservationism or a "Paradise" of a truly natural environment that we have now lost. Although present in popular thinking and literature for a long time, these issues crystallized in debates over the Columbian Quincentennial. The effort to bring out the contributions and viewpoints of Native Americans in the development of American society was a very important activity and one to which archaeology contributed heavily. Unfortunately, some writers oversimplified the data to make what became political statements rather than observations based on an accurate reconstruction of prehistory. The results in the popular press and some scholarly works were characterizations of all Native Americans as near perfect "primitives" who treaded lightly on their environment, and of Europeans and their modern descendants as evil exploiters (Ford 1973; Martin 1992; Alvard 1993; Baleé 1998a). Without accepting or rejecting this characterization, we must move beyond this type of statement to examine what archaeology has revealed about the empirical situation and to identify the social forces that might have influenced a statement such as this.

In 1992 William Denevan, a geographer, published an article, "The pristine myth: the landscape of the Americas in 1492," as part of a special journal issue on that general topic. Using early historical accounts and archaeological evidence, Denevan suggests that the North American landscape at the time of Columbian contact was almost everywhere a humanized landscape and that the view of it as pristine was to a large extent an invention of nineteenth century romantic writers. This wilderness image became a key part of the American heritage, associated with a heroic pioneer past; the land was empty, wild, and needed taming. The image was often taken to suggest that the few Indians that were there had not used (i.e., farmed) its resources, and hence, really did not own the land or need it. The acceptance of this "empty, natural, pristine, paradise" image of the lands to the west was important in the early years of our country for glorifying the role of the pioneer (so more people would do it) and for justifying the taking of the land once settlers arrived. The very imagery that is being used in recent years to suggest that Native Americans were more in tune with their environment and hence more noble than their Euro-American counterparts, originated in an effort to show how irrelevant the indigenous peoples were in terms of their relationship to the land. Clearly this idea originated with racial intentions and may still have similar undertones.

Looked at closely, through the various case studies presented in this volume, it is clear that the question of whether Indians, as a people, lived in a special harmony with nature and with a sustainable system of resource management is not a productive line of inquiry. Sometimes they did and sometimes they did not, similar to many other premodern societies around the globe. The more interesting possibility that Denevan and others suggest is that the Indians of North America, and premodern peoples in many other regions of the world, did alter their environment in significant ways in nearly every location open to human settlement. His hypothesis is that the Indian landscape of 1492 was thoroughly humanized, having been transformed through land clearance, farming practices, and intentional brush fires. Moreover, by 1750, due to the small numbers of surviving Indians, these anthropogenically degraded landscapes had largely regenerated themselves and appeared quite wild and well forested by the time most Europeans saw them.

What makes this hypothesis reasonable is a careful examination of the archaeological and early historical data on the population densities in the various regions of the Americas before and following Columbian contact. Denevan musters evidence that Pre-Columbian populations were surprisingly high throughout the Americas and that the decline in population in the century following contact was dramatic. He estimates that there were over 50 million people living in the New World at the time of contact, with the following distribution: 3.8 million in North America; 17.2 million in Mexico; 5.6 million in Central America; 3.0 million in the Caribbean; 15.7 million in the Andes; and 8.6 million in lowland South America. If these estimates are anywhere near correct, they would dispel any notion of an "empty continent." These numbers are similar to, if not greater than, those we project for many areas of the Old World.

Hand in hand with these high estimates for before contact, there is strong evidence for dramatic declines in population in all regions of the hemisphere from disease and social upheaval after European contact. This may have been one of the greatest demographic disasters of all times. Denevan estimates an overall drop from 54 million in A.D. 1492 to 5.6 million in 1650, a fall of 89%. He suggests that in the tropics the proportion is higher, variously in the low 90% range, while in North America where population was lower and more scattered, it was about 75%. Replacement with Europeans and regeneration of indigenous populations were very slow processes and even after 250 years most people remained clustered along the coastlines and in certain highland areas. In A.D. 1750 the total New World population may have only been 30% of what it was in 1492.

When looked at from this perspective, there is little question that the density level of pre-Columbian population estimated here, most of whom had practiced agriculture for 1000 years or more, would have led to widespread environmental impacts. In the vicinity of most settlements, this would have meant land clearance of large areas for planting corn. In some regions where more advanced irrigation and terracing technologies were practiced, such as in central Mexico, in the Andes, or with the Hohokam in Arizona, thousands of hectares of land near each population center would have been completely transformed. Archaeological evidence, extending well beyond the cases cited in this book, has documented that farming practices in many parts of the New World had led to prehistoric deforestation of landscapes and episodes of soil erosion serious enough to ultimately undermine the productive potential of the region. In the eastern woodlands of North America, it is assumed that pre-Columbian agricultural clearing and burning had converted much of the forest into earlier successional communities and semi-permanent grassy openings, resulting in a forest of large, widely spaced trees, few shrubs, and much grass and herbage. This created a mosaic quality to the ecosystem, favoring a landscape that would have been more open than would be the case without human intervention. This may have had the effect of diminishing the extent of climax communities and old-growth forests, but it also shifted the mix of plants towards those more resistant to fire and those adaptable to open space, offering some improved habitats for wildlife. There is little question that in the vicinity of settlements, some wildlife would be seriously suppressed both from hunting and habitat destruction. However, in the more distant areas, the opening up of the forest, increased length of the edge of the forest, and the spread of grassy areas would have been strongly favorable for herbivores such as deer, antelope, and elk.

In other areas of the New World, the impact of hunters and more mobile agriculturists may have largely been felt through their use of fire to clear the land, drive wild herds, and improve the growth of fodder for these herds. It is still a controversial issue, but the weight of scientific opinion agrees that fires caused by the prehistoric inhabitants both in the New and Old World extended the prairies and savannas by inhibiting the active regeneration of forests. The opening up of the mid–United States grasslands by the Native Americans and then the drastic decline in the population of Native Americans may have been major factors in the spread and population increase of bison in the centuries before settlement of the Great Plains by Euro-Americans and their subsequent hunting to near extinction. Just as the bison may have increased their numbers rapidly when the hunting pressure of Native Americans was dramatically reduced, so might the forests have returned to many of their native habitats once the pressures that accompanied agricultural settlements were reduced.

The Maya of Central America provide a fine prehistoric example of forest regeneration following population decline (Rice 1996). The Maya developed a spectacular civilization based on agriculture and trade that attained a zenith of organization, population, and construction around A.D. 700 to 900. This was followed by a rapid depopulation of many of the ceremonial centers, especially those in the highland regions. Archaeologists estimate that fully 75% of the Maya's environment was humanized and cleared for agriculture at their peak, yet by the time of the first Spanish explorers in the sixteenth century, the terrain was covered with an almost unbroken forest.

Denevan reports that the very first explorers who reached the New World usually reported amazement at the presence of Indian villages and their farming of plants new to the Europeans. However, explorers and colonists who visited 100 years later, more often cited the bounteous forests. When James Fenimore Cooper wrote about the "forest primeval" of the interior of the eastern seaboard in the early 1800s, it was an accurate description of the regenerated forests and should not have been thought of as a model for what had existed there in 1492 and before. When Columbus reported to Queen Isabelle that he had discovered a "paradise," he clearly meant a human paradise, where the land was actively cultivated and there were abundant people available for exploitation.

Is There a Natural or "Best" Environment?

I believe that most people, both lay public and environmental land managers, assume there is a best environment that should be the goal when making environmental decisions. To many, this best environment is synonymous with a natural or untouched environment, one that has not been sullied by human actions. To others, the best environment would be one that had very pleasing aesthetic features, a criterion that would vary depending on one's sense of beauty or at least of appropriateness. For others still, the best environment would be one that had been modified to produce the maximum value of goods or recreation. Each of these perspectives on the environment is held by major segments of the population and finds support among policy makers, the media, and in the arts. It is obvious, however, that these positions are quite different from each other, and decisions based on one would often conflict with the goals of another. I believe that even if people do not adhere to one view to the exclusion of the other two, they hold these in a priority sequence and formulate their opinions accordingly. In this chapter I try not to champion one of these views over the others, but to provide some insights into them from the perspective of an archaeologist.

The perspective held by many who identify themselves as environmentalists, and probably by most readers of this book, is that a return to a natural environment — that is, one unaffected by humans — would be the best in most circumstances. Although this remains an absolutely reasonable objective, insights reported in this book should convince the reader that a "natural environment" does not exist in an absolute sense. The first problem in identifying the "natural environment" for a particular landscape is that environments are constantly undergoing change. Change is the natural state. Some of this is predictably cyclical, such as climate changes that coincide with the seasons. Other climate changes may also be cyclical, but are not easily predictable, such as warming trends, *El Niño* effects, etc. These types of major climate changes have been a primary force in the transformations of plant and animal communities around the world, with the ebb and flow of the last several ice ages during the Quaternary. Careful scientific reconstructions of paleoenvironments have shown radical changes in the distribution of animals, such as the presence of hippos in Europe and temperate zone animals in the Sahara within the past quarter million years, as well as changing forest cover, and the rise and disappearance of lakes. These climate changes have led to replacements of some species in a region by species better adapted to the new conditions, and it also has favored evolutionary changes in species.

In any particular environment, there are also constant changes occurring to the biota of the region without there being any climate changes. The successional progression of plant communities as they change over time was discussed in chapter 3. Given the characteristics of the local climate and landscape and the extant biological communities, the composition of subsequent successional stages can be predicted within limits. Plant communities, and their associated fauna, move through successional stages in a rational order, but natural forces frequently impede this development or even set it back to a beginning stage, such as what happens after a forest fire. In addition, the actual composition of the plant and animal community will be affected by the specific organisms present at the beginning of the cycle and any intrusions by competitors or pests. Hence, even in a region with no human presence and no major climate changes, one would not see a homogeneous environment, but a mosaic of patches at different successional stages. These patches also vary due to impacts of stochastic biological events like pests, seed distributions, and changing distribution of surface water. Therefore, if we are to use the natural, unaffected by humans, environment as the objective for decision-making, it is at least necessary to understand that it is a moving target that itself has considerable inherent variability.

This brings us to a salient issue — whether we can reconstruct, even on paper, such a thing as an environment "unaffected by humans." Among today's popular icons of the natural environment are the old-growth forests of the temperate zones, the rain forests of the tropics, and the tall grass prairies of the drier regions. When one looks closely at the regions where today's old-growth forests exist, one discovers the presence and impact of humans on the region. For those of us who live in densely settled urban enclaves, it is difficult to conceptualize the dispersed, small-scale pattern of human settlement that characterized much of the world for most of its history. Yet as the reader has seen from earlier chapters, even in relatively small communities, people were capable of transforming their surroundings. My own favorite setting of natural beauty, Yosemite Valley seen from a high enough viewpoint so that the buildings on the floor of the valley are obscured by the dense stand of ponderosa pines and only the great monoliths of granite are visible, did not look the same even two centuries ago. Up until very recent times, the natural cover was a grassland with a forest of widely spaced oak trees. The valley was home to groups of the Ahwahnechee Indians who lived by collecting acorns, hunting, and farming on a small scale. Frequent fires were set because they maintained the open forest setting, but slowly they led to the replacement of oaks with the more fire-resistant ponderosa. Today there is barely a single oak that remains of the native forest; they have been replaced by nature — in response to human pressures — with the magnificent ponderosa pines of today.

Don Rice, who has conducted extensive fieldwork investigating the Maya of Central America, has considered the evidence on whether the rain forests of that region as well as Amazonia should be considered "pristine" (1994, 1996). He persuasively argues that too often ecologists look at the environment from a static, synchronic, twentieth century perspective alone. Contemporary habitats are substantially affected by their history and much of that history has involved human manipulation (Russell 1997). To understand the human impact on a particular environment, it is necessary to take a diachronic perspective and to evaluate the nature and persistence of human impacts. Rice finds that humans have been in the Central and South American rain forest regions since between 10,000 and 12,000 years ago. Specific evidence is only now coming to light, but already there is a strong suggestion of forest disturbance in Panama as early as 11,000 years ago and in Amazonia by 8000 years ago (Roosevelt et al. 1996). These rain forests probably were of a much different composition when people first began to occupy them. Evidence points to the now tropical rain forest regions being four to six degrees centigrade cooler during the last ice age and drier as well (Hodell, Curtis, and Brenner 1995). The implication of all this research is that the tropical rain forests of the Americas (and certainly those of the Old World) developed and reached their current form during Holocene times in relatively constant association with, and under the selective pressures of, human groups.

The first humans to enter the Americas and to utilize the regions that are now rain forests would have been hunters and gatherers. It can be argued that their impact would have been modest and that they might not have significantly changed the course of forest development. However, it is suggested that charcoal found in deposits that date to these early years are the result of human-induced fires (Pyne 1998). By 8000 B.P. there is evidence for sedentary occupations in Amazonia, and by 5000 B.P. village agriculture is documented throughout Amazonia (Roosevelt 1998). Moreover, by 2000 B.P. there is good evidence for a dramatic growth in population in many areas of the region, dependent on intensive seed agriculture. Only with recent evidence in hand is it possible to make overall population estimates for this part of the world, and they are surprising. Numerous sites are being discovered and some of them are so large that they must have held thousands of inhabitants. Archaeologist Anna Roosevelt estimates that on the island of Marajó in the heart of Amazonia, where she has worked, the density may have reached 50 people per square kilometer, with a total population for that vicinity approaching a million people (1991:38).

Regionwide estimates are still at the level of speculation, but William Denevan has tried to bring together travelers' reports, early censuses, and archaeological data in order to make a serious attempt (1976, 1992). The result is that Denevan suggests that Greater Amazonia may have held 6.8 million people at the time of first European contact. As we discussed above, once contacted by Europeans with new diseases, this population fell dramatically. The impact of Old World diseases may have been most severe in the densely settled tropical lowlands, with Denevan estimating that from peak to low point the population dropped by at least 35 to 1, if not 50 to 1 (1976:212–213). This type of population decrease must have led to the breakdown in social organization and the abandonment of most settlements, especially the large centers. Only now are archaeologists beginning to find major sites in the flood plains of most of the major rivers in Amazonia. These were not simple folks, but organized societies that altered their landscapes with terraces, irrigation, raised fields, dams, and reservoirs, all in order to improve their agricultural yield (Denevan 1992:375). It is only after the demographic disaster of the sixteenth century that it is possible to suggest that these forests developed with only modest impact from humans. Up until then they had evolved in close association with sedentary intensive agriculturists who clearly transformed their surroundings and strongly influenced the biological basis of today's tropical rain forests.

The point of the above examples is not to challenge the value of wilderness areas or to assert that there is no difference between areas that have not suffered degradation at human hands versus those that have. Clearly, human impact on the environment is a serious threat to natural settings as most of us recognize them. Rather, I hope that two important points have become clear to the reader that I believe are essential for effective environmental decision-making. First, *there is no absolute when one refers to the natural state of the environment*. Nature, herself, works continual change on every local environment through rhythmic cycles, long-term processes, and evolutionary change. Moreover, if that was not enough, humans have had a role in transforming virtually every environment and locale on this earth (Crumley 1994a; Vitousek et al. 1997). The human role is an old one wherein most environments, as we now see them, have developed under pressures created by the presence of humans. Sometimes the transformations have been radical and obvious as in the clearing of forests for agricultural fields. In other instances the changes are more subtle and difficult to recognize, such as species replacement in forests due to human-induced fires or browsing of domestic animals.

The second essential point for environmental decision-making that I hope has become clear from this book is that a definition of *an ideal, or best, environment is conditioned by human values and objectives.* For many environmentalists the best environment is one that is "untouched by human hands," or in pristine condition. If one accepts my first point, then this type of environment does not exist and one probably should substitute for it the very real alternative of an environment that has been *minimally* affected by human hands. This is clearly the objective defined by many seeking to preserve or restore *wilderness* areas. Although it minimizes the magnitude of the many ambiguities and problems with introduced species and altered ecological relationships, it is a viable objective and one that in many cases I would personally endorse. However, when one gets down to the details of implementation, one finds that people do not always seek to convert open spaces into wildernesses. In those situations where wilderness is the objective, it is usually defined in terms of suitability for recreation and not solely in terms of the ecology itself. Hence, there are two aspects to this issue: first, what is intended by the concept *wilderness;* and second, whether we can restore environments to conditions that are preferable to wilderness.

Wilderness is not an easy-to-observe ecological condition as much as it is the interplay between the constantly changing state of nature and the constantly changing state of the human mind (Pyne 1998:98). Disagreements emerge quickly once one tries to get specific about restoring a wilderness. First is the very real question of just what that wilderness should be composed of and how much effort should be invested in eliminating exotic species, especially if they are appropriate to the climate and terrain. Moreover, does one artificially aid the growth of some species, such as by feeding mammals during the winter, or protecting plants from a pest or blight? Some may believe that introduced sport fish, such as trout, are an appropriate part of the wilderness, while others would argue strongly for their removal. And then there is the fundamental question of access and facilities for visitors. How should that be restricted? It may enhance the minimally affected by human hands aspect of the landscape to keep out as much human modification as possible, but then how many people will actually be able to *enjoy* the landscape?

An even more fundamental question is whether wilderness is, in fact, the optimal way to transform a landscape. It is possible to observe how people make this decision for themselves by looking at how people deal with their own yard, how they convince local officials to deal with parks and open spaces in real estate developments, and how they vote to administer public lands. Issues such as access, activities, personal aesthetics, safety, and maintenance all play a role in determining the *best use* of "open" space. When one looks at the results of these deliberations, it is often not transforming the landscape into a wilderness, but into an aesthetically pleasant, recreational, outdoor zone.

On the level of an individual family yard or city park, this often involves the installation of tracts of neatly cropped lawn, not a very natural landscape. Trees and shrubs often are set as borders or scattered widely in the lawn area. Exotic flowers and decorative plants are often introduced to enhance the aesthetic appeal of the terrain. All of this is laid out with varying degrees of geometric order depending on personal taste and other criteria. Interestingly, there is some consistency in how people of a particular culture have chosen to transform their local environments as witnessed in the changing styles of parks and gardens (Westoff 1983). These outdoor spaces often reflect both practicalities of their use, but also some aspects of the worldview of their creators. Formal French gardens, British wooded park lands, and carefully orchestrated Oriental wilderness gardens each capture widely held ideals and allow their visitors to relate effectively with *nature*.

The transformation of landscapes also resulted from attempts to recreate what was familiar for people who had newly settled in a region. Just as the Polynesians brought their pigs and breadfruit to New Zealand and other islands, so did the later British settlers bring their wheat fields, sheep, green lawns, and white picket fences. Throughout history people have *transported landscapes* to new areas of settlement partly to ensure a productive environment according to their past experience, and partly to provide a comfortable aesthetic setting. Sometimes these exotic landscapes were suitable to the new climate and thrived in their new setting, and sometimes they were poorly suited and required major investment of labor to maintain. The lawns, parks, and woodlands of Britain were easily transported to New England and the Mid-Atlantic states, but as the descendants of these people moved to settings such as the deserts of central Arizona, these environments became less practical, yet still are installed with great frequency. One could debate how important these landscapes are to the new settlers and whether over time they fade and cease to be created, but given their expense in many settings and their durability in some localities, I believe that we are looking at a powerful impetus. This sense of an *appropriate environment* that is culturally defined probably is just as powerful a force in environmental decision-making as is the concept of returning land to its pristine condition as determined through some sort of historical, ecological study.

The notion of appropriate environment can be expanded to include decisions on how landscapes should be used in a more general sense. This brings us to the fundamentally important issue of *productivity*. There is a vast, yet finite amount of land surface available for human use on our planet. How much of that should be consumed by urban construction, how much devoted to industry and transportation, how much to agrarian production, how much to recreation, and how much should be reserved for wilderness or returned to pristine conditions? This question is asked and answered hundreds of times every day across the globe in the context of great tracts of land or the use of a small parcel of personal property. Obviously, economics, community needs, and local regulations all play an important role in deciding land use, but here I want to focus on what people value when thinking of land use. As a metaphor for popular beliefs, one only has to look at the song "America." America's beauty is composed of such disparate metaphors as "purple mountains majesty . . . amber waves of grain." Wilderness is certainly seen as beautiful and valuable, but agricultural fields also have a beauty beyond their economic value. In American history great value is bestowed upon those who "settled" the West; that is, those who transformed apparent wilderness into orderly productive agrarian landscapes. The term wilderness has serious negative connotations in world literature as well, including in the Bible where having to wander in the wilderness was employed as a grave punishment. Civilizing the savage wilderness was a national priority in early U.S. history, as it was elsewhere, and ownership of land was often based on doing something *useful* with it, such as clearing trees, building structures, farming, grazing, or mining. In fact, for the first century of our country's existence, there was little interest in preserving open spaces or wilderness areas — quite the opposite was valued. Not surprisingly, given our economic system, land was assigned a value based on its potential economic uses, rather than its role as a wilderness reserve or in maintaining the viability of an ecosystem.

It is only just over 100 years ago with the establishment of our National Park system that official sanction was given to preserving natural wonders and special landscapes as national treasures with real value. Somewhat later, with the establishment of the National Forest Service, our government recognized there may be significant value in managing large tracts of land to insure the integrity of watersheds feeding the great reservoirs being created behind the new dams. It was an important step forward to acknowledge that serious management of catchments was required if water in reservoirs was to be useable. Unfortunately, the government bowed to other influences and agreed that this land could be used for a variety of purposes at the same time, thereby enhancing its traditionally recognized economic value as well. Outside of the park and forest systems, governments at all levels have time and again demonstrated that land is to be used in ways that maximize its economic value. Given how pervasive this pattern is, one can only assume that they have been carrying out the will of the people. Only recently have regulations been adopted that protect public lands from the worst abuses and balance the economic motive with some concern for aesthetics, health, and ecological viability.

Private, nongovernmental, organizations have also arisen in the United States and elsewhere with the express purpose of preserving habitats and the ecological viability of threatened species. One of these, The Nature Conservancy, combines the economic realities of today with their desire for habitat preservation by purchasing key tracts of land and organizing local groups to act as stewards for this land. They have adopted a long-term perspective by working to define key "ecoregions" of the country and then working with local partners to preserve the diversity of each region (Sawhill 1998). Although organizations like The Nature Conservancy are having a significant impact, they are by no means holding their own against the tide of economic development. As an example, in the Phoenix area of central Arizona, it is estimated that every hour another acre of former desert or farmland is converted to residential or commercial construction (Morrison Institute 1997:29). For better or worse, most people still perceive the primary value of a parcel of land as what economic or personal use it can provide. Is this inherent in the nature of the human species? Perhaps it is this perspective of viewing everything in terms of its potential value if maximally exploited, that has defined us as a species and led to our spectacular success on this planet.

Just as economic success drives the human existence, so does pursuit of knowledge. Whether this is knowledge for its own sake or knowledge to be used to improve our success is not as important as the fact that we are a highly inquisitive species and that we do in fact employ our knowledge to improve our chances of survival. Hopefully this book and all of the archaeological investigations that it summarizes are contributions to enhancing the knowledge base for decisions about the future. As rich as this database already is, we must take strides to improve it. Most of the research reported in this volume is the result of hardworking investigators with small research teams, dedicating themselves to fieldwork and analysis. However, it is increasingly necessary to assemble large-scale interdisciplinary projects like the Archaeomedes Project described in chapter 5, the Central Petén Historical Ecology Project described in chapter 6, and the North Atlantic Biocultural Organization described in chapter 7. If we are to answer the questions of greatest interest, we need the full range of natural scientists working together with archaeologists, historians, and geographers. These projects had to look beyond the normal sources of archaeological funding to underwrite these types of endeavors and to attract the needed scientists. Happily, funding agencies are beginning to recognize these demands. The National Science Foundation (NSF) has provided leadership in this area by establishing several programs to sponsor long-term ecological research. The NSF asserts that long-term data are crucial to our understanding of environmental change and our attempts at management (Gosz 1998:3).

In 1980 a network of sites dedicated to long-term ecological research in the United States was founded and has grown steadily to include 21 research sites (Waide 1998:74). The concept is collaborative interdisciplinary research into the fundamental operation of these ecosystems, always with a strong interest in the historic trajectory of the system. Increasingly it became apparent to these researchers that even in seemingly isolated locations, human activities would have profound impacts on the functioning of the ecosystem. This culminated in 1997 with the expansion of the network of sites to include two in explicitly human-dominated urban ecosystems (NSF 1997:1). This has brought together on a large scale biologists, earth scientists, engineers, urban planners, social scientists, and archaeologists. The human impact on ecosystem function, the necessity of social science perspectives on ecosystem operation, and the need for a long-term historic perspective have opened the door for meaningful archaeological input into the conduct of future environmental science.

Coevolutionary Trends

This is not meant to be a book on human evolution nor on what has led to the human species being able to outcompete so many other species to become dominant on this planet, yet some of those issues may also be tied to how our interaction with the environment has developed. The increasing use of tools to extend our physical abilities, the reliance on organizational abilities to direct cooperative efforts, and the domestication of other species to our direct benefit are each a cornerstone in building the human career. Our success has derived from these abilities to expand our procurement base beyond what is available to us as individual animals, and to devise other means to aid survival and suppress competitors. These approaches are learned from experience and then encoded and passed on to the next generation and to neighboring humans through culture. Culture-based behavior can be adapted to changing conditions and opportunities far more quickly than natural selection can act to guide genetically based behavior. This provided humans with the ability to adjust to changing climates, so they could survive global change, and to conditions in neighboring zones, so they could spread quickly to occupy new regions. All of these advantages have led to tremendous demographic and geographic success for humans despite our relatively slow rate of individual reproduction and maturation.

To take full advantage of these human potentials, certain behaviors would be favored over others. In this way, each of the advantages cited above would have coevolutionary implications for the likely development of human society. As tools became more central to the human existence, they required a greater investment of labor to manufacture and favored a sedentary existence, so they did not need to be continually transported. The most effective use of cooperative action and planning would occur in relatively large groups of humans who maintained their cooperative relationships over time. The reliance on domesticated plants and animals necessitated major investments of labor and in most cases encouraged a sedentary existence that was tied to fields planted in crops. The enormous importance of cultural knowledge for guiding activities required increasing effort to digest and encode this knowledge and mechanisms to distribute it to others. Although individual situations have been diverse, in simplest terms the overall trend has been for these forces to favor humans that did the following:

1. organized themselves into larger groups;

2. established sedentary settlements where tools and facilities could be increased and agriculture pursued; and

3. developed cultural mechanisms for effectively assembling and redistributing knowledge essential to productive success and survival.

Each of these three sets of forces exerted a strong influence on which societies were most successful and, consequently, on the general direction of social change, particularly during the past 5000 to 10,000 years as agriculture became widespread and urban society developed.

Urban society emerged out of these developments about 5000 years ago in a few regions at first, and has slowly grown since then to become the dominant way of life across the globe, and in the course of that, established a new set of human-environmental interactions. Archaeology can provide important insights into the operation of early urban societies and the environmental relationships that they engendered. Although aspects of urban society have changed since its inception, many of the basic relationships were formed early on, establishing a new society-environment stability that in many respects still rules the world today. More than half of the population of the globe live in cities today and that proportion is expected to grow in the coming decades

Among the many changes that urban life has been associated with, there is one other new innovation in thought that I believe is fundamental to human-environmental relationships. The development of a socially sophisticated concept of value is essential to urban society as we know it and has had profound effects on the environment. Although it is variously referred to as wealth, status, or property, I think they are all manifestations of the same fundamental change in human perception. Concepts such as social hierarchy, value, and property are as old as human society and perhaps existed in prehuman behavior as well, yet about 5000 years ago their meanings were transformed. Certainly social hierarchies existed before this time, but as far as we can tell they were based on the specific abilities or strengths of the individuals and changed as those attributes changed. Value was almost certainly closely related to aspects of subsistence and survival. In fact, one would expect that the procurement of food would be closely related to the amount that could be consumed or stored. In a mobile, preagricultural society, storage would be minimal, so production goals would be closely tied to extant population needs. So we could assume that what could be eaten or what might contribute to reproductive success or defense very closely conditioned the value of goods or activities. Since the amount of food that could be consumed by a set number of people is relatively inelastic, it would mean that there would be little incentive to expend the labor to procure excess food or produce goods that were not immediately necessary. Similarly, the concept of property or ownership may have existed in early societies, but it probably was poorly developed and implied a temporary, nonenduring relationship. It is also likely that for categories such as land or other environmental resources, the ownership was vested in the larger corporate group such as the community, rather than with the individual or single family.

With the onset of sedentary living and agrarian systems of food procurement, all of this seems to have changed. With permanence in settlement there would be less restriction on the quantity of goods one might keep, and a greater incentive to invest effort to create labor-saving tools and facilities. There also would be more incentive to produce food beyond one's immediate needs if it was possible to store this food against the possibility of future shortages. I think we can rightly assume that in most circumstances, human decisions have been governed by a desire to minimize risks to survival. In preagricultural times modest quantities of food could be stored, but shortages were probably met by expanding the categories of food one was willing to eat, or by moving to a new territory where resources were more available. With sedentism it was possible to store more food, and it was a more costly decision to relocate the settlement, abandoning all of the permanent facilities constructed there.

With agriculture, differences in the productive potential of varying tracts of land must have become obvious and encouraged communities to delimit their territory more clearly and to defend it against encroachment. This stimulus toward restrictive ownership of land would be further encouraged by the use of irrigation agriculture. At some point this process of formal ownership was extended down to corporate groups within the community, extended families, and ultimately to individuals. The land had value in terms of what resources could be extracted from it or produced on it, but at some point it must have become recognized that the land would have this potential value whether it was used or not. It is not difficult to understand why one community would defend its land against another, but it is intriguing to contemplate when and why societies were willing to allow specific members to hold land privately and enforce those advantages against other members of that same society. In this way, a community or specific members of a community could accumulate land, tools, and facilities beyond their own immediate needs. But why would any individual or group be inclined to do this?

Accumulation beyond one's immediate needs makes little sense unless a society recognizes the abstract concept of *value* and links it with something desired; in this case *privilege, power and status*. The possibility that items could be valued beyond their immediate use as food, clothing, shelter, etc. was a true revolution in society. This is the driver behind surplus production, the cornerstone of urban society. There was little incentive to produce more than one could easily consume (you can only eat so much, and storage was limited by deterioration) until there came a way to convert that produce into something that also had value to you. Extra food could be used to support traders to secure exotic raw materials and craftspeople to transform them into recognized prestige goods. A system where one might be able to trade these goods to neighboring groups when one's own food supply was short is a very logical step in producing a surplus. But this was only one of what became many important reasons to encourage surplus production among all members of an agrarian society.

The accumulation of goods, especially prestige goods that were without immediate value for sustenance or survival, was prompted by their role in maintaining differences in status and power within society. The advantage of accumulating prestige goods over foodstuffs and common tools is that it is more possible to limit the availability of prestige goods if they are made from exotic raw materials and/or by a craft or technology that is only known to a few in the society. Prestige goods also were advantageous because they were often long-lived and could be exchanged for foodstuffs if one faced a food shortfall. These characteristics of prestige goods and the status associated with them created a strong positive feedback situation, wherein those who had power over others were in a position to encourage additional surplus production that would allow the creation of more prestige goods, that in turn would help extend or solidify these positions of power. Producing food and goods that could be transformed into items of recognized value that would not deteriorate like food does provided the elite with not only a source of extending their control, but also a means of deterring risk by being able to offer these up in times of trouble and a means of conveying their status to their descendants. Concomitant with the advantages that the existence of prestige goods might confer on an elite, they also require excessive production in a society, an issue of great importance in this book.

Urban Society as a Sustainable Solution?

Given the fact that urban society quickly spread throughout the world and has continued to exist until today, it is clear that the relationships it engendered among people and between society and the environment must have been highly adaptive. In some very real sense equilibrium at a new level has been obtained, and perhaps it has promise of continuing well into the future. The survival of our ecosystem, or any system in general, emanates from two basic elements: first, the availability of sufficient energy and other resources; and second, effective self-regulating processes that keep in balance the various flows of energy and life-forms that comprise the system.

In most business and civic decisions, the environment is seen as an element of the economy, a factor to be calculated in figuring the cost of a product or a new urban development (Prugh 1995:17). Raw materials are valued by the cost of extraction, land modification by the cost of moving the earth, and loss of habitat or scenic views may be given no value at all. In these computations, replacement of nonrenewable resources or even the full cost of renewable resources are seldom considered. If one assumes that the natural capital of the earth's ecosystem is limitless or at least that it can be replaced by human-produced goods, then this approach may be reasonable.

This very shortsighted perspective has led to the rise of a group of scholars who refer to themselves as ecological economists and assert the primary importance of preserving the natural capital of the earth (Costanza et al. 1997). Their view is that the global ecosystem provides an array of indispensable resources and services to humans and, viewed in this way, the environment should be thought of as a vast, but ever-diminishing store of natural capital (see fig. 2.3; Prugh 1995:xix). They argue that mainstream economics does not take into account the "environmental" costs of virtually any activities, and as we deplete the store of natural capital, the sustainability of the global economy is at serious risk. To reorient modern economics and decision-making to utilize this perspective would require an enormous transformation of contemporary society, but the risk of continuing with the status quo is ominous.

When considered against many measures, urban society is very successful, but according to ecological economists and other scholars, its future is in peril due to troublesome aspects of its systemic relations. As discussed in chapters 3 and 7, maladaptations reduce the survival chances of a system not by subjecting the system to stress, but by impeding the effectiveness of its responses to stress (Rappaport 1978:58). The growth of organizational structure in an urban society often leads to higher level decision makers no longer being in close contact with productive situations or the changing aspects of the environment it relies upon. Problems of these sorts, associated with the increasing scale and complexity of society, could include the following:

1. delay in the passage of information up the hierarchy and adaptive decisions back down so that the response is no longer timely;

2. distortion of information as it is conveyed up the hierarchy or back down;

3. failure of higher level decision-makers to understand the productive situation or the requirements of the environment;

4. a divergence in the objectives of the differing groups in the society, so that certain institutions or groups of people may thrive at the expense of the well-being of the majority and/or the environment.

If these types of problems are inherent in the growth of urban society, are advanced civilizations themselves maladaptive? And if civilization and cities are the inevitable outcome of basic cultural forces, are culture and the very nature of human purposefulness maladaptive? In the face of potential risks from the biotic, abiotic, and human environment, people shape their culture to buffer themselves against these threats to their continued existence, and devise ideologies to mask the maladaptiveness of these contradictory institutions. Yet, despite these problems, humans as a species and civilization as an advanced organizational structure have thrived by almost any conceivable measure. Are we on the brink of disaster, being held together by obfuscation, or is this a finely tuned solution to the problems of survival on this planet that will be sustainable well into the future?

The Past as Prologue: A Personal Viewpoint

One of the fundamental working principles of anthropology is that humans, like other species, act directly to ensure their survival and indirectly to ensure the survival of their species. In this way, we consider human actions to be adaptive in a general sense, even if they appear to be counterproductive or irrelevant to survival in certain details. This could lead the reader to the logical conclusion that what people have been doing during the past 10,000 years has been adaptive and guided by enhancing the chances of survival of the species. In fact, if we can extend evolutionary principles to human behavior and combine that with cultural transmission of ideas and the human ability to plan, then it would be reasonable to assert that during the past millennia, human actions have been increasingly refined responses to the conditions of their environment, oriented at insuring the survival of the individual and of the species. Looking at demographic estimates for the continually increasing rate of human population growth and maps of the expansion of humans into virtually all regions on the earth, it is fair to say that as a species we have been very successful when measured by normal biological indicators. Moreover, if we accept the widely held proposition that knowledge of the world is gained through human perception and consequently is evaluated in human-defined terms, then it is likely that any measure of the condition of the environment should indicate a high state of health as well. Therefore, it could be expected that the result of the coevolutionary process of human-environmental interaction over the past millennia has resulted in favorable conditions for all parties concerned. More than that, given the special human attributes of holding ethical values, conceptual planning for the future, and being able to act in order to operationalize our plans, it might be safe to paraphrase Voltaire's Dr. Pangloss and others by saying that *we live in the best of all possible worlds,* utopia has arrived, and we are well on our way to having created a paradise here on Earth.

This may all sound logical in the abstract, but countless individuals in science, media, government, and the general public have decried the condition of the environment, claiming that we have not created a utopia but are propelling ourselves toward the edge of a cliff. Among the grave problems that are attributed to human action are numerous species extinctions, deforestation on a vast scale, soil degradation and erosion, air and water pollution, and possibly a changing global climate. Taken together, these disastrous human impacts on the environment threaten the health and continued survival not only of the human species, but of all living creatures. The imputed causes are various, but among the most often repeated are the unconstrained growth in human population, the unlimited human hunger for energy and natural resources, and the apparent lack of concern over the increasingly polluted air we breathe and water we drink. Those who adhere to this perspective can point to endless examples of localized environmental disasters and general environmental deterioration on a continental, if not global, scale. So what is the correct answer: Are we cruising along on a smooth highway toward a human-defined paradise or are we speeding with reckless abandon toward the final apocalypse for the human species?

I do not believe that there is a simple response to this question, and perhaps there is not a single answer at all. As I have argued from the early chapters of this book, your attitude toward the environment — that is, what you expect of it — has a great deal to do with your judgment of its condition. What I have attempted to add to this is an historical perspective. Countless societies have coped with their environment and with what I am sure they perceived as environmental crises. For many these responses meant the end of their settlement or even their society as they knew it. For many others it meant continued survival or even increasing success for many generations. I am not so naïve as to suggest that we can derive specific strategies for the future or even answer today's challenges by looking to the past, but I do believe that it enriches our perspectives and illuminates some basic relationships between humans and their environment that are useful for each of us in formulating our own attitudes and decisions about the environment.

For me the lessons of the past are manifold, but do not conclusively lead to a course for action. Without trying to impose these on the reader, let me suggest some of my personal responses to the kind of information presented in this book and challenge you to formulate your own.

1. For a very long time and in every part of the globe, humans have demonstrated that they are extraordinarily talented, able to understand the intricacies of their environment, and willing to take action to promote their continued survival.

214

2. Humans have developed cultural traditions and technological innovations that have allowed them to successfully exist in virtually every locality on Earth, in ever-increasing numbers and in more densely packed settlements.

3. Whether the problems confronting them were a changing climate, deteriorating soil fertility, or too many people to feed, human groups have reorganized themselves to meet these challenges, and in most circumstances and by most measures they have succeeded.

4. Responses to environmentally related stresses have included new techniques of subsistence, new modes of transport and exchange, new social organizational forms, changes in residential mobility, downsizing of communities, and outright abandonment of regions.

5. Local environments, in virtually all cases, have been significantly altered by human presence. Prehuman ecosystemic balances have been replaced by new sets of relationships, with their own balances and trajectories that include human impacts. Many of these local situations have demonstrated a degree of sustainability, at least on the time scale of human generations.

6. Human impacts on the environment vary with each situation, but in general they transform biota so that their net yield for human consumption is increased and native plant and animal conditions often are degraded.

7. Human decisions about resource use and the environment are usually predicated on maximizing short-term returns, and only secondarily take into account long-term consequences of these actions.

8. The trajectory of the human career appears to be irreversible. The factors that give rise to the social condition at any point in time are so complex that attempting to reconstruct former conditions in the present is almost impossible. Social change, like biological evolution, will not allow the recreation of extinct conditions, although it may be possible to duplicate some of their characteristics in a new form.

   With these general points in mind, let me give my own answer to that most seminal question: Are we, as humans, a part of nature or outside of it? And then, were we set here on Earth to exploit it, to serve as its steward, or to be just another species in the natural order? I firmly believe that we are 100% a part of nature, created by natural forces, and subject to the continuing "laws" of nature. However, I also believe that there are no similar organisms left in the natural world, as was the case 5 or 10 million years ago when other primates shared so many characteristics with our ancestors. Consequently, we do not have facile models to measure our behavior against.

As wondrous as we all find nature, it is not a benign agent when it comes to governing the continuing survival of species. As Charles Darwin codified in the Law of Natural Selection, intra-species competition for reproductive rights, and inter-species competition for resources to consume govern the changing membership in the natural world. Individual losers in these competitions cease to contribute to the continuing gene pool of their species, while population losers either find their condition modified in future generations or they cease to exist. The risks to continued survival in these competitions of nature are enormous and the results are final. The result of several million years of this competition is that we have no really close relatives in the animal kingdom, and that we have both destroyed those that were close to us and have ourselves evolved into a new, more distinct species. There is nothing inherently *unnatural* about humans, but the fact is that we are vastly different from any other surviving animal species, and it is not especially useful to insist we behave in a manner suggested by observing other animals. If we are to judge behavior according to a code, it must be a code that takes into recognition the very traits that have made us human.

From the beginning, humans have been successful competitors in nature's struggle. Our abilities to perceive potential sources of food and devise means of securing them were matched by a willingness to suppress competitors, even those closely related to us. I believe the single most important key to the success of the human species was our ability to reduce our risks in the struggles of nature. This took many forms, but simply put, it meant first, we found ways to procure an ample and continuous food supply; second, we defended ourselves and our offspring from danger of attack from competitors; and third, we altered our immediate environment to lessen the exposure to harsh climatic conditions. To meet these challenges, humans developed technology, both tools and the strategies to use them effectively. We also devised increasingly complex means of organizing ourselves to achieve greater and greater security of survival. Some of the changes became a part of the species through selective pressures slowly favoring certain genetic compositions over others, while the most striking human achievements can be traced to the accumulation and transmission of cultural knowledge. Past experience could be used to avoid mistakes and refine successful strategies. Through culture, these innovations in technology and organization could be perpetuated to future generations and disseminated to other groups. Throughout the thousands of generations of humans, two basic struggles defined by nature have exerted immense influence on cultural development: first, individuals effectively situating themselves to maximize their reproductive success, and second, acting as a group to insure their survival versus other groups. Producing a surplus of food, converting excess food into prestige goods, and organizing groups for efficient production and effective defense all have contributed to human success and have become a part of our character, our very existence.

If one accepts the above line of reasoning, then it seems as though our current human-environmental relations have to be seen as the logical outcome of thousands of generations of successful experiments. At some level I am forced to agree with this conclusion and to acknowledge the world as we see it to be perfectly suited for humans, and our environmental relations to be highly acceptable, because they are the products of the cumulative decisions of millions of rational humans. While accepting this logic and its optimism about the condition and future of the world, I also recognize that just because humans have made a decision and survived does not mean it is the *correct* decision in a larger sense. The case studies presented in this book are ample documentation that human groups in all parts of the world have developed and made decisions in such a manner that they were not in concert with the requirements of their environment, and consequently, they have failed as social and sometimes as biological communities. The marvel has been that in the aggregate, the species has survived and flourished in the face of these many and diverse failures.

The basic questions remain: Have we learned from these many disasters? Are we refining and improving our strategies for living sustainably in our world? Or are we destined to repeat these failures on an ever-increasing scale, ultimately leading to the extinction of our species or at least of our way of life? When I weigh my often contradictory viewpoints on this question, I come out in favor of the first answer. Seeing the world through the eyes of a human, it is a good world, because we have acted to make it so. That does not mean we will not continue to have failures or face serious threats to our existence. That also does not mean that the environment we live in or the ways we relate to it will remain static even as we know it today in its already substantially altered form. But I do hold a fundamentally optimistic view that despite the maladaptations we have created in developing the urban society of today, we also have built in balances that continue to bring the system back in line.

Being optimistic about the problem-solving ability of humans does not mean that there is no need to be constantly vigilant about human actions and their impact on the environment. Critics of growth, advocates of wilderness, and balladeers of nature have all contributed to the state of the world as we know it and are essential parts of the decision-making process. Moreover, there is the possibility that I have misread the past, and that we are in fact on a collision course with environmental disaster unless drastic changes are implemented. I see two basic issues that the past does not adequately address: first, has the scale of the problem in the past always been too small to be globally threatening and only now is it approaching a true crisis; and second, are the nature of human impacts themselves changing so that they are of a far more threatening nature? Certainly, the scale has changed, with global population approaching six billion people and per capita consumption of energy and reliance on food higher on the trophic pyramid increasing, especially in key countries like China. Moreover, in prehistory there were substantial areas of unoccupied land that could be moved to if people degraded their own land. The filling up of the potentially productive land, plus problems of private property and national boundaries put limits on what problems can now be solved by mobility. Yet, in the face of the enormous threat posed by growth, humans have been incredibly inventive in finding ways to live together densely, to produce more food and products from available resources, and to move the food and products from those who produce more than they need to those who need more than they produce (albeit with some serious implications for the social order). The issue here is can we keep ahead of the curve?

History provides us little insight into the second question: Are there new threats that never existed in the past? There are many who argue that the nature of technology in our times and the enormity of the demands humans put on the natural systems of the world are more than can be handled either by humans or nature. Although there are precedents for most of these problems in the past, they occurred at a different scale and certainly did not threaten the basic life-supporting systems of the earth. The question is, do they now? Nuclear weaponry, hazardous wastes, chemical water and air pollutants, massive deforestation, the extinction of species with great medical potential, global warming, and ozone depletion are all candidates for global disaster, yet will it happen? Although each one poses a distinctly real threat, I doubt any one of these will lead to the demise of urban society.

To put this into a perspective that has more immediate relevance for most of us, I will conclude this book with a hypothetical situation. What if your confidence in technology and human organization was so high that you estimated that there was only a one in ten chance of a global environmental disaster occurring? Given all the risks that we do face, I would say that is a very optimistic view of our problem-solving abilities. Knowing that the costs of taking an alternate course of action that would minimize human impacts would be high in both economic and social terms and that success by that route was not certain, it might be tempting to allow growth to proceed on its current course unchecked despite the potential dangers. But let me pose a question to you: Would you board an airplane to reach your destination if you knew there was a 10% chance of a fatal air disaster? I doubt it. Would you instead take another more arduous, expensive means of transport? Probably. When the threat is to your life, just as the environmental threat is to the existence of the human species, no significant level of risk is acceptable, no cost of remedy too high.

With the continued pressure on the decision-makers of our society by those who are concerned with environmental preservation, I predict that there is a substantially better chance than ever for us to survive each threat. But that is not a reason to celebrate or to diminish our resolve to minimize harmful human impacts. The stakes are very high when we are taking chances with the world's environment. I do not think we can treat these decisions as we would evaluate risks in a normal game of chance.

Works Cited

Abbott, David R.
1994   *Hohokam Social Structure and Irrigation Management: The Ceramic Evidence From the Central Phoenix Basin.* Ph.D. Dissertation, Department of Anthropology, Arizona State University, Tempe.

Abrams, Elliot M., and David J. Rue
1988   The Causes and Consequences of Deforestation Among the Prehistoric Maya. *Human Ecology* 16(4): 377–395.

Adams, Robert McC.
1966   *The Evolution of Urban Society.* Aldine Publishing Company, Chicago.
1974   Anthropological Perspectives on Ancient Trade. *Current Anthropology* 15(3): 239–258.
1977   World Picture, Anthropological Frame. *American Anthropologist* 79(2): 265–279.
1978   Strategies of Maximization, Stability and Resilience in Mesopotamian Society, Settlement, and Agriculture. *Proceedings of the American Philosophical Society* 122(5): 329–335.

Algaze, Guillermo
1989   The Uruk Expansion: Cross-cultural Exchange in Early Mesopotamia Civilization. *Current Anthropology* 30: 571–608.

Alvard, Michael S.
1993   Testing the "Ecologically Noble Savage" Hypothesis: Interspecific Prey by Piro Hunters of Amazonian Peru. *Human Ecology* 21(4): 355–387.

Athens, J. Stephen, and Jerome V. Ward
1993   Environmental Change and Prehistoric Polynesian Settlement in Hawai'i. *Asian Perspectives* 32: 205–224.

Bahn, P., and J. R. Flenley
1992   *Easter Island, Earth Island.* Thames and Hudson, London.

Baleé, William
1998a   Historical Ecology: Premises and Postulates. In *Advances in Historical Ecology*, edited by William Baleé, pp. 13–29. Columbia University Press, New York.

Baleé, William (ed.)
1998b   *Advances in Historical Ecology.* Columbia University Press, New York.

Barker, Grahame
1995   Land Use and Environmental Degradation in Biferno Valley (Central Southern Italy) from Prehistoric Times to the Present Day. *L'Homme et la Dègradation de l'Environ-*

ment. XVe Rencontres Internationales d'Archéologie d'Histoire d'Antibes. Editions APCDA, Juan-les-Pins.

Bell, Martin, and Michael J. C. Walker
1992   *Late Quaternary Environmental Change: Physical and Human Perspectives.* Long-man Scientific & Technical, John Wiley & Sons, New York.

Bennett, John
1976   *The Ecological Transition: Cultural Anthropology and Human Adaptation.* Perga-mon Press, New York.

Binford, Michael W., and Barbara Leyden
1987   Ecosystems, Paleoecology and Human Disturbance in Subtropical and Tropical America. Quaternary Science Reviews 6: 115–128.

Black, Francis L.
1975   Infectious Diseases in Primitive Societies. *Science* 187: 515–518.

Black, John
1970   *The Dominion of Man: The Search for Ecological Responsibility.* Edinburgh University Press, Edinburgh.

Boserup, Ester
1965   *The Conditions of Agricultural Growth.* Aldine Publishing Company, Chicago.
1981   *Population and Technological Change: A Study of Long-term Trends.* University of Chicago, Chicago.

Boyden, S. V. (ed.)
1970   *The Impact of Civilization on the Biology of Man.* Australian National University Press, Canberra.

Braudel, Fernand
1972   *The Mediterranean and the Mediterranean World in the Age of Phillip II,* Vol. 1. Translated by Siân Reynolds. Harper & Row, Publishers, New York.

Bronson, Bennet
1972   Farm Labor and the Evolution of Food Production. In *Population Growth: Anthro-pological Implications,* edited by B. Spooner, pp. 190–218. MIT Press, Cambridge.

Brown, Lester R.
1995   *State of the World.* W. W. Norton & Company, New York.

Butzer, Karl W.
1982   *Archaeology as Human Ecology: Method and Theory for a Contextual Approach.* Cambridge University Press, Cambridge.
1996   Ecology in the Long View: Settlement, Agrosystem Strategies, and Ecological Perfor-mance. *Journal of Field Archaeology* 23(2): 141–150.

Catton Jr., William R.
1993   Carrying Capacity and the Death of a Culture: A Tale of Two Autopsies. *Sociological Inquiry* 63(2): 200–223.

Chadderton, Thomas J.
1994   Tin Production and Deforestation in Anatolia During the Early Bronze Age. Manu-script on file at Arizona State University.

Chisholm, Michael
1968   *Rural Settlement and Land Use: An Essay in Location.* Hutchinson & Co., London.

Clark, G. A., and C. M. Willermet
1997   *Conceptual Issues in Modern Human Origins Research.* Aldine de Gruyter, New York.

Coe, Michael D.
1964   The Chinampas of Mexico. *Scientific American* 211(1): 90–98.
1982   *Mexico.* Thames and Hudson, New York.

Cohen, Mark Nathan
1989   *Health and the Rise of Civilization.* Yale University Press, New Haven, Conn.

Cohen, Mark Nathan, and George J. Armelagos
1984   Paleopathology at the Origins of Agriculture: Editor's Summation. In *Paleopathology at the Origins of Agriculture,* edited by M. N. Cohen and G. J. Armelagos, pp. 585–601. Academic Press, New York.

Costanza, Robert
1996   Ecological Economics: Reintegrating the Study of Humans and Nature. *Ecological Applications* 6(4): 978–990.

Costanza, Robert, John Cumberland, Herman Daly, Robert Goodland, and Richard Norgaard
1997   *An Introduction to Ecological Economics.* St. Lucie Press, Boca Raton, Fla.

Cowgill, George L.
1975   On Causes and Consequences of Ancient and Modern Population Changes. *American Anthropologist* 77(3): 505–573.
1993   Distinguished Lecture in Archaeology: Beyond Criticizing New Archaeology. *American Anthropologist* 95(3): 551–573.
1996   Population, Human Nature, Knowing Actors, and Explaining the Onset of Complexity. In *Debating Complexity — Proceedings of the 26th Annual Chacmool Conference,* edited by D. A. Meyer, P. C. Dawson, and D. T. Hanna, pp. 16–22. The Archaeological Association of the University of Alberta, Calgary, Alberta, Canada.

Crosby, Alfred W.
1993   *Ecological Imperialism: The Biological Expansion of Europe, 900–1900,* CANTO edition. Cambridge University Press, Cambridge.

Crown, Patricia L., and James Judge (eds.)
1991   *Chaco and Hohokam: Prehistoric Regional Systems in the American Southwest.* School of American Research Press, Santa Fe, N.Mex.

Crumley, Carole L.
1994a   Historical Ecology: A Multidimensional Ecological Orientation. In *Historical Ecology: Cultural Knowledge and Changing Landscapes,* edited by C. L. Crumley, pp. 1–16. School of American Research Press, Santa Fe, N.Mex.

Crumley, Carole L. (ed.)
1994b   *Historical Ecology: Cultural Knowledge and Changing Landscapes.* School of American Research Press, Santa Fe, N.Mex.

Culbert, T. Patrick (ed.)
1973   *The Classic Maya Collapse.* University of New Mexico Press, Albuquerque.

Deevey, E. S., D. S. Rice, P. M. Rice, H. H. Vaughan, M. Brenner, and M. S. Flannery
1979   Mayan Urbanism: Impact on a Tropical Karst Environment. *Science* 206: 298–306.

Denevan, William M.
1970   Aboriginal Drained Field Cultivation in the Americas. *Science* 169: 647–654.
1976   The Aboriginal Population of Amazonia. In *The Native Population of the Americas in 1492,* edited by W. M. Denevan, pp. 205–234. University of Wisconsin Press, Madison.
1992   The Pristine Myth: The Landscape of the Americas in 1492. In *The Americas Before and After Columbus: Current Geographical Research,* edited by Karl W. Butzer. *Annals of the Association of American Geographers* 82(3): 369–385.

Diamond, Jared
1984   Historic Extinctions: A Rosetta Stone for Understanding Prehistoric Extinctions. In *Quaternary Extinctions: A Prehistoric Revolution,* edited by Paul S. Martin and Richard G. Klein, pp. 824–862. University of Arizona Press, Tucson.
1995   Easter's End. *Discovery: The World of Science* 16(5): 62–69.
1997   *Guns, Germs, and Steel: The Fates of Human Societies.* W. W. Norton & Company, New York.

Dickson, Bruce D.
1987   Circumscription by Anthropogenic Environmental Destruction: An Expansion of Carneiro's (1970) *Theory of the Origin of the State. American Antiquity* 52(4): 709–716.

Dillehay, T. D., G. Ardilla Calderon, G. Politis, and M. C. Beltrão.
1992   Earliest Hunters and Gatherers of South America. *Journal of World Prehistory* 6(2): 145–203.

Durham, William H.
1991   *Coevolution: Genes, Culture, and Human Diversity.* Stanford University Press, Stanford, Calif.

Edzard, Dietz O.
1967   The Third Dynasty of Ur: Its Empire and Its Successor States. In *The Near East: The Early Civilizations,* edited by J. Bottéro, E. Cassin, and J. Vercoutter, pp. 133–176. Delacorte Press, New York.

Ehrlich, Paul R., and Peter H. Raven
1964   Butterflies and Plants: A Study in Coevolution. *Evolution* 18: 586–608.

English, P. W.
1966   *City and Village in Iran: Settlement and Economy in the Kirman Basin.* University of Wisconsin Press, Madison.

Euler, Robert C., and George J. Gumerman
1978   *Investigations of the Southwestern Anthropological Research Group: An Experiment in Archaeological Cooperation.* Museum of Northern Arizona, Flagstaff.

Falconer, Steven E., and Patricia L. Fall
1995   Human Impacts on the Environment During the Rise and Collapse of Civilization in the Eastern Mediterranean. In *Late Quaternary Environments and Deep History: A Tribute to Paul S. Martin,* edited by David W. Steadman and Jim. I. Mead. Scientific Papers, Vol. 3, pp. 84–101. Mammoth Site of Hot Springs, South Dakota, Hot Springs.

Fish, Paul R., and Suzanne K. Fish
1992   Prehistoric Landscapes of the Sonoran Desert Hohokam. *Population and Environment: A Journal of Interdisciplinary Studies* 13: 269–283.

Flenley, John R., and Sarah M. King
1984   Late Quaternary Pollen Records from Easter Island. *Nature* 307: 47–50.

Ford, Richard I.
1973   Archaeology Serving Humanity. In *Research and Theory in Current Anthropology*, edited by C. L. Redman, pp. 83–93. John Wiley & Sons, New York.

Forman, Richard T. T., and Michael Gordon
1986   The Human Role in Landscape Development. In *Landscape Ecology*, pp. 273–311. John Wiley & Sons, New York.

Geertz, Clifford
1963   *Agricultural Involution*. University of California Press, Berkeley.

Gelburd, Diane E.
1985   Managing Salinity: Lessons from the Past. *Journal of Soil and Water Conservation* 40(4): 329–331.

Gibson, McGuire
1974   Violation of Fallow and Engineered Disaster in Mesopotamian Civilization. In *Irrigation's Impact on Society: Anthropological Papers of The University of Arizona, No. 25*, edited by Theodore E. Downing and McGuire Gibson, pp. 7–19. University of Arizona Press, Tucson.

Glacken, Clarence J.
1956   Changing Ideas of the Habitable World. In *Man's Role in Changing the Face of the Earth*, edited by William L. Thomas, pp. 70–92. University of Chicago Press, Chicago.

Gladwin, Christina H.
1980   A Theory of Real-life Choice: Applications to Agricultural Decisions. In *Agricultural Decision Making: Anthropological Contributions to Rural Development*, edited by P. F. Barlett, pp. 45–85. Academic Press, New York.

Goldsmith, Edward, Peter Bunyard, Nicholas Hildyard, and Patrick McCully
1990   *Imperiled Planet: Restoring Our Endangered Ecosystems*. MIT Press, Cambridge.

Gosz, James R.
1998   Long-term Research on a Global Scale. In *The International Long-Term Ecological Research Network 1998*, edited by Patricia Sprott, pp. 3–6. U.S. LTER Network Office, Albuquerque, N.Mex.

Goudie, Andrew
1993   *The Human Impact on the Natural Environment*, 4th Edition. Blackwell Publishers, Cambridge.

Grayson, D. K.
1977   Pleistocene Avifaunas and the Overkill Hypothesis. *Science* 195: 691–693.

Green, Stanton W.
1980   Broadening Least-Cost Models for Expanding Agricultural Systems. In *Modeling*

Change in Prehistoric Subsistence Economics, edited by Timothy K. Earle and Andrew L. Christenson, pp. 209–241. Academic Press, New York.

Gumerman, G. J. (ed.)
1991   *Exploring the Hohokam: Prehistoric Desert Peoples of the American Southwest.* Amerind Foundation Publication, Dragoon. University of New Mexico Press, Albuquerque.

Haggett, Peter
1979   *Geography: A Modern Synthesis.* Prentice Hall, London.

Heyerdahl, Thor
1950   *Kon-Tiki: Across the Pacific by Raft.* Translated by F. H. Lyon. Rand McNally, Chicago.

Higgs, Eric S., and Claudio Vita-Finzi
1970   Prehistoric Economies in the Mt. Carmel Area Palestine: Site Catchment Analysis. *Proceedings of the Prehistoric Society of London* 36: 1–37.
1972   Prehistoric Economies: A Territorial Approach. In *Papers in Economic Prehistory,* edited by E. S. Higgs, pp. 27–36. Cambridge University Press, Cambridge.

Hillel, Daniel
1991   *Out of the Earth: Civilization and the Life of the Soil.* University of California Press, Los Angeles.
1994   *Rivers of Eden: The Struggle for Water and the Quest for Peace in the Middle East.* Oxford University Press, Oxford.

Hodder, Ian
1982   *The Present Past.* Batsford, London.

Hodell, David A., Jason H. Curtis, and Mark Brenner
1995   Possible Role of Climate in the Collapse of Classic Maya Civilization. *Nature* 375(6530): 391–394.

Hong, Sungmin, Jean-Pierre Candelone, Clari C. Patterson, and Claude F. Boutron
1994   Greenland Ice Evidence of Hemispheric Lead Pollution Two Millennia Ago by Greek and Roman Civilizations. *Science* 265: 1841–1843.

Huntington, Ellsworth
1934   *Mainsprings of Civilization.* New American Library, New York.

Islebe, Gerald A., Henry Hooghiemstra, Mark Brenner, Jason H. Curtis, and David A. Hodell
1996   A Holocene Vegetation History from Lowland Guatemala. *Holocene* 6(3): 265–271.

Ives, Vickie Souza
1994   Urbanization, Irrigation and Environment: Malaria in the Ur III and Sasasian Periods of Southern Mesopotamia. Manuscript on file at Arizona State University.

Jacobsen, Thorkild
1982   Salinity and Irrigation Agriculture in Antiquity; Diyala Basin Archaeological Projects: Report on Essential Results, 11957–58. *Biblioteca Mesopotámica* 14. Undena Publications, Malibu.

Jacobsen, Thorkild, and Robert McC. Adams
1958   Salt and Silt in Ancient Mesopotamian Agriculture. *Science* 128(3334): 1251–1258.

Jacobson, Judith E., and John Firor (eds.)
1992   *Human Impact on the Environment: Ancient Roots, Current Challenges.* Westview Press, Boulder, Colo.

James, Steven R.
1994   Hunting, Fishing, and Resource Depletion: Prehistoric Cultural Impacts on Animals in the Southwest. Paper presented at the 1994 Southwest Symposium, January 7–8, 1994, Arizona State University, Tempe.

Jarman, M. R.
1977   Early Animal Husbandry. In *The Early History of Agriculture,* edited by J. Hutchinson, J.G.G. Clark, E. M. Jope, and R. Riley, pp. 85–97. Oxford University Press, Oxford.

Jennings, Jesse D.
1978   Origins. In *Ancient Native Americans,* edited by J. D. Jennings, pp. 1–41. W. H. Freeman and Company, San Francisco.

Kempton, Willett, James S. Boster, and Jennifer A. Hartley
1995   *Environmental Values in American Culture.* MIT Press, Cambridge.

Khaldun, Ibn
1967   *The Muqaddimah.* Translated by F. Rosenthal. Princeton University Press, Princeton, N.J.

Kirch, Patrick V.
1982   The Impact of the Prehistoric Polynesians on the Hawaiian Ecosystem. *Pacific Science* 36(1): 1–14.
1989   Non-marine Molluscs from the Rockshelter Sediments. In *Prehistoric Hawaiian Occupation in the Anahulu Valley, O'ahu Island: Excavations in Three Inland Rockshelters,* edited by P. V. Kirch, pp. 73–82. Contributions of the University of California Archaeological Research Facility No. 47, Berkeley.
1990   The Evolution of Sociopolitical Complexity in Prehistoric Hawaii: An Assessment of the Archaeological Evidence. *Journal of World Prehistory* 4: 311–346.

Kirch, Patrick V., J. R. Flenley, David Steadman, F. Lamont, and S. Dawson
1992   Ancient Environmental Degradation. *National Geographic Research and Exploration* 8(2): 166–179.

Klein, Richard G.
1992   The Impact of Early People on the Environment: The Case of Large Mammal Extinctions. In *Human Impact on the Environment: Ancient Roots, Current Challenges,* edited by Judith E. Jacobsen and John Firor, pp. 13–34. Westview Press, Boulder, Colo.

Kohler, Timothy A.
1992   Prehistoric Human Impact on the Environment in Upland North American Southwest. *Population and Environment: A Journal of Interdisciplinary Studies.* 13(4): 255–268.

Köhler-Rollefson, Ilse, and Gary O. Rollefson
1990   The Impact of Neolithic Subsistence Strategies on the Environment: The Case of Ain Ghazal, Jordan. In *Man's Role in the Shaping of Eastern Mediterranean Landscape,* edited by S. Bottema, G. Entjes-Niegorg, and W. van Zeist, pp. 3–14. Rotterdam, The Netherlands.

Komarek, E. V.
1983   Fire as an Anthropogenic Factor in Vegetation Ecology. In *Man's Impact on Vegetation,* edited by W. Hozner, M.J.A. Werger, and I. Ikusima, pp. 77–82. Dr. W. Junk Publishers, London.

Le Houérou, Henri Noel
1981   Impact of Man and His Animals on Mediterranean Vegetation. In *Mediterranean Type Ecosystems,* edited by F. DiCastri and H. A. Hooney, pp. 479–521. Springs, New York.

Leyden, Barbara W., Mark Brenner, Tom Whitmore, Jason H. Curtis, Dolores R. Piperno, and Bruce H. Dahlin
1996   A Record of Long- and Short-Term Climatic Variation from Northwest Yucatán: Cenote San José Chulchacá. In *The Managed Mosaic: Ancient Maya Agricultural and Resource Use,* edited by Scott L. Fedick, pp. 30–50. University of Utah Press, Salt Lake City.

Little, Michael A., and George E. B. Moren Jr.
1976   *Ecology, Energetics, and Human Variability.* Wm. C. Brown Company Publishers, Dubuque, Iowa.

Malthus, Thomas
1878   *An Essay on the Principle of Population; or, A View of Its Past and Present Effects on Human Happiness.* Reeves & Turner, London.

Marsh, George Perkins
1864   *Man and Nature.* Cambridge Belknap Press of Harvard University Press, Cambridge.

Martin, Calvin Luther
1992   *In the Spirit of the Earth: Rethinking History and Time.* Johns Hopkins University Press, Baltimore.

Martin, Paul S.
1972   The Discovery of America. In *Science* 179: 969–974.
1984   Prehistoric Overkill: The Global Model. In *Quaternary Extinctions: A Prehistoric Revolution,* edited by Paul S. Martin and Richard G. Klein, pp. 354–403. University of Arizona Press, Tucson.

Martin, Paul S., and Richard G. Klein
1984   *Quaternary Extinctions: A Prehistoric Revolution,* edited by Paul S. Martin and Richard G. Klein. University of Arizona Press, Tucson.

Martin, Paul S., and Christine Szuter
1994   Deep History and Wild Arizona. Paper presented at the 1994 Southwest Symposium, January 7–8, 1994, Arizona State University, Tempe.

Matson, P. A., W. J. Parton, A. G. Power, and M. J. Swift
1997   Agricultural Intensification and Ecosystem Properties. *Science* 277: 504–509.

McGovern, Thomas H.
1994   Management for Extinction in Norse Greenland. In *Historical Ecology: Cultural Knowledge and Changing Landscapes,* edited by Carole L. Crumley, pp. 127–154. School of American Research Press, Santa Fe, N.Mex.

McGovern, Thomas H., Gerald Bigelow, Thomas Amorosi, and Daniel Russell
1988   Northern Islands, Human Error, and Environmental Degradation: A View of Social and Ecological Change in the Medieval North Atlantic. *Human Ecology* 16(3): 225–270.

Mikesell, M.
1974   Geography as the Study of Environment: An Assessment of Some Old and New Commitments. In *Perspectives on Environment*, edited by Ian R. Manners and Marvin W. Mikesell, pp. 1–23. Association of American Geographers Publication 13, Washington.

Miller, Naomi
1985   Paleoethnobotanical Evidence for Deforestation in Ancient Iran: A Case Study of Urban Malyan. *Journal of Ethnobiology* 5(1): 1–19.
1992a   Clearing Land for Farmland and Fuel: Archaeobotanical Studies of the Ancient Near East. In *Economy and Settlement in the Near East: Analyses of Ancient Sites and Materials,* edited by Naomi F. Miller, pp. 71–78. MASCA, University Museum of Archaeology and Anthropology. University of Pennsylvania, Philadelphia.
1992b   Archaeobotanical Perspectives on the Rural-Urban Connection. In *Economy and Settlement in the Near East: Analyses of Ancient Sites and Materials,* edited by Naomi F. Miller, pp. 79–83. MASCA, University Museum of Archaeology and Anthropology. University of Pennsylvania, Philadelphia.

Montgomery, Carla W.
1992   *Environmental Geology.* Wm. C. Brown Publishers, Dubuque, Iowa.

Moore, A. M. T.
1985   The Development of Neolithic Societies in the Near East. In *Advances in World Archaeology,* Vol. 4, edited by F. Wendorf and A. E. Close, pp. 1–69. Academic Press, New York.

Moran, Emilio F. (ed.)
1990   *The Ecosystem Approach in Anthropology: From Concept to Practice.* University of Michigan Press, Ann Arbor.

Morrison Institute for Public Policy
1997   *What Matters in Greater Phoenix: 1997 Indicators of Our Quality of Life.* Arizona Board of Regents, Arizona State University, Tempe.

National Science Foundation (NSF)
1997   Fifth Competition for Long-Term Ecological Research (LTER): Urban LTER. NSF 97-53. National Science Foundation, Arlington, Va.

Netting, Robert McC.
1977   *Cultural Ecology.* Cummings Publishing Company, Menlo Park, Calif.
1993   *Smallholders, Householders: Farm Families and the Ecology of Intensive, Sustainable Agriculture.* Stanford University Press, Stanford, Calif.

Newson, Linda A.
1998   A Historical-Ecological Perspective on Epidemic Disease. In *Advances in Historical Ecology,* edited by W. Baleé, pp. 42–63. Columbia University Press, New York.

Nials, Fred L., David A. Gregory, and Donald A. Graybill
1989   Salt River Stream Flow and Hohokam Irrigation Systems. In *The 1982–1992 Ex-*

cavations at Las Colinas: Environment and Subsistence, Vol. 5., edited by D. A. Graybill, D. A. Gregory, F. L. Nials, S. Fish, R. Gasser, C. Miksicek, and C. Szuter, pp. 59–78. Arizona State Museum Archaeological Series, No. 162.

Nissen, Hans J.
1988 *The Early History of the Near East 9000–2000* B.C. Translated by E. Lutzeier. University of Chicago Press, Chicago.

Norgaard, Richard B.
1994 *Development Betrayed: The End of Progress and A Coevolutionary Revisioning of the Future.* Routledge, London.

Nriagu, Jerome O.
1983 *Lead and Lead Poisoning in Antiquity.* Wiley, New York.

Odum, Eugene P.
1963 *Ecology.* Holt, Rinehart and Winston, New York.

O'Hara, Sara L., F. Alayne Street-Perrott, and Timothy P. Burt
1993 Accelerated Soil Erosion Around a Mexican Lake Caused by Prehispanic Agriculture. *Nature* 362: 48–51.
1994 "O'Hara, Street-Perrott and Burt Reply." Correspondence. *Anthropology Newsletter* 35(3): 4.

Peterson, Jane
1994 *Changes in the Sexual Division of Labor in the Prehistory of the Southern Levant.* Ph.D. Dissertation, Department of Anthropology, Arizona State University, Tempe.

Polish Army Topographical Service
1968 *Pergamon World Atlas.* Pergamon Press, Oxford, New York.

Ponting, Clive
1991 *A Green History of the World: The Environment and the Collapse of Great Civilizations.* Penguin Books, New York.

Posey, Darrell A.
1998 Diachronic Ecotones and Anthropogenic Landscapes in Amazonia: Contesting the Consciousness of Conservation. In *Advances in Historical Ecology*, edited by W. Baleé, pp. 104–108. Columbia University Press, New York.

Powell, Marvin A.
1985 Salt, Seed, and Yields in Sumerian Agriculture: A Critique of the Theory of Progressive Salinization. In *Zeitschrift fuer Assyriolgie und Vorderasiatische Archaeologie* 75(1): 7–38.

Pringle, Heather
1997 Death in Norse Greenland. *Science* 275: 924–926.

Prugh, Thomas
1995 *Natural Capital and Human Economic Survival.* International Society for Ecological Economics Press, Solomons, Md.

Pyne, Stephen J.
1997 *America's Fires: Management on Wildlands and Forests.* Forest History Society Issues Series. Durham, N.C.

1998   Forged in Fire: History, Land, and Anthropogenic Fire. In *Advances in Historical Ecology*, edited by W. Baleé, pp. 64–103. Columbia University Press, New York.

Rappaport, Roy A.
1978   Maladaptations in Social Systems. In *The Evolution of Social Systems*, edited by J. Friedman and M. J. Rowlands, pp. 49–87. University of Pittsburgh Press, Pittsburgh.

Redman, Charles L.
1973   *Research and Theory in Current Anthropology*. John Wiley & Sons, New York.
1978   *The Rise of Civilization: From Early Farmers to Urban Society in the Ancient Near East*. W. H. Freeman and Company, San Francisco.
1992   The Impact of Food Production: Short-Term Strategies and Long-Term Consequences. In *Human Impact on the Environment: Ancient Roots, Current Challenges*, edited by J. F. Jacobsen and J. Firor, pp. 35–49. Westview Press, Boulder, Colo.

Renfrew, Colin, J. E. Dixon, and J. R. Cann
1966   Obsidian and Early Cultural Contact in the Near East. *Proceedings of the Prehistoric Society* (London) 32: 30–72.

Rice, Don S.
1994   The Human Impact on Lowland Mesoamerican Environments. Paper presented at the Society for American Archaeology 59th Annual Meeting, April 20–24, 1994, Anaheim, Calif.

Rice, Don Stephen
1996   Paleolimnological Analysis in the Central Petén, Guatemala. In *The Managed Mosaic: Ancient Maya Agricultural and Resource Use*, edited by Scott L. Fedick, pp. 193–206. University of Utah Press, Salt Lake City.

Rice, Don Stephen, and Prudence M. Rice
1984   Lessons from the Maya. *Latin American Research Review* 19(3): 7–34.

Rice, Donald S., Prudence M. Rice, and Edward S. Deevey, Jr.
1985   Paradise Lost: Classic Maya Impact on a Lacustrine Environment. In *Prehistoric Lowland Maya Environment and Subsistence Economy*, edited by M. Pohl, pp. 91–105. Peabody Museum Papers, Vol. 77, Cambridge.

Ricklefs, Robert E.
1993   *The Economy of Nature*. W. H. Freeman, New York.

Rindos, David
1984   *The Origins of Agriculture: An Evolutionary Perspective*. Academic Press, San Diego.

Rollefson, Gary O., and Ilse Köhler-Rollefson
1992   Early Neolithic Exploitation Patterns in the Levant: Cultural Impact on the Environment. *Population and Environment: A Journal of Interdisciplinary Studies* 13(4): 243–254.

Roosevelt, Anna C.
1991   *Moundbuilders of the Amazon: Geophysical Archaeology on Marajó Island, Brazil*. Academic Press, San Diego.
1998   Ancient and Modern Hunter-Gatherers of Lowland South America: An Evolutionary Problem. In *Advances in Historical Ecology*, edited by W. Baleé, pp. 190–212. Columbia University Press, New York.

Roosevelt, Anna C., M. Lima da Costa, C. Lopes Machado, M. Michab, N. Mercier, H. Valla-das, J. Feathers, W. Barnett, M. Imazio da Silveira, A. Henderson, J. Silva, B. Chernoff, D. S. Reese, J. A. Holman, N. Toth, and K. Schick
1996   Paleoindian Cave Dwellers in the Amazon: The Peopling of the Americas. *Science* 272: 373–384.

Russell, Emily W. B.
1997   *People and the Land through Time: Linking Ecology and History.* Yale University Press, New Haven, Conn.

Sahlins, Marshall, and Patrick V. Kirch
1992   *Anahulu: The Anthropology of History in the Kingdom of Hawaii.* University of Chicago Press, Chicago.

Sanders, William T., and Barbara J. Price
1968   *Mesoamerica: The Evolution of a Civilization.* Random House, New York.

Sandor, J. A., and N. S. Eash
1991   Significance of Ancient Agricultural Soils for Long-Term Agronomic Studies and Sustainable Agricultural Research. *Agronomy Journal* 83: 29–37.

Sandor, J. A., and P. L. Gersper
1988   Evaluation of Soil Fertility in Some Prehistoric Agricultural Terraces in New Mexico. *Agronomy Journal* 80: 846–850.

Sauer, Carl O.
1956   The Agency of Man on the Earth. In *Man's Role in Changing the Face of the Earth,* Vol. 1, edited by William L. Thomas, Jr., pp. 49–69. University of Chicago Press, Chicago.

Sawhill, John C.
1998   After the Flood. In *Nature Conservancy* 48(5): 5.

Schreiber, Katherine J., and Josué Lancho Rojas
1988   Los puquios de Nasca: un sistema de galerías filtrantes. *Boletin de Lima* 59(10): 51–63.

Sears, Paul B.
1956   The Processes of Environmental Change by Man. In *Man's Role in Changing the Face of the Earth,* Vol. 2, edited by William L. Thomas, Jr., pp. 471–484. University of Chicago Press, Chicago.

Simmons, I. G.
1989   *Changing the Face of the Earth: Culture, Environment, History.* Basil Blackwell, Oxford.

Simon, H. A.
1957   *Models of Man: Social and Rational; Mathematical Essays on Rational Human Behavior in Society Settings.* Wiley, New York.

Spoehr, Alexander
1956   Cultural Differences in the Interpretation of Natural Resources. In *Man's Role in Changing the Face of the Earth,* Vol. 2, edited by W. L. Thomas, pp. 93–102. University of Chicago Press, Chicago.

Steadman, David W.
1995   Prehistoric Extinctions of Pacific Island Birds: Biodiversity Meets Zooarchaeology. *Science* 267: 1123–1131.

Steadman, David W., and Patrick Kirch
1990   Prehistoric Extinction of Birds on Mangaia, Cook Island, Polynesia. *Proceedings of the National Academy of Sciences* 87: 9605–9609.

Steadman, David W., and Paul S. Martin
1984   Extinction of Birds in the Late Pleistocene of North America. In *Quaternary Extinctions,* edited by Paul S. Martin and Richard G. Klein, pp. 466–477. University of Arizona Press, Tucson.

Steadman, David W., and Jim I. Mead (eds.)
1995   *Late Quaternary Environments and Deep History: A Tribute to Paul S. Martin.* Scientific Papers, Vol. 3. Mammoth Site of Hot Springs, South Dakota, Hot Springs.

Steward, Julian
1955   *Theory of Culture Change: The Methodology of Multilinear Evolution.* University of Illinois Press, Urbana.

Thirgood, J. V.
1981   *Man and the Mediterranean Forest: A History of Resource Depletion.* Academic Press, London.

Thomas, William L. (ed.)
1956   *Man's Role in Changing the Face of the Earth.* Published for the Wenner-Gren Foundation for Anthropological Research and the NSF by the University of Chicago Press, Chicago.

Toynbee, Arnold Joseph
1934   *A Study of History.* Oxford University Press, Oxford.

Tuan, Yi-Fu
1970   Our Treatment of the Environment in Ideal and Actuality. *American Scientist* 58: 244–249.

van Andel, Tjeerd H., Curtis N. Runnels, and Kevin O. Pope
1986   Five Thousand Years of Land Use and Abuse in the Southern Argolid, Greece. *Hesperia* 55: 103–128.

van Andel, Tjeerd H., Eberhard Zangger, and Anne Demitrack
1990   Land Use and Soil Erosion in Prehistoric and Historical Greece. *Journal of Field Archaeology* 17: 379–396.

van der Leeuw, Sander E. (ed.)
1998a   *The Archaeomedes Project: Understanding the Natural and Anthropogenic Causes of Land Degradation and Desertification in the Mediterranean Basin.* European Communities, Luxembourg.
1998b   Introduction. In *The Archaeomedes Project: Understanding the Natural and Anthropogenic Causes of Land Degradation and Desertification in the Mediterranean Basin,* pp. 1–22. European Communities, Luxembourg.

van Zeist W., H. Woldering, and D. Stapert
1975   Late Quaternary Vegetation and Climate of Southwestern Turkey. *Palaeohistoria* 17: 53–143.

Vita-Finzi, Claudio
1969   *The Mediterranean Valleys: Geological Changes in Historical Times.* Cambridge University Press, Cambridge.

Vitousek, Peter M., Carla M. D'Antonio, Lloyd L. Loope, and Randy Westbrooks
1996   Biological Invasions as Global Environmental Change. *American Scientist* 84: 468–478.

Vitousek, Peter M., Harold A. Mooney, Jane Lubchenco, and Jerry M. Melillo
1997   Human Domination of Earth's Ecosystems. *Science* 277: 494–499.

von Daniken, Erich
1968   *Chariots of the Gods? Unsolved Mysteries of the Past.* Putnam, New York.

von Thünen, Johann Heinrich
1966   *Isolated State: An English Edition of* Der isolierte Staat. Translated by Carla M. Wartenberg. Edited with an introduction by Peter Hall. Pergamon Press, Oxford.

Waide, Robert B.
1998   Status of the U.S. Long-Term Ecological Research Network. In *The International Long-Term Ecological Research Network 1998,* edited by Patricia Sprott, pp. 74–85. U.S. LTER Network Office, Albuquerque, N.Mex.

Waters, Michael R.
1991   The Geoarchaeology of Gullies and Arroyos in Southern Arizona. *Journal of Field Archaeology* 18(2): 141–159.

Westoff, V.
1983   Man's Attitudes Towards Vegetation. In *Man's Impact on Vegetation,* edited by M.J.A. Werger and I. Ikusima, chapter 1. Dr. W. Junk Publishers, Boston.

White Jr., Lynn
1967   The Historical Roots of Our Ecological Crisis. *Science* 155(3767): 1203–1207.

Whitmore, Thomas M., B. L. Turner II, Douglas L. Johnson, Robert W. Kates, and Thomas R. Gottschang
1990   Long-Term Population Change. In *The Earth as Transformed by Human Action,* edited by B. L. Turner II, William C. Clark, Robert W. Kates, John F. Richards, Jessica T. Mathews, and William B. Meyer, pp. 25–39. Cambridge University Press, Cambridge.

Woods, C. S.
1979   *Human Sickness and Health: A Biocultural View.* Mayfield Publishing Company, Mountain View, Calif.

Wright, Henry T., and Gregory A. Johnson
1975   Population, Exchange, and Early State Formation in Southwestern Iran. *American Anthropologist* 77(2): 267–289.

Zipf, G. K.
1949   *Human Behavior and the Principle of Least Effort.* Cambridge University Press, Cambridge.

Index

About the Author

Charles Redman received his bachelor of arts degree from Harvard University and his master of arts and Ph.D. degrees in anthropology from the University of Chicago. He taught at New York University and at SUNY-Binghamton before taking a position at Arizona State University in 1983. Since then, he has served as chair for the Department of Anthropology and recently assumed the directorship of the Center for Environmental Studies.

Redman's interests include archaeological research design, environmental education, the rise of civilization, historical ecology, human impacts on the environment, and public outreach. The author or coauthor of eight books including *Explanation in Archaeology, The Rise of Civilization,* and *People of the Tonto Rim,* he has directed archaeological field projects in the Near East, North Africa, and Arizona.

Redman has served as principal investigator or coprincipal investigator on 35 research grants from federal, state, and private agencies totaling over $20 million. This past year he began codirecting the Central Arizona—Phoenix Long-Term Ecological Research Project, the first project of its kind established by the National Science Foundation in an urban arid locale.

Redman is also a founding member of the Southwest Center for Education and the Natural Environment (SCENE), a member of the board of trustees of the Museum of Northern Arizona and of the state chapter of The Nature Conservancy, and a member of the Science Advisory Committee of Biosphere 2 and the Wenner-Gren Foundation. He has served as a member of several state councils and as chair of the state's Archaeology Advisory Commission and the Arizona Advisory Council on Environmental Education.